TEACHING IN THE KNOWLEDGE SOCIETY

Education in the Age of Insecurity

TEACHING
IN THE
KNOWLEDGE SOCIETY

Education
in the
Age of Insecurity

Andy Hargreaves

Teachers College
Columbia University
New York and London

Published by Teachers College Press, 1234 Amsterdam Avenue,
New York, NY 10027

Library of Congress Cataloging-in-Publication Data

Hargreaves, Andy.
    Teaching in the knowledge society : education in the age of insecurity /
Andy Hargreaves.
        p.   cm.
    Includes bibliographical references and index.
    ISBN 0-8077-4360-7 (cloth : alk. paper) — ISBN 0-8077-4359-3 (pbk. :
alk. paper)
    1. Effective teaching.   2. Education—Curricula—Standards.   3. Compe-
tency based education.   4. Education—Social aspects.   I. Title.
LB1025.3.H366   2003
371.102—dc21   2002035459

ISBN 0-8077-4359-3   (paper)
ISBN 0-8077-4360-7   (cloth)

Printed on acid-free paper
Manufactured in the United States of America

10   09   08   07   06   05   04   03   8   7   6   5   4   3   2   1

To Pauline

—humanity and integrity personified—

with great love

CONTENTS

ACKNOWLEDGMENTS

This has been a demanding book to write. It almost certainly would never have come to print had it not been for the benefits of a Rockefeller Foundation writing residency at the Villa Serbelloni in Bellagio, Italy, in fall 2001. On the edge of Lake Como the foundation has created a remarkable intellectual oasis where academic dedication and humanitarian contribution are brought together as one. I am immensely grateful to the foundation for the precious opportunity it has provided to me and to others like me.

The core of the book is based on research evidence from two large-scale projects concerned with high-school improvement and reform. The study of eight Canadian and U.S. secondary schools in *Change over Time?* was funded by the Spencer Foundation of the United States. The five-year improvement project with six Ontario secondary schools was supported through partnership funding from the Peel Board of Education where the schools were located and the Ontario Ministry of Education and Training. On behalf of my colleagues and myself, I extend my very great thanks to the time and goodwill that teachers, principals, and district staff gave freely to participate in these projects in a reform climate that was professionally difficult and sometimes overwhelming for many of them.

The work on these projects has benefited from collaboration with a range of colleagues and fellow researchers who have influenced my thinking in many ways. They include Carol Beynon, Dean Fink, Corrie Giles, Sonia James-Wilson, Susan Lasky, Shawn Moore, Michele Schmidt, and Paul Shaw at the International Center for Educational Change in Toronto, along with Colin Biott at the University of Northumbria in England, who contributed to one of the projects as a visiting scholar. My co-investigator Ivor Goodson and his researchers, Michael Baker and Martha Foote at the University of Rochester, New York, also worked with me as supportive and stimulating colleagues on one of the key projects. Those whose case-study analyses are most strongly represented in the text of this book are listed as co-authors of chapters 3, 4, and 5. An analogy I draw between public-education reform and the privatization of the railways in Britain owes much to Ivor Goodson's paper *The Personality of Change,* presented at the invitational conference Social Geographies of Educational Change (funded by the Spencer Foundation) in Barcelona in March 2001, in which this parallel was drawn for the first time.

Interactions with a number of colleagues have challenged and pushed my thinking about the potential and the limits of large-scale educational reform. They are Amanda Datnow, Lorna Earl, and Michael Fullan at the International Center for Educational Change, Toronto; Alma Harris and David Hopkins at the University of Nottingham, England, where I have spent part of my academic time each year; and Brahm Fleisch at the University of Witwatersand, South Africa, for his ideas and experiences concerning large-scale reform in less-developed countries. Brahm also drew my attention to—and, indeed, purchased a copy for me of—Richard Sennett's *Corrosion of Character,* which became one of the major theoretical influences on this book. These people will not agree with all of the views in this book, but whether their work has prompted reinforcement or reaction, it has undoubtedly influenced my own.

One important strand of thinking in this book concerns the nature and impact of professional learning and professional development in teaching. In these areas, I am grateful to the influence and support of Steve Anderson and Shawn Moore in Toronto and of Christopher Day and others at Nottingham University in the projects we have undertaken together on the long-term effects of professional development on teachers and teaching. These projects have been supported by the Learning First Alliance in the United States, a consortium of the nation's most influential organizations in education, and the Department for Education and Skills in the United Kingdom. I particularly value the patience and support of my former colleagues in the School of Education and the National College for School Leadership at Nottingham University, who heard me rehearse some of the key ideas in this book in a series of seminars in spring 2002.

No book writes or formats itself. Leo Santos has once again miraculously processed the interminable drafts and redrafts of my barely legible text. Karen Shooter provided invaluable support in assembling the final version. In moving to my new Chair at Boston College, I miss both of them dreadfully.

Last, but by no means least, I acknowledge the contribution and support of my wife, Pauline, to whom this book is dedicated. Not only does she serve as a living model of a dedicated educator, but her unswerving support, her enduring love, and her insistence on always demanding the best of me (none of which are easy when you have me for a partner) sustain me and my work beyond measure.

INTRODUCTION

We live in a knowledge economy, a knowledge society. Knowledge economies are stimulated and driven by creativity and ingenuity. Knowledge-society schools have to create these qualities; otherwise, their people and their nations will be left behind. Like other kinds of capitalism, the knowledge economy is, in Joseph Schumpeter's terms, a force of creative destruction. It stimulates growth and prosperity, but its relentless pursuit of profit and self-interest also strains and fragments the social order. Along with other public institutions, our schools must therefore also foster the compassion, community, and cosmopolitan identity that will offset the knowledge economy's most destructive effects. The knowledge economy primarily serves the private good. The knowledge society also encompasses the public good. Our schools have to prepare young people for both of them.

Schools today serve and shape a world in which there can be great economic opportunity and improvement if people can learn to work more flexibly, invest in their future financial security, reskill or relocate themselves as the economy shifts around them, and value working creatively and collaboratively. The world that schools serve is also characterized by growing social instability. The bonds among citizens are increasingly strained by the fragmenting effects of economic flexibility. People who spend most of their time producing and consuming find less time for family or community. There is a loss of trust in and growing suspicion about political, corporate, and professional integrity. The widening gaps between rich and poor fan the flames of terrorism, crime, and mounting insecurity.

Yet instead of fostering creativity and ingenuity, more and more school systems have become obsessed with imposing and micromanaging curricular uniformity. In place of ambitious missions of compassion and community, schools and teachers have been squeezed into the tunnel vision of test scores, achievement targets, and league tables of accountability. And rather than cultivating cosmopolitan identity and the basic emotion of sympathy, which Adam Smith called the emotional foundation of democracy,[1] too many educational systems promote exaggerated and self-absorbed senses of national identity.

1

In many parts of the world, the rightful quest for higher educational standards has degenerated into a compulsive obsession with standardization. By and large, our schools are preparing young people neither to work well in the knowledge economy nor to live well in a strong civil society. Instead of promoting economic invention and social integration, too many schools are becoming mired in the regulations and routines of soulless standardization.

We are living in a defining moment of educational history, when the world in which teachers do their work is changing profoundly, and the demographic composition of teaching is turning over dramatically. The vast cohort of teachers who entered the profession in the expansionist decades of the 1960s and 1970s are retiring. Teaching is becoming a young person's profession again. Whoever enters teaching and however he or she approaches the work will shape the profession and what it is able to achieve with our children for the next 30 years.

If we capitulate to the idea that public education can only be a low-cost system running on low-skilled, poorly paid, and overloaded teachers whose job is to maintain order, teach to the test, and follow standardized curriculum scripts, then teachers for the next three decades will be neither capable of nor committed to teaching for and beyond the knowledge society. They will instead become the drones and clones of policymakers' anemic ambitions for what underfunded systems can achieve.

Alternatively, we can promote a high-investment, high-capacity educational system in which highly skilled teachers are able to generate creativity and ingenuity among their students by experiencing creativity and flexibility themselves in how they are treated and developed as knowledge-society professionals. In this second scenario, teaching and teachers will reach far beyond the technical tasks of producing acceptable test results to pursuing teaching as a life-shaping, world-changing social mission again.

In their preparation, their professional development, and their working lives, today's teachers must get a grasp of and a grip on the knowledge society in which their students live and will work. If teachers do not understand the knowledge society, they cannot prepare their students for it. As a traditional Irish saying proclaims, "You have to listen to the river if you want to catch a trout."

Teachers must take their place again among society's most respected intellectuals—moving beyond the citadel of the classroom to being, and preparing their students to be, citizens of the world. They must do their best to ensure that their students promote and prosper from the private goods of the knowledge economy. They must also help their students commit to the vital public goods that cannot be taken care of by the corporate interests of the knowledge economy—a strong and vigorous civil society, developing the character that promotes involvement in the community, and cultivating the dispositions of sympathy and care for people in other nations and cultures that are at the heart of cosmopolitan identity. These are the challenges facing teachers in the knowledge society today and that are the focus of this book, which deals with the changing world as well as the changing work of teaching.

The term *"knowledge society"* is actually a misnomer. I stick with it in this book because of its widespread and accepted use. In truth, though, a knowledge society is really a learning society. In chapter 1, I argue that knowledge societies process information and knowledge in ways that maximize learning, stimulate ingenuity and invention, and develop the capacity to initiate and cope with change. In the knowledge economy, wealth and prosperity depend on people's capacity to out-invent and outwit their competitors, to tune in to the desires and demands of the consumer market, and to change jobs or develop new skills as economic fluctuations and downturns require. In the knowledge economy, these capacities are the property not just of individuals, but also of organizations. They depend on collective as well as individual intelligence. Knowledge-society organizations develop these capacities by providing their members with extensive opportunities for up-skilling and retraining; by breaking down barriers to learning and communication and getting people to work in overlapping, flexible teams; by looking at problems and mistakes as opportunities for learning more than as occasions for blame; by involving everyone in the "big picture" of where the organization is going; and by developing the "social capital" of networks and relationships that provide people with extra support and further learning.

Teaching for the knowledge society, I argue, involves cultivating these capacities in young people—developing deep cognitive learning, creativity, and ingenuity among students; drawing on research, working in networks and teams, and pursuing continuous professional learning as teachers; and promoting problem-solving, risk-taking, trust in the collaborative process, ability to cope with change and commitment to continuous improvement as organizations.

Chapter 2 then turns to the costs of the knowledge economy—to a public good for which it has no capacity to care. The knowledge economy drives people to put their self-interest before the social good, to indulge in consumption instead of involving themselves in community, to enjoy the buzz of temporary teamwork more than to develop the long-term emotions of loyalty and perseverance that sustain the enduring commitments of group life.

The knowledge economy is necessarily hungry for profit. Left to itself, it drains resources from the state and erodes the institutions of public life, including public schools themselves. In its most extreme forms of what I call *market fundamentalism,* the knowledge economy drives wedges between rich and poor, within nations and among them, creating anger and despair among the excluded. Exclusion exacerbates crime as people steal what they cannot earn. It creates societies of suspicious minds—walled within their gated communities, watched by endless security cameras, and protected in private schools that keep out the excluded. The knowledge economy also sows the seeds of ethnic and religious fundamentalism as some people turn away from the market to find other sources of hope, meaning, and certainty in their lives. In rebuffing the market, they also reject democratic reason and cosmopolitan tolerance—persecuting outsiders and repressing their own women in their opposition to dominant Western values. Insecurity, crime, and terrorism are the predictable (though never just) desserts of knowledge societies that have little desire to redistribute resources to improve the quality of life domestically, and that neglect their humanitarian and democratic responsibilities internationally. One-sided globalization produces lopsided societies. As the international financier and philanthropist George Soros has put it:

> Globalization also has a negative side. . . . Many people, particularly in less developed countries have been hurt by globalization without being supported by a social safety net; many others have been marginalized by global markets. Globalization has [also] caused a misallocation of resources between private goods and public goods. Markets are good at creating wealth but are not designed to take care of other needs. The heedless pursuit of profit can hurt the environment and conflict with other social values.[2]

The challenge, says Soros, is not to attack globalization or destroy the knowledge economy. Its economic benefits are too great for that. Instead, we have to commit more resources and pay better global attention to the other social needs. In preparing the generations of the future, public education is in a pole position to teach values,,dispositions and senses of global responsibility that extend beyond the bounds of the knowledge economy.

Chapter 2 argues that teaching beyond the knowledge economy entails developing the values and emotions of young people's character; emphasizing emotional as well as cognitive learning; building commitments to group life and not just short-term teamwork; and cultivating a cosmopolitan identity that shows tolerance of race and gender differences, genuine curiosity toward and willingness to learn from other cultures, and responsibility toward excluded groups within and beyond one's own society. Among teachers, this means committing to personal development as well as formal professional learning, working with colleagues in long-term groups as well as short-term teams, and having opportunities to teach (and therefore learn) in other contexts and countries. For the organization, the challenge is to balance the chaotic forces of risk and change with a work culture that has elements of continuity, a foundation of trust and a capacity to create coherence among the many initiatives the school is pursuing. Most of all, in an educational world dominated by standards, test scores, and achievement targets, teaching beyond the knowledge economy means retrieving and rehabilitating the idea of teaching as a sacred vocation that pursues a compelling social mission. The cliché of "making a difference" no longer suffices as a moral purpose for teaching. What difference, in what kind of world, and for what reasons? These are the issues that count in today's high-stakes, high-risk knowledge society.

Chapters 3 and 4 discuss the evidence of New York State and Ontario, Canada, to show that key reform imperatives are preparing people neither for the knowledge economy nor for public life beyond it. The chapters present survey and interview data from high schools in these two contexts to show that curriculum standards have largely degenerated into soulless standardization. The standards are irrelevant to the highest-achieving schools, which feel that they are already meeting them. In the schools with high numbers of special education or vocational students, the standards are depressingly unattainable. These students are denied graduation in exchange for degradation, and their teachers are thrust into spectacles of failure and shame, building up dams of frustration that will surely burst when vast numbers of students fail to graduate. At best, the standards suit only the students in the middle, but they are applied insensitively to the rest.

Even in the middle, the regimes of teaching and learning that the standards have created are largely undesirable. Improving standards in the form of subject-based targets, or putting excessive emphases on math and literacy, marginalizes the attention to personal and social development that is the foundation of community and eliminates interdisciplinary attention to global education that is at the heart of cosmopolitan identity. More than this, in standardized reform teachers are treated and developed not as high-skill, high-capacity knowledge workers, but as compliant and closely monitored producers of standardized performances. Teachers with over-examined professional lives complain of eroded autonomy, lost creativity, restricted flexibility, and constrained capacity to exercise their professional judgment.

They keep their heads down, struggle along alone, and withdraw from work with their colleagues. Professional community collapses, time to reflect evaporates, and the love of learning disappears. Teachers lose faith in their governments, grasp at opportunities for resignation and retirement, and even urge their own children not to follow in their footsteps. Standardized educational reform is as valuable for a vigorous knowledge economy and a strong civil society as locusts are for a cornfield.

There are exceptions, though. Chapter 5 describes a school that has managed to construct itself as a vibrant knowledge-society school. From the outset, it established itself as a learning organization and a professional learning community. The school promotes professional learning teams, involves everyone in the "big picture" of where the school is going, uses technology to promote personal and organizational learning, bases decisions on shared data, and involves parents in determining student outcomes when they leave the school. The school is a caring community as well as a learning community—giving prime value to family, relationships, and a cosmopolitan concern for others in the world. It teaches beyond the knowledge economy as well as for it. But standardized reform threatens this knowledge-society school, as well, by recycling back into the school policy changes that it originally invented in rigid formats that make the changes unworkable. Soulless standardization threatens even those few knowledge-society schools that already exist.

The school described in chapter 5 is not alone in its efforts. At their own instigation, or because of the support of North America's many philanthropic foundations, more than a few schools and their districts have developed their own purposes and strengthened themselves as professional communities in order to run against and around government currents of standardization. Much of what we know about successful school change springs from their work. But foundations do not have enough resources for everyone; it is often the same innovative and entrepreneurial schools and districts that keep applying for the funds that are available; many initiatives fade when the discretionary funding disappears; and governments are reluctant to fill the funding gap to implement what has been learned across whole systems or nations. Thus, although exceptions to standardization are always evident, the overall trend continues to exert and reassert its influence on most of our schools—increasingly so, as compliance with statewide standards is enforced.

These exceptions remain important. They create new memories of what knowledge-society schools can look like. But their overall numbers are lower than the numerous research studies written about them imply.

Research dollars tend to follow examples of optimistic innovation or entrepreneurial initiative. The accumulated publication of these studies can distort their authors', and our own, perceptions of how widespread innovation actually is. Studies of how regular schools and systems deal with policy change are not so abundant. Although exceptions have a lot to teach us and are a constant source of hope, the pervasive threat posed by standardization to knowledge-society schools, and to their ability to spread across systems and sustain themselves over time, remains substantial.

Chapters 6 and 7 search for a way through this impasse. Chapter 6 reviews the policies of nations outside North America and districts within it that have experienced years of standardization and now grasp the urgency of moving beyond it—especially when in the face of a teacher-recruitment crisis and the need to attract able people to, and retain them within, the profession. These nations and districts are facing the need for more generosity toward the new teaching force. Some developments are promising. In places, there will be more autonomy, flexibility, and professional community for teachers who are doing well. These developments demand what I call a "grown-up" profession, with grown-up professional norms of teaching where teachers are as much at ease with demanding adults as they are with problem children; where professional disagreement is embraced and enjoyed rather than avoided; where conflict is seen as a necessary part of professional learning, not a fatal act of personal betrayal.

Other educational change trends are more disturbing. Teachers and schools in poorer nations and communities are being subjected to micromanaged interventions in the basic areas of math and literacy. These take the form of what I call performance training sects that provide intensive implementation support for teachers but only in relation to highly prescriptive interventions in "basic" areas of the curriculum that demand unquestioning professional compliance. But the real danger is that performance training sects may be viewed as the end of improvement in poor communities, locking teachers and students into cycles of low-level dependency rather than offering a first step toward something better. Inadvertently, I argue, we may be creating a system of professional development apartheid where the rich and successful will enjoy the privilege of professional learning community, while most of the poor and unsuccessful are subjected to sectarian performance training (except in those cases funded by foundation incentives).

Chapter 7 advocates against an apartheid of professional development and school improvement. It questions a world and a school system that divides those who learn how to create the high-skill knowledge society from those who learn only how to cater to it through lower-level service jobs in the consumer and hospitality industries. The essential task, I argue, is to redesign school improvement on developmental lines to make professional community ultimately available to everyone, and to end the educational and social impoverishment that undermines many nations' and communities' capacity to improve at all. Pursuing improvement is not a substitute for ending impoverishment. Both have to be tackled together. This should be one of the central social and professional missions of educational reform in the twenty-first century, one of its greatest projects of social ingenuity.

It should be evident that the style of this book is not clinically dispassionate. The research on which it is based has been undertaken thoroughly, and the evidence has been treated seriously. My research colleagues and I have had to shift our understandings and perceptions several times because of it. But professors of education are also ultimately public intellectuals. Our work enters a field of action that changes students' and teachers' lives. It is a moral and not just a technical endeavor. My moral stance is therefore evident throughout the text, and the issues raised by the evidence are discussed in a spirit of engagement, not detachment. It would make no sense to urge teachers to treat their work as a social mission if, as educators, we failed to do so ourselves.

Last, because of its knowledge-society orientation, the book sometimes moves away in its first two chapters from the immediate world of schools to provide a thorough analysis of the nature of the knowledge society and the challenges it presents to teachers and their schools. After chapter 2, the text returns to and stays within the world of schools and teaching, tracing how knowledge-society influences, on the one hand, and the trends toward standardization, on the other, make themselves felt in the everyday world of teaching.

NOTES

1. Smith, A., *The Theory of Moral Sentiments* (12th ed.; first published in 1759), Glasgow, R. Chapman, 1809.
2. Soros, G., *George Soros on Globalization,* New York, Perseus Books, 2002.

1

TEACHING FOR
THE KNOWLEDGE SOCIETY
Educating for Ingenuity

THE PARADOXICAL PROFESSION

Teaching is a paradoxical profession. Of all the jobs that are or aspire to be professions, only teaching is expected to create the human skills and capacities that will enable individuals and organizations to survive and succeed in today's knowledge society. Teachers, more than anyone, are expected to build learning communities, create the knowledge society, and develop the capacities for innovation, flexibility and commitment to change that are essential to economic prosperity. At the same time, teachers are also expected to mitigate and counteract many of the immense problems that knowledge societies create, such as excessive consumerism, loss of community, and widening gaps between rich and poor. Somehow, teachers must try to achieve these seemingly contradictory goals at the same time. This is their professional paradox.

Meanwhile, public expenditure, education, and welfare have been the first casualties of the slimmed-down state that knowledge economies have often required. Teachers' salaries and work conditions have been among the most expensive items at the top of the public-service casualty list.

In the industrial revolution, resources of human labor moved from the country to the city. This mass migration filled the Dickensian factories and dark Satanic mills of the period with labor power. But in the face of overcrowding and urban squalor, this movement also prompted the creation of great institutions of public space and public life such as state education, public libraries, and the great municipal parks. The economic explosion of the industrial revolution was not limitless. It was counterbalanced by acts of civic and philanthropic responsibility that provided learning, schooling, and green urban space that would benefit the people.

The knowledge revolution has been redirecting resources once more, this time from the public purse to private pockets as a way to boost consumer

9

spending and stimulate stock-market investment in a global casino of end-less speculation. There is little sign of social compensation or counterbalancing in this second revolution. Indeed, its drain on public spending and its championing of private choice is placing many of our public institutions, including public education, in jeopardy. Just as we are expecting the very most from teachers to prepare children for the knowledge society, their total salary costs, a result of having become a mass profession, have driven many governments to limit or withhold the resources and support their need to be more effective. In damaging the teachers of the next generations, the knowledge economy is eating its young.

The knowledge society finds it difficult to make teaching a true learning profession. It craves higher standards of learning and teaching. Yet it has also subjected teachers to public attacks; eroded their autonomy of judgment and conditions of work; created epidemics of standardization and over-regulation; and provoked tidal waves of resignation and early retirement, crises of recruitment, and shortages of eager and able educational leaders. The very profession that is so often said to be of vital importance for the knowledge economy is the one that too many groups have devalued, more and more people want to leave, less and less want to join, and very few are interested in leading. This is more than a paradox. It is a crisis of disturbing proportions.

Teachers today thus find themselves caught in a triangle of competing interests and imperatives:

- To be *catalysts* of the knowledge society and all the opportunity and prosperity it promises to bring;
- To be *counterpoints* for the knowledge society and its threats to inclusiveness, security and public life;
- To be *casualties* of the knowledge society in a world where escalating expectations for education are being met with standardized solutions provided at minimum cost.

The interactions and effects of the three forces shown in Figure 1.1 are shaping the nature of teaching, what it means to be a teacher, and the very viability of teaching as a profession in the knowledge society.

BEFORE THE KNOWLEDGE SOCIETY

Since the emergence of compulsory schooling and its spread across the world, public education has repeatedly been expected to save society. Schools and

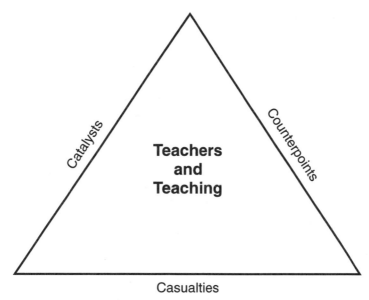

FIGURE 1.1. The Knowledge Society Triangle.

their teachers have been expected to rescue children from poverty and destitution; to rebuild nationhood in the aftermath of war; to develop universal literacy as a platform for economic survival; to create skilled workers even when little suitable employment has beckoned them; to develop tolerance among children in a world where adults are divided by religious and ethnic conflict; to cultivate democratic sentiments in societies that bear the scars of totalitarianism; to keep developed nations economically competitive and help developing ones become so; and to eliminate drugs, end violence, and make restitution for the sins of the present generation by reshaping how educators prepare the generations of the future.

Expectations for public education have always been high, but they have not always been expressed in the same way. In the 30 years following World War II, education in the world's leading economies was widely viewed as an investment in human capital, in scientific and technological development, in a commitment to progress.[1] Booming demographics in what Eric Hobsbawm calls "the golden age of history"[2] led to a call for more teachers, optimism about the power of education, and pride in being a professional as a young and expanding generational cohort of teachers developed the bargaining power to raise their salaries, became an increasingly well qualified and more graduate-based profession, and were accorded greater status and sometimes flexibility and discretion in how they performed their work. In this *age of the autonomous professional,* as I have called it, many teachers in developed, democratic countries benefited from expanding populations, prosperous economies, and benign states.[3]

Although all this optimism, expansion, and autonomy increased people's access to public education, it did little to change the fundamental nature of the education provided or the way in which teachers taught. Few innovations lasted for long, and the rhetoric of classroom change usually outstripped the reality.[4] Behind all the autonomy, attempted innovation, and educational expansion, a basic "grammar" of teaching and learning persisted in which most teachers taught as they had for generations—from the front of the classroom; through lecturing, seat work, and question-and-answer methods; and in separate classes of children of the same age, evaluated by standard paper-and-pencil methods.[5]

Less-developed countries inherited different economic and cultural legacies and had a disproportionately tiny share of the world's wealth with which to address them. Aid was largely directed toward establishing and extending basic primary or elementary education and creating the fundamental literacy levels that were seen as essential for economic "lift off" and independence. But resources were limited; class sizes were (and mainly still are) overwhelming; technology could be basic in the extreme, with stones for seats and sand for chalkboards; and teachers' qualifications, expertise, and salaries were poor.[6] In secondary schools, smaller elites often learned the curricula of their colonial masters; they were taught it in didactic ways and were separated from their experience and drawn away from their own people as a result.[7] Teaching here remained confined to what I have called a *pre-professional age,* where poorly paid and prepared teachers were able to master and use only a restricted range of teaching strategies.[8] These strategies—little more than strategies for coping with and surviving the situations they faced[9]—might have suited the constraining circumstances and finances of less-developed countries, but they also became ingrained in teachers' and other people's imaginations as the only possible ways to teach.

The oil crisis of 1973 and the collapse of Keynesian economics brought an end to optimistic educational assumptions in many of the developed economies of the West. Education suddenly became the problem, not the solution. In debt-burdened economies, welfare states began to collapse, and resources for education went with them. Western nations turned inward, and many lost their confidence as they became overshadowed by Asian "Tiger" economies. Meanwhile, demographics went into reverse: student populations shrank, teachers lost their market attraction and bargaining power, and the bulk of the remaining teaching force began to show its age.

In academic circles, pessimism about the power of education as an agent of social change defined the mood of the times. Christopher Jencks argued, on the basis of large statistical data sets, that education did little to remedy social inequalities.[10] Basil Bernstein's seemingly prophetic argument that "education cannot compensate for society" began to strike many chords,[11] and Tom Popkewitz observed in retrospect that history repeatedly assigned misplaced faith in schools as agents of social redemption.[12]

Once the crucible of social optimism, education became a target of purging, despair, and panic. In the United States, the dramatic report *A Nation at Risk* proclaimed, in bellicose language, that Americans would be outraged if growing foreign superiority in educational achievement and economic performance had instead been one of military might.[13] Meanwhile, in Britain the incoming Conservative government of the late 1980s used the deliberately misspelled slogan "Education Isn't Wurking" as its election votegrabber. Governments started to link education more closely to business, work, science, and technology.[14] Structures were reorganized, resources were pegged back, and policies of market choice and competition between schools began to proliferate. Curriculum control was often tightened and, in some places, linked to the explicit task of re-establishing pride in the nation.[15] Change became ubiquitous and was implemented, "just in time," with an escalating sense of urgency. And teachers were blamed for everything—by governments, media, and newly instituted league tables of school performance that shamed the "worst" of them (usually those in the poorest communities) for failing their students.[16] According to some critics, these developments were deliberate measures designed to make teaching and public schooling unpopular, to encourage many parents to fund their own children's education privately, and to force older, expensive teachers, who were impeding the new reform agenda, into early retirement.[17]

By the 1990s, the average age of teachers in many Organization for Economic Cooperation and Development (OECD) countries was well into the 40s.[18] Under the pressures of reform, morale problems, stress levels, and rates of teacher burnout all increased[19]—even in countries such as Japan, where educational-reform cycles had started later.[20] Many teachers started to feel deprofessionalized as the effects of reform and restructuring began to bite.[21] Teachers experienced more work, more regulation of their work, and more distractions from what they regarded to be core to their work (teaching children) by the bureaucratic and form-filling burdens of administrative decentralization.[22] The funeral pyre of public education was starting to smolder.

One of the strongest pretexts for school reform in Western nations was the introduction of international test comparisons. The economic miracle of the Asian "Tigers"—Hong Kong, Singapore, Korea, and Taiwan—along with the rising sun of Japan, led Western policymakers to oversimplify the contributions of these societies' educational systems to their economic success. International test results in mathematics and science provoked public anxiety and provided ammunition for many Western governments to reform their educational systems. This then led to greater standardization and micro-management of teaching and learning through tightened inspection systems, performance-related pay, and closely scripted curriculum reforms that severely reduced the latitude of teachers' pedagogical decisions—as in the widely used "Success for All" literacy program in the United States and the United Kingdom's National Literacy Strategy in primary schools. Ironically, however, the emerging knowledge economy actually needs much more flexibility in learning and teaching than these trends have allowed—as the unexpected economic downturns in and collapses of Asian currencies in the late 1990s belatedly led people to recognize.[23]

Meanwhile, the educational downsizing and restructuring seemed no more helpful in reversing or ameliorating educational and social inequality than the movement of deck chairs might have been in saving the *Titanic*. Rates of child poverty expanded and exploded in Britain, the United States, and elsewhere.[24] Restructuring measures showed little sign of narrowing the learning gap between schools in rich and poor communities.[25] In sub-Saharan Africa and parts of South America especially, a Fourth World of absolute destitution began to emerge.[26] Here, strings of famines, disease, and other ecological disasters, as well as inter-tribal genocide, tragically characterized a postcolonial era in in which political dictatorships with corrupt regimes (often supported by Western governments) divided their nations, marginalized their poor, and personally sequestered most of the educational and other resources that economic aid agencies tried to give them. Teachers' hopes for enhanced professionalism were rarely being realized in developed nations. Elsewhere, they were an unattainable dream.

PROFITING FROM THE KNOWLEDGE SOCIETY

These have been the dubious educational legacies of the dying industrial and imperial era of modernization in the final quarter of the twentieth century. But at century's turn, a new economy and society, emerging from the ashes of old industrialism, began to take shape.

In 1976, the American sociologist Daniel Bell first foretold this coming social age and invented a new phrase to describe it: the *knowledge society*.

Bell's book, *The Coming of Post-Industrial Society,* charted an economic shift that had already begun, from an industrial economy in which most people were engaged in producing things, to a post-industrial economy in which the workforce was increasingly concentrated in services, ideas, and communication.[27] Much of this new emphasis, Bell argued, would be increasingly dependent on people and institutions that produced knowledge—in science, technology, research, and development. "The post-industrial society," he said,

> is a knowledge society in a double sense: first the sources of innovation are increasingly derived from research and development . . . second, the weight of the society—measured by a larger proportion of Gross National Product and a larger share of employment—is increasingly in the knowledge field.[28]

The educational sphere alone, he argued, would mushroom as part of this trend so that, "by the year 2000, the United States will have become . . . a mass knowledge society," with rocketing rates of enrollment in higher education.[29]

Bell's prophecy was partly correct. Access to more years of public education, higher education, and adult education continues to expand everywhere. Young people stay in school longer, enter higher education in greater numbers, and start full-time paid employment and careers later.[30] But whether all this leads to a greater, better, more widely distributed knowledge society as a whole is an open question. More schooling does not always amount to better learning.

Today's widespread talk about the knowledge society among politicians, bureaucrats, educators, and entrepreneurs broadens its meaning considerably beyond Bell's. Today's knowledge society is not just represented in the growth of particular expert sectors such as science, technology, or education. It is not just a resource for work and production. It permeates all parts of economic life, characterizing the very way in which corporations and many other kinds of organizations operate.

The economist and nonagenarian futurist Peter Drucker has best captured and popularized this newer, more powerful and pervasive idea of the knowledge society. The basic economic resource of society, he says, is no longer capital or labor. Instead

> it is and will be knowledge. . . . Value is now created by "productivity" and "innovation," both applications of knowledge to work. The leading groups of the knowledge society will be "knowledge workers." . . . The economic challenge . . . will therefore be the productivity of knowledge work and the knowledge worker.[31]

In his brilliant trilogy *The Network Society,* Manuel Castells, an adviser in high-level expert think tanks on social reform in Eastern Europe and the less-developed world, uses the term *informational society* to describe this new social and economic order.[32] For Castells, this society is rooted in and driven by the development, expansion, and circulation of globalized electronic, computer-based, and digital information and entertainment. He writes:

> In the industrial mode of development, the main source of productivity lies in the introduction of new energy sources, and in the ability to decentralize the use of energy throughout the production and circulation processes. In the new informational mode of development, the source of productivity lies in the technology of knowledge generation, information processing and symbolic communication. . . . What is specific to the informational mode of development is the action of knowledge upon knowledge itself as the main source of productivity . . . in a virtuous circle of interaction.[33]

In this constantly changing, self-creating informational society, knowledge is a flexible, fluid, ever-expanding, and ever-shifting resource. In the knowledge economy, people do not just draw on and use outside "expert" knowledge from the universities and elsewhere. Knowledge, creativity and invention are intrinsic to everything people do. Knowledge is not only a support for work and production, as Bell first argued, but the key form of work and production itself, as more educated people work in the fields of ideas, communication, selling, marketing, counseling, consultancy, tourism, event organizing, and so forth. In one of Ian Rankin's popular detective novels, his aging protagonist, Inspector Rebus, scans the avant-garde occupations of the tenants of a fashionable Edinburgh apartment block where he is interviewing suspects and sarcastically wonders whether "anybody has real jobs anymore."[34]

In the knowledge society, how we produce is linked to how we consume. Jeremy Rifkin's *The Age of Access* illustrates that, while the downpayment prices for many of the things we purchase, such as cars, computers, and telephones, are falling or disappearing altogether, the services these things lock us into—car leasing, Internet access, telephone plans—are eating up more of our personal budgets.[35] Service is at the core of economic success.

Robert Reich, President Bill Clinton's former Secretary of Labor, describes how profitability in the new economy depends not on old industrial economies of scale, with their techniques of mass production and marketing.[36] Rather, in a world of spiraling and capricious consumer choice, companies stay profitable and viable by inventing new products and services more quickly than their rivals. Competitive companies therefore rely on building cultures and systems of "continuous innovation"[37] where "speed and cleverness . . . count far more than production."[38] In this culture, "geeks" who can invent, create, and take all-consuming pleasure in novelty and seeking out new possibilities are at a premium. So, too, are employees and experts who can empathize with client's needs—who can anticipate and foresee their future desires, and who can figure out what is most likely to titillate their consumer taste buds.

All this innovation and market anticipation calls for knowledge, and the greatest entrepreneurial geniuses, such as Thomas Edison, today's Stephen Spielberg, or Oprah Winfrey, says Reich, possess both kinds.[39] But individual geniuses are rare. Successful corporations therefore bring innovators and marketers together, breaking down the old departmental divisions between marketing, on the one hand, and research and development, on the other, that characterized corporations in the older industrial era.

The best corporations in the knowledge economy therefore operate as learning organizations where innovators and marketers work in teams, enjoy ease of communication with one another, have regular access to outside knowledge, and are able to generate and apply new ideas together.[40] These organizations build their capacity to share, create, and apply new knowledge continuously over time. As Reich observes, "mutual learning that leads to continuous innovation tends to be informal, unplanned, serendipitous."[41] The organizational challenge is to create the groups and cultures in which this mutual, spontaneous learning can thrive. The success of Silicon Valley sprang from this very principle—a community that brought together Stanford University researchers, technical innovators, and venture capitalists in a newly developed industrial park that would have a historic worldwide impact on economic and technological change.[42] More recently, the Santa Fe Institute draws on strong corporate financing from organizations such as Motorola to bring together theoretical physicists, economists, and others to discover the secrets of the networks and patterns that evolve in chaotic and complex systems. It is understanding these emergent patterns in economic and social networks, the funders believe, that holds the key to future economic success.[43]

So the knowledge society has three dimensions. First, it comprises an expanded scientific, technical, and educational sphere, in the way Bell described. Second, it involves complex ways of processing and circulating knowledge and information in a service-based economy. Third, it entails basic changes in how corporate organizations function so that they enhance continuous innovation in products and services by creating systems, teams, and cultures that maximize the opportunities for mutual, spontaneous learning.

The second and third aspects of the knowledge society depend on having a sophisticated infrastructure of information and communication technology that makes all this learning faster and easier. This informational infrastructure is crucial—and not only in the leading economies. Castells demonstrates that becoming electronically switched on to the knowledge or informational society is just as important a priority in less-developed countries.[44] Those countries most excluded from the informational economy, or that have been the latest starters with information technology, he shows, have fared least well economically. Indeed, failure to invest in information technology and to spread its access (with accompanying free flows of information) beyond the military to civil society, was one of the prime causes of the collapse of Soviet communism. Nations and groups that do not or cannot participate in the informational society become increasingly marginalized by it.

The key to a strong knowledge economy, though, is not only whether people can access information but also how well they can process that information. The OECD has been one of the prime movers behind new knowledge-economy initiatives. In a significant position paper for OECD, Martin Carnoy and Castells describe the information age as being centrally concerned with knowledge and learning:

> The distinguishing feature of work in the information age is the centrality of knowledge, especially "transportable" general knowledge that is not specific to a single job or firm. The best jobs are those that require high levels of education (high levels of general knowledge) and provide opportunities to accumulate more knowledge. The best firms are those that create the best environment for teaching, learning, and interchanging information. It is knowledge and information that creates flexibility in work—the capacity of firms to improve product lines, production processes, and marketing strategies, all with the same work force; and the capacity of workers to learn new processes as they change; to shift jobs several times in the course of a work life; to move geographically, and, if necessary, to learn entirely new vocations.[45]

DEVELOPING THE KNOWLEDGE SOCIETY

The knowledge society is a learning society. Economic success and a culture of continuous innovation depend on the capacity of workers to keep learning themselves and from one another. A knowledge economy runs not on machine power but on brain power—the power to think, learn, and innovate. Industrial economies needed machine workers; knowledge economies need knowledge workers.[46] As Drucker puts it, " Knowledge workers will give the emerging knowledge society its character, its leadership and its profile. They may not be the ruling class of the knowledge society, but they are already its leading class."[47]

The influential OECD report *Knowledge Management in the Learning Society* links knowledge management to the challenges created by the acceleration of change:

> We are moving into a "learning economy" where the success of individuals, firms, regions and countries will reflect, more than anything else, their ability to learn. The speeding up of change reflects the rapid diffusion of information technology, the widening of the global marketplace . . . and deregulation of and less stability in markets.[48]

These trends, the OECD points out elsewhere, raise "profound questions for the kinds of knowledge students are being equipped with, and ought to be equipped with, by schools."[49]

The international educational-change expert Michael Fullan concludes that "knowledge-creation using the world of ideas about learning"—including the best of brain research, cognitive science, and so on—must be at the heart of teaching and schooling.[50]

Leading social theorists and policy advisers of all political stripes are recognizing that high-quality public education is essential to developing knowledge workers and the knowledge society everywhere. Castells advises that

> education is the key quality of labor; the new producers of informational capitalism are those knowledge generators and information processors whose contribution is most valuable to the firm, the region and the national economy.[51]

Anthony Giddens, a leading "guru" of British Prime Minister Tony Blair, also asserts that "improved education and skills training" are essential, "particularly as far as poor groups are concerned"—if they, too, are to benefit from and be included in the new economy. "Investment in education," he continues, "is an imperative of government today, a key basis of the redistribution of possibilities."[52] The Australian reform consultants Brian Caldwell and Jim Spinks argue that, after years of reform in education that have concentrated on making schools more self-managing, then directing their efforts to reaching performance targets and improving learning standards, the focus of policy efforts worldwide is shifting to creating schools for the knowledge society.[53]

As I complete this book, I am speaking at the ceremonial opening of the National Institute of Education building in Singapore. Singapore is a tiny, young nation of 3 million people; barely a dot on the map. Having built its success on the large-scale production of electronic goods, Singapore faces particularly severe challenges in rebounding from the 1997 Asian economic and currency collapse, which hit the electronics sector especially hard. Singapore's neighbors can offer much cheaper labor to the international economy, and, in China's case, vast domestic markets.

The Singapore government realizes that its future prosperity depends not on educating its people in the knowledge and skills for a particular kind of economy but in developing its people's capacity for learning and dealing with change so they can respond quickly and flexibly, adapting and retraining as future economic opportunities or recessions arise.[54] Singapore's educational vision is therefore one of becoming a society that is composed of "Thinking Schools, [in a] Learning Nation." The national curriculum is being cut back; flexibility and creativity are being encouraged; and a number of schools are being established and architecturally refitted as learning organizations. Almost $50 million has been dedicated to educational research. At other universities I have visited, improved buildings in engineering or science symbolize the belief of government that the future depends on technology. The creation of the Singapore National Institute of Education, with more than 360 faculty and 7,000 students, symbolizes its government's belief that the nation's future depends on its people. Many other Asian nations, such as Japan—whose models of standardized competitiveness the West has tried so hard to emulate—are now also reducing the quantity of prescribed curriculum content, promoting teachers' flexibility, and urging greater classroom creativity.

National educational policies that are driven by market fundamentalism— the unshakable belief, even against the evidence, that unfettered markets offer the best path to prosperity—downsize their systems to produce basic, standardized achievements and reduce costs to free up the economy. But an advanced knowledge economy needs an educational system built by the state that will actively fuel, not merely free up, the economy. Phillip Brown and Hugh Lauder argue that, "in a knowledge-driven economy characterized by rapid change, adequate job performance cannot easily rely on external controls, as people need to be proactive, solve problems and work in teams."[55] Classroom performance can no longer rely on these controls, either.

Writers and policymakers of quite different ideological persuasions increasingly concur that a strong and improved public educational system is essential to producing a vigorous knowledge economy and to enabling poorer communities and countries to participate in and not be marginalized by it. In later chapters, we will see that all that glitters in the knowledge economy is not gold, and that the age of information brings real threats as well as benefits to human experience and opportunity. But schools and their teachers cannot and should not stand aside from their responsibilities to promote young people's opportunities in, engagements with, and inclusion within the high-skill world of knowledge, information, communication, and innovation. All children must be properly prepared for the knowledge society and its economy.

More education in existing forms is not the answer, though. More efficient classrooms that concentrate on teaching and learning rather than behavior management; more time spent on literacy and other basics; more summer schools and Saturday schools for students who are slow in learning; more hours in the school day and more days in the school year—all these things do help increase students' achievement, but only achievement of existing kinds. Subjecting them to more of the same does not change what students are achieving at.

In an earlier book, I described how schools that were preparing young people for the rapid change and complexity of a postmodern, postindustrial world were actually locked in modern—even premodern—principles of the factory and the monastery.[56] Schools were still ruled by clocks and bells, periods and classes; children were grouped by age and taught memorizable knowledge via a standardized curriculum that was conventionally tested. Much of this conventional "modernism" of our school systems persists through the actions of professionals and bureaucrats who look inward to the custom and certainty of their own expertise and routines rather than outward to the concerns of students, families, and communities.

Today's schools and school systems are a tragic example of what the Canadian political scientist Thomas Homer-Dixon calls an "ingenuity gap" in society.[57] Building on current thinking in geography, environmental studies, political science, and brain psychology,[58] Homer-Dixon argues that our world is increasingly complex, interdependent, and fast-paced—generating a profusion of urgent and unpredictable problems that demand instant and effective responses. Instantaneous and endless stock-market trading and speculation across the globe means that currency crises in Thailand or Argentina can immediately undermine confidence in economies elsewhere.

Global warming produced by carbon dioxide in one part of the planet, and the disappearance of rain forests in another, create floods and gales in a third. The frog population is disappearing everywhere, and we have no idea why. The world is more interdependent. So are its problems. In the computer age, more and more information and data are available to help people address and respond to these problems, but this information glut, or "data smog,"[59] can itself become part of the problem as it assails us in ever greater quantities with increasing rapidity. Stock-market traders and even advertising executives are getting younger, as the brains of only the young and the nimble can manage the multiple channels of data, ideas, and communications that make up their workplace. In organizations critical to society's economic well-being, key workers may be smarter and able to work faster but are less wise and less capable of drawing on experience and institutional memory to influence their judgment.

What the knowledge society needs, says Homer-Dixon, is lots of ingenuity. He defines *ingenuity* as

> ideas that can be applied to solve practical, technical and social problems, such as the problems that arise from water pollution, cropland erosion and the like. Ingenuity includes not only truly new ideas—often called "innovation"—but also ideas that though not fundamentally novel are nevertheless useful.[60]

Ideas, says Homer-Dixon, "are a factor of economic production just like labor and capital."[61] What matters is getting an "adequate flow of the right kind of ideas" and understanding the factors that govern that flow.[62] Ingenuity can be technical in dealing with the physical world or social in dealing with organizations, institutions, and communities. The fundamental problem, Homer-Dixon concludes, is that, although we need a greater supply of social ingenuity in particular in today's complex world, the ingenuity we can create is falling far short of the overwhelming demand for it. The "shortfall between" [the] "rapidly rising need for ingenuity [and its] "inadequate supply" is what Homer-Dixon means by the ingenuity gap.[63] Carnoy and Castells make the same point in their OECD position paper when they remark that "men's and women's work is being transformed by new technologies but the social institutions needed to support this change are lagging far behind."[64]

The integration (or non-integration) of information and computer technology into high schools provides a striking example of the failure of ingenuity in educational change. At one level, the growth of computer technology in schools has been phenomenal. As recently as the mid-1980s, when my children attended a highly innovative primary school in England, they were sent once or twice a week by their teacher to bring the solitary school computer on its trolley from the other side of the building—and they used it to work with small groups of peers, just 5 or 6 years old, to compose and redraft pieces of writing. In England and many other developed Western nations, almost every school is now directly wired to the Internet. The problems of technical ingenuity in using information technology in schools are no longer great. The major problems are with social and organizational ingenuity.

Elementary schools especially have often shown great ingenuity in putting computers into regular classrooms and integrating them within flexible processes of teaching and learning. In high schools, however, computers have usually been installed not in classrooms but in separate computer laboratories. Why? Because in this way, the traditional grammar of schooling—with its one-subject, one-teacher, one-class system—is left intact. Students' computer use is confined to special sessions during the week in which particular classes are all scheduled into the computer lab together, or to assignments that students undertake individually, after school, in their own time. The rest of the time, teaching and learning proceed as they have done for decades. The absent computer safely locked in its laboratory provides no challenge to them.

The regulations and routines of factories, monasteries, and self-perpetuating bureaucracies provide young people with poor preparation for a highly innovative, flexible, and team-based knowledge economy where routine is the enemy of risk.

TEACHING FOR THE KNOWLEDGE SOCIETY

What might it mean in practical terms for teachers to be catalysts of the knowledge society; to be the key agents who can bring it into being? How would this mandate affect their role, as well as their own and other people's understanding of what being a professional entails?

In general, as catalysts of successful knowledge societies, teachers must be able to build a special kind of professionalism. This cannot be the professionalism of old, in which teachers had the autonomy to teach in the ways they wished or that were most familiar to them. There is no value in reviving the Julie Andrews curriculum—"these are few of my favorite things"—in which teachers could teach anything they liked. Rather, teachers who are catalysts of the knowledge society must build a new professionalism where they:

- Promote deep cognitive learning;
- Learn to teach in ways they were not taught;
- Commit to continuous professional learning;
- Work and learn in collegial teams;
- Treat parents as partners in learning;
- Develop and draw on collective intelligence;
- Build a capacity for change and risk; and
- Foster trust in processes.

More and more governments, businesses, and educators are urging teachers in the knowledge society to commit themselves to standards-based learning in which all students (not just a few) achieve high standards of cognitive learning; they also create knowledge, apply it to unfamiliar problems, and communicate it effectively to others, instead of treating knowledge as something that students should simply memorize and regurgitate.[65] New approaches to learning necessitate new approaches to teaching. These include teaching that emphasizes higher-order thinking skills, metacognition (thinking about thinking), constructivist approaches to learning and understanding, brain-based learning, cooperative learning strategies, multiple intelligences and different "habits of mind," employing a wide range of assessment techniques, and using computer-based and other information technology that enables students to gain access to information independently.

For many teachers, the impact of new developments in the science of learning has meant learning to teach differently from how they were taught as students.[66] In the past, teachers learned the rudiments of teaching by watching the teachers who taught them. Teaching for today's knowledge society is technically more complex and wide-ranging than teaching has ever been. It draws on a base of research and experience about effective teaching that is always changing and expanding. Today's teachers therefore need to be committed to and continually engaged in pursuing, upgrading, self-monitoring, and reviewing their own professional learning. This includes but is not restricted to participating in face-to-face and virtual professional learning networks,[67] adopting continuous professional-development portfolios in which teachers accumulate and review their own professional learning,[68] consulting and critically applying the evidence of educational research so their practice is always informed by it,[69] undertaking action research and inquiry of their own, and connecting professional learning with levels of reward in teacher pay.[70]

Teachers can no longer take refuge in the basic premises of the pre-professional age: that teaching is managerially hard but technically simple; that once you have qualified to teach, you know the basics of teaching forever; and that from then on, teaching is something you work at improving by yourself, through trial and error, in your own classes. I would be horrified if my dentist approached his professional learning this way. From time to time, when my mouth is not stuffed with instruments and padding, I ask him how he goes about improving as a dentist over time. As he tells me to "open wide," I am relieved that he does not reveal that he improves mainly by trial and error and that, if his innovations do not generate shrieks of pain, he knows he is probably on the right track. Instead, he reports that he gets better by reading new research about dentistry, undertaking training in new technology or pain management, watching expert dentists practice at the hospital, and talking about dentistry with his colleagues.

If my dentist does not pursue his own learning, his insurance premiums skyrocket. He becomes a liability to his patients. Teachers who do not keep learning by more than trial and error are a liability to their students. For this reason, professional learning in teaching is an individual obligation as well as an institutional right.

Learning to improve as a teacher needs to look like learning to get better as a dentist—and more, because teachers work in large communities, not just among small groups of individuals. Gary Hoban argues that schools, like other workplaces, must become sophisticated professional learning systems that are organized and structured to encourage professional learning for teachers, so that it becomes an endemic and spontaneous part of their work.[71] In the complex, fast-changing knowledge society, teachers, like other workers, cannot work and learn entirely alone or in separate training courses after school. No one teacher knows enough to cope or improve by himself or herself. It is vital that teachers engage in action, inquiry, and problem-solving together in collegial teams or professional learning communities.[72] Through such teams, teachers can undertake joint curriculum development, respond effectively and creatively to external reform imperatives, engage in collaborative-action research, and analyze students' achievement data together in ways that benefit their students' learning.[73]

Knowledge economies and knowledge-economy organizations operate not just by sponsoring know-what, know-why, or know-how; they also operate by developing the capacities of what the OECD calls "know-who." Know-who involves the methods and dispositions of accessing explicit and tacit knowledge from others. In the OECD's words, "Know-who involves information about who knows what and who knows what to do. But it also involves the social ability to cooperate and communicate with different kinds of people and experts."[74]

Over the past decade, teachers in many countries have indeed become more expert at and experienced in working with their colleagues. They have helped to re-culture the profession so that working effectively with adults outside the classroom is as essential as working effectively with children within it. But while teachers have made great strides at developing learning relationships with their colleagues, they have been much less effective at doing so with parents. As we reach for higher standards and deeper learning in the knowledge society, treating parents as indispensable assets who support their children's learning is essential.[75] Some practical steps include developing interactive report cards, sharing computerized student- and school-performance data openly and instantly with parents, creating schemes that promote parents' involvement in their children's literacy, setting shared homework assignments to be undertaken by children and their parents together, and offering workshops to parents on new developments in curriculum, teaching, and learning.[76] Specific measures can vary. What matters in the knowledge society is that parents become part of the school's extended web of learning and that teachers extend their sense of professionalism to include and embrace these broader learning partnerships.

Developing and managing effective teamwork, problem-solving, and mutual learning among adults calls for a high degree of what Daniel Goleman calls *emotional intelligence*.[77] In his best-selling texts, Goleman argues that mastering a set of emotional competences significantly improves work performance and personal relationships. Emotional intelligence, he claims, adds value to cognitive intelligence. It distinguishes leaders who are stars from those who are merely adequate. The five basic competences that make up emotional intelligence are:

- Knowing and being able to express one's own emotions;
- Being able to empathize with others' emotions;
- Being able to monitor and regulate one's emotions so they do not get out of control;
- Having the capacity to motivate oneself and others; and
- Possessing the social skills to put the first four competences into action.

All these aspects of emotional intelligence enable workers and managers to motivate and improve their relationships with colleagues, to bounce back from adversity, to work through the difficulties and disappointing moments of change, to build high-performing teams, to solve problems effectively, to value the diverse learning styles and cultural backgrounds of teammates, and to resolve conflicts when they arise. Emotional intelligence is as important in a school classroom or staffroom as it is in a corporate office. Emotional competences, says Goleman, improve our organizations and relationships. In the knowledge society, they are an essential end of classroom learning, not just a context or climate for that learning. Emotional intelligence provides the emotional foundations for shared professional learning and teamwork among teachers.[78] This is why Michael Fullan and I explicitly advocate that teachers and leaders develop their own and others' emotional intelligence.[79]

Phillip Brown and Hugh Lauder expand this argument and claim that successful, high-skill knowledge economies depend on their societies' ability to create and pool what they call *collective intelligence:*

> Collective intelligence involves a transformation in the way we think about human capability. It suggests that all are capable rather than a few; that intelligence is multiple rather than a matter of solving puzzles with only one right answer; and that our human qualities for imagination and emotional engagement are as important as our ability to become technical experts.[80]

The development and pooling of collective intelligence, they say, "will . . . become the ultimate source of economic security in a global economy."[81] The key for the high-skill economy and its educational system is grasping that intelligence is not scarce, singular, fixed, and individual. Collective intelligence, rather, is universal, multiple, infinite, and shared. Schools that are learning organizations for everyone build the capacity to develop these essentials of collective intelligence.

The knowledge society is a changing society in which information expands rapidly and circulates continuously around the globe; money and capital flow in a restless and relentless search for new investment opportunities; organizations continually restructure themselves; government policies undergo volatile shifts as electorates become more and more capricious; and multicultural migration keeps reconstituting the communities in which we live. Schools are not immune to all of this, and in a constantly changing world with expanding knowledge, shifting communities, and volatile seesaw politics in education, teachers in the knowledge society must therefore develop and be helped to develop capacities for taking risks, dealing with change, and undertaking inquiries when new demands and novel problems repeatedly confront them.[82] There is no creativity without risk—the risk of trying a new idea, experimenting with an unfamiliar practice, being prepared to fail or look silly when trying something new, not taking setbacks to heart, being responsive rather than overly sensitive to critical feedback, working with and seeking advice from colleagues who are different as well as from colleagues who share one's convictions, and so on. If we are to encourage students to be risk-takers, teachers must be risk-takers, too. Teaching is not a place for shrinking violets, for the overly sensitive, for people who are more comfortable with dependent children than they are with independent adults. It is a job for grown-ups, requiring grown-up norms of how to work together.

In teaching, risk requires a special kind of trust in processes, as well as in people.[83] This *professional trust* is not a matter of passive blind faith in others. It involves active commitments to shared work, openness, and reciprocal learning.[84] This means teachers trusting people who may not be well known to them, who are not familiar friends, whose predictability and reliability have not been proved many times in the past. In large, complex, and rapidly changing organizations, it is not enough to trust and work closely with only small circles of friends, such as a well-liked team-teaching partner.[85]

In another study, in which I examined the emotional aspect of teachers' relationship with their colleagues, one of the strongest causes of positive emotion came when teachers' colleagues agreed with them, shared the same goals, completed each other's sentences, or felt as if they were in a marriage. What teachers disliked most was conflict with their colleagues. So they learned to avoid situations that might expose differences or provoke disagreement among them.[86]

Recently, I was taken to a game reserve in Africa. Our tracker stopped by a herd of impala. Nearby, we heard the blood-curdling call of a jackal. "Why's he howling?" we asked. "The jackal is calling for the cheetah," the tracker replied, "to show him where the game is." The cheetah needs the jackal to find his game. The jackal needs the cheetah to kill it for him. They need each other to survive. This collaborative animal behavior demonstrates the basics of professional trust.

If teachers want to make progress as professionals and have an impact in the complex world of schools, they must learn to trust and value colleagues who are distant and different from them as well as those who are the same. This professional trust moves people into the realm of the uncertain and unknown, and in that sense it "involves a willingness to take risks or to place oneself in a vulnerable situation."[87] Teamwork, learning from people who are different, sharing information openly—all of these essential ingredients of the knowledge society involve vulnerability, risk, and a willingness to trust that the processes of teamwork and partnership ultimately will work for the good of all, including oneself.

Professional learning can take many forms—informal learning from colleagues or more formal learning from data and evidence. David Hargreaves complains that the practice of teaching has not been as well grounded in research evidence as the practice of doctors.[88] This, he says, is partly a problem of the teacher culture that has looked askance at research evidence compared with teachers' own experiential judgements. However, it is also a fault of the educational research community, whose work often has little direct value for or accessibility to practitioners. More evidence-based or evidence-informed practice need not lead to dependence on and deference to outside research, though. Teachers themselves, says Hargreaves, can be more involved in teacher research than they have been. As strong communities, teachers can also have the competence and confidence to engage critically, not compliantly, with the research that informs their practice. In a knowledge society, evidence as well as experience must significantly inform schools' efforts to improve.

Teachers who are catalysts of the knowledge society must therefore try to make their schools into learning organizations where capacities to learn and structures that support learning and respond constructively to change are widespread among adults as well as children.[89] Schools that are good learning institutions for children must be effective learning organizations for teachers and leaders, too.[90] Chapter 5 will look in detail at a school that has been established deliberately as a learning organization.

In all, teaching in and for the knowledge society is concerned with sophisticated cognitive learning; an expanding and changing repertoire of research-informed teaching practices; continuous professional learning and self-monitoring; teamwork; learning partnerships with parents; developing and using collective intelligence; and cultivating a profession that values problem-solving, risk-taking, professional trust, coping with change, and committing to continuous improvement. In short, teaching for the knowledge economy fosters and thrives on:

- Creativity
- Flexibility
- Problem-solving
- Ingenuity
- Collective intelligence
- Professional trust
- Risk-taking
- Continuous improvement

Although they may be difficult to put into practice, these qualities seem to make up a set of professional virtues that are beyond argument. Who would not want learning and teaching to be like this? The problem, it would seem, is not adjudicating on the merits of these components. It is figuring out how to bring them into being. This is a dangerous and misleading assumption, though, as we shall see.

NOTES

1. Halsey, A. J., Floud, J. & Anderson, C. A., *Education, Economy and Society,* London, Collier-Macmillan, 1961.

2. Hobsbawm, E., *Age of Extremes: The Short Twentieth Century, 1914–1991,* London, Abacus, 1995.

3. Hargreaves, A., "Four Ages of Professionalism and Professional Learning," *Teachers and Teaching: Theory and Practice* 6(2), 2000, 151–182.

4. Fullan, M. & Stiegelbauer, S., *The New Meaning of Educational Change,* New York, Teachers College Press, 1991.

5. Tyack, D. & Tobin, W., The Grammar of Schooling and Why It Has Been So Hard to Change, *American Educational Research Journal* 31(3), 1994, 453–480.

6. Torres, R. M., *What Works in Education: Facing the New Century,* Buenos Aires, Argentina, International Youth Foundation, 2001; Bray, M., *Educational Planning in Small Countries* (research report), Paris, United Nations Educational, Scientific, and Cultural Organization (UNESCO), 1992.

7. Willinsky, J., *Learning to Divide the World: Education at Empire's End,* Minneapolis, University of Minnesota Press, 1998.

8. Hargreaves, *op. cit.,* note 3.

9. Hargreaves, A., The Significance of Classroom Coping Strategies, in L. Barton & R. Meighan (eds.), *Sociological Interpretations of Schooling and Classrooms: A Reappraisal,* Driffield, Nafferton Books, 1978; Woods, P., "Teaching for survival," in P. Woods & M. Hammersley (eds.), *School Experience,* London, Croom Helm, 1977.

10. Jencks, C., *et al., Inequality: A Reassessment of the Effect of Family and School in America,* New York, Basic Books, 1972.

11. Bernstein, B., *Class, Codes and Control* (vol. 3), London, Routledge & Kegan Paul, 1976.

12. Popkewitz, T., "Educational reform and its millennial quality: The 1980s," *Journal of Curriculum Studies* 18(3), 1986, 267–283.

13. National Commission on Excellence in Education, *A Nation at Risk: A Report to the Nation and the Secretary of Education,* Washington, DC, U.S. Department of Education, 1983.

14. Developments in the United Kingdom during this period are described more fully in Hargreaves, A. and Reynolds, D. (eds.), *Educational policy: Controversies and Critiques,* New York and Philadelphia, Falmer Press, 1989.

15. See Hargreaves, A., *Curriculum and Assessment Reform,* Milton Keynes, Open University Press, 1989; Goodson, I. F., Anstead, C. & Morgan, J. M., *Subject Knowledge: Readings for the Study of School Subjects,* London, Falmer Press/Routledge, 1998.

16. Stoll, L. & Myers, K., *No Quick Fixes: Perspectives on Schools in Difficulty*, London, Falmer Press, 1998.

17. Barlow, M. & Robertson, H. J., *Class Warfare: The Assault on Canada's Schools*, Toronto, Key Porter Books, 1994.

18. Organization for Economic Cooperation and Development (OECD), *Quality of Teaching*, Paris, OECD, 1994.

19. Dinham, S. & Scott, C. . *The Teacher 2000 Project: A Study of Teacher Motivation and Health*, Perth, University of Western Sydney, Nepean, 1997; Huberman, M. & Vandenberghe, R., "Introduction: Burnout and the teaching profession," in R. Vandenberghe & A. M. Huberman (eds.), *Understanding and Preventing Teacher Burnout: A Sourcebook of International Research and Practice* (pp. 1–13), Cambridge, Cambridge University Press, 1999.

20. Fujita, H. & Wang, S.-Y. (eds.), *Teacher Professionalism and the Culture of Teaching in Japan: The Challenge and Irony of Educational Reform and Social Change*, Tokyo, Tokyo University Press, 1997.

21. Jeffrey, B. & Woods, P., "Feeling deprofessionalized: The social construction of emotions during an OFSTED inspection," *Cambridge Journal of Education* 126(3), 1996, 235–343; Nias, J., "Changing times, changing identities: grieving for a lost self," in R. G. Burgess (ed.), *Educational Research and Evaluation: For Policy and Practice*, London, Falmer Press, 1991; Hargreaves, A. & Goodson, I., "Teachers' professional lives: Aspirations and actualities," in I. Goodson & A. Hargreaves (eds.), *Teachers' Professional Lives*, New York, Falmer Press, 1996.

22. Hargreaves, A., *Changing Teachers, Changing Times: Teachers' Work and Culture in the Postmodern Age*, London, Cassell and New York, Teachers College Press, 1994; Helsby, G., *Changing Teachers' Work and Culture*, Buckingham, Open University Press, 1998.

23. Shimahara, K., "Japanese lessons for educational reform," in A. Hargreaves & R. Evans (eds.), *Beyond Educational Reform*, Buckingham, Open University Press, 1997.

24. These trends are widely remarked on in many contemporary texts, but among the most thorough documentation of the evidence is Castells, M., *The Rise of the Network Society*, Oxford, Blackwell, 1996.

25. Wylie, C., *Self-Managing Schools in New Zealand: The Fifth Year*, Wellington, New Zealand Council for Educational Research, 1994; Whitty, G., Power, S. & Halpin, D., *Devolution and Choice in Education: The School, State, the Market*, Buckingham, Open University Press, 1998.

26. This is described and documented in Castells, M., *End of Millennium*, Oxford, Blackwell, 1998.

27. Bell, D., *The Coming of Post-industrial Society*, New York, Basic Books, 1976.

28. Ibid., p. 212.

29. Ibid., p. 242.

30. Handy, C., *The Empty Raincoat: Making Sense of the Future*, London, Hutchison Press, 1994; Carnoy, M. & Castells, M., "Sustainable flexibility: A prospective study on work, family and society in the information age," *OECD Working Papers*, 5(29), 1997, OECD, Paris.

31. Drucker, P., *Post-capitalist Society*, New York, HarperCollins, 1993, p. 8.

32. Castells, *op. cit.,* note 24; Castells, M., *The Power of Identity,* Oxford, Blackwell, 1997; Castells, *op. cit.,* note 26.

33. Castells, *op. cit.,* note 24, pp. 16–17.

34. Rankin, I., *The Falls,* London, Orion Books, 2001, p. 372.

35. Rifkin, J., *The Age of Access: The New Culture of Hypercapitalism Where All Life Is a Paid-For Experience,* New York, J. P. Tarcher/Putnam Books, 2000.

36. Reich, R., *The Future of Success,* New York, Alfred Knopf, 2001.

37. Ibid., p. 49.

38. Ibid., p. 41.

39. Ibid., p. 58.

40. Senge, P., *The Fifth Discipline: The Art and Practice of the Learning Organization,* New York, Doubleday, 1990; Nonaka, I. & Takeuchi, H., *The Knowledge-Creating Company: How Japanese Companies Create the Dynamics of Innovation,* New York, Oxford University Press, 1995; Leonard-Barton, D., *Wellsprings of Knowledge: Building and Sustaining Sources of Innovation,* Boston, Harvard Business School Press, 1995; Leadbeater, C., *The Weightless Society: Living in the New Economy Bubble,* New York and London, Texere, 2000.

41. Reich, *op. cit.,* note 36, p. 64.

42. Castells, *op. cit.,* note 24.

43. The information is available on the Santa Fe Institute's Web site. Available at: <http://www.santafe.edu/sfi/indexPublications.html>.

44. Castells, *op. cit.,* note 24.

45. Carnoy & Castells, *op. cit.,* note 30, p. 33.

46. One of the first writers to discuss the idea of knowledge workers in educational contexts was Schlechty, P., *Schools for the Twenty-First Century: Leadership Imperatives for Educational Reform,* San Francisco, Jossey-Bass, 1990.

47. Drucker, P., "The age of social transformation," *Atlantic Monthly* 27, 1994, 53–80.

48. OECD, *Knowledge Management in the Learning Society,* Paris, OECD, 2000, p. 29.

49. OECD, *Schooling for Tomorrow: What Schools for the Future?* Paris, OECD, 2001, p. 29.

50. Fullan, M., *Change Forces: Probing the Depths of Educational Reform,* London, Falmer Press, 1993, p. 80.

51. Castells, *op. cit.,* note 24, p. 345.

52. Giddens, A., *The Third Way,* Cambridge, Polity Press, 1998.

53. Caldwell, B. & Spinks, J., *Leading the Self-Managing School,* London, Falmer Press, 1992.

54. Gopinathan, S. & Sharpe, S., "The teacher is the key: Professionalism and the strategic state," in E. Thomas (ed.), *Teacher Education: Dilemmas and Prospects, World Yearbook of Education,* London, Kogan Page, 2002.

55. Brown, P. & Lauder, H., *Capitalism and Social Progress: The Future of Society in a Global Economy,* Basingstoke, Hampshire, and New York, Palgrave, 2001.

56. Hargreaves, *op. cit.,* note 22.

57. Homer-Dixon, T., *The Ingenuity Gap: Can We Solve the Problems of the Future?* Toronto, Alfred A. Knopf, 2000.

58. For example, Harvey, D., *The Condition of Postmodernity,* Oxford, Blackwell, 1989. These and other texts on the growing complexity of society in the postmodern age and its implication for schools are described more fully in Hargreaves, *op. cit.,* note 22.

59. Shank, D., *Data Smog: Surviving the Information Glut,* New York, Harper-Collins, 1997.

60. Homer-Dixon, *op. cit.,* note 57, p. 21.

61. Ibid.

62. Ibid.

63. Ibid., p. 1.

64. Carnoy & Castells, *op. cit.,* note 30, p. 9.

65. For development of this argument and of evidence related to it, see Hargreaves, A., Earl, L., Moore, S. & Manning, S., *Learning to Change: Teaching Beyond Subjects and Standards,* San Francisco, Jossey-Bass/Wiley, 2001.

66. McLaughlin, M. & Talbert, J., *Professional Communities and the Work of High School Teaching,* Chicago, University of Chicago Press, 2001.

67. Lieberman, A. & Wood, D., "From network learning to classroom teaching," *Journal of Educational Change* 3(3–4), 2002.

68. Day, C., *Developing Teachers: The Challenges of Lifelong Learning,* London, Falmer Press, 1998.

69. Hargreaves, D., "Revisiting educational research: Past lessons and future prospects," in M. Fielding (ed.), *Taking Education Really Seriously: Four Years' Hard Labor,* London, Routledge/Falmer Press, 2001.

70. West, M., "Reforming teachers' pay," in Fielding, *op. cit.,* note 69.

71. Hoban, G., *Teacher Learning for Educational Change: A Systems Thinking Approach,* Buckingham, Open University Press, in press.

72. McLaughlin & Talbert, *op. cit.,* note 66.

73. Newmann, F., & Wehlage, G., *Successful School Restructuring,* Madison, WI, Center on Organization and Restructuring of Schools, 1995.

74. OECD, *op. cit.,* note 48, p. 15.

75. Epstein, J., "Perspectives and previews on research and policy for school, family and community partnerships," in A. Booth & J. Dunn (eds.), *Family–School Links: How Do They Affect Educational Outcomes?* (pp. 204–246), Hillsdale, NJ, Lawrence Erlbaum Associates, 1996.

76. These strategies are discussed more fully in Hargreaves, A. & Fullan, M., *What's Worth Fighting for Out There?* Toronto, Elementary Teachers Federation of Ontario; New York, Teachers College Press; and Buckingham, Open University Press, 1998.

77. Goleman, D., *Emotional Intelligence,* New York, Bantam Books, 1995; Goleman, D., *Working with Emotional Intelligence,* New York, Bantam Books, 1998.

78. Day, *op. cit.,* note 68.

79. Hargreaves & Fullan, *op. cit.,* note 76.

80. Brown & Lauder, *op. cit.,* note 55, p. 8.

81. Ibid., 10.

82. Fullan, *op. cit.*, note 50; Fullan, M., *Change Forces: The Sequel,* London, Falmer/Routledge Press, 1999; Stoll, L., Earl, L. & Fink, D., *It's about Learning: It's about Time,* London, Falmer Press, 2002.

83. Hargreaves & Fullan, *op. cit.*, note 76. Discussions about changes in the experience of trust in society were first raised in Giddens, A., *Modernity and Self-Identity,* Cambridge, Polity Press, 1990. For an extended discussion of the collapse of traditional forms of trust in contemporary society, read Fukuyama, F., *Trust: The Social Virtues and the Creation of Prosperity* (3rd ed.), New York, Free Press, 2000. See also Hargreaves, A., "Teaching and betrayal," *Teachers and Teaching: Theory and Practice,* in press.

84. Sachs, J., *The Activist Teaching Profession,* Buckingham, Open University Press, 2003.

85. Hargreaves, D., "The new professionalism: The synthesis of professional and institutional development," *Teaching and Teacher Education* 10(4), 1994, 423–438; Fielding, M., "Radical collegiality: Affirming teaching as an inclusive professional practice," *Australian Educational Researcher* 26(2), 1999, 1–33.

86. Hargreaves, A., "The emotional geographies of teachers' relations with colleagues," *International Journal of Educational Research* 35(5), 2001, 503–527.

87. Toole, J., *Framing the Role of Trust in School Reform: Case Studies of Service Learning,* Paper presented at the American Educational Research Association, New Orleans, April 2000.

88. Hargreaves, D., "The production, mediation and use of professional knowledge among teachers and doctors: A comparative analysis," in OECD, *op. cit.*, note 48.

89. The classic works on learning organizations are Senge, P., *The Fifth Discipline: The Art and Practice of the Learning Organization,* New York, Doubleday, 1990; and Senge, P., Cambron-McCabe, N., Lucas, T., Smith, B., Dutton, J. & Kleiner, A., *Schools That Learn: A Fifth Discipline Fieldbook for Educators, Parents, and Everyone Who Cares about Education,* New York, Doubleday/Currency, 2000.

90. See Barthes, R., *Improving Schools from Within: Teachers, Parents and Principals Can Make a Difference,* San Francisco, Jossey-Bass, 1990; Crowther, F., Kaagan, S., Hann, L. & Ferguson, M., *Developing Teacher Leaders: How Teacher Leadership Enhances School Success,* Thousand Oaks, CA, Corwin Press, 2002.

2

TEACHING BEYOND
THE KNOWLEDGE SOCIETY
Dealing with Insecurity

THE SOUTH SEA BUBBLE

Three centuries ago, in 1711, a business called the South Sea Company was established to assume 10 million pounds of Great Britain's national debt, at 6 percent interest. In exchange, the company was granted a monopoly by the British government to trade in the South Seas. In these times preceding the voyages of Charles Darwin and the explorations of Captain James Cook, the very notion of the South Seas conjured up exotic images to the British of distant worlds where unimaginable trading opportunities could be had. Investors began to be lured by the company with grand ideas that the solid and reliable products of English manufacturing could be exchanged for bounteous Spanish gold from the South American continent. This international alchemy promised to convert iron and cloth into gold and silver, and it captured the public imagination—particularly when the British government offered to pay off its debt to people in South Sea Company shares. The value of the company's shares soon rose dramatically, and in less than a decade their market value had increased tenfold.

The prospects of increased wealth flowing from South Seas ventures seemed imminent and instant, and anyone who could began to invest. Numerous other companies quickly emerged to feed this frenzy of speculation. Some promised mining for gold, others offered trading in silk and tobacco, more than a few held out the most evanescent prospects—for transmuting quicksilver into a malleable fine metal, creating a wheel for perpetual motion and, most improbably of all, "for carrying on an undertaking of great advantage: but nobody to know what it is."[1] This period of delirious, widespread speculation in ventures of questionable substance and merit came to be known as the "South Sea bubble."

In practice, the trading realities fell far short of their grandiose publicity. The king of Spain restricted trading in South America to just three British shiploads per year. The promised fountain of wealth was never more than a trickle. The South Sea Company did not produce a real profit; neither did many of the companies that rode briefly on its coattails. By 1720, the over-reaching of speculative investment and the dawning realization that the South Sea companies would produce little of any consequence became evident to almost everyone. Quickly and desperately, those who could withdrew what remained of their investments.

Just nine years after its emergence, the South Sea bubble finally burst. By December 1720, the South Sea Company's shares had returned to their original value. Thousands of people suffered financial ruin. In his ballad on the issue, the satirist Jonathan Swift proclaimed:

> *Thus the deluded Bankrupt raves;*
> *Puts all upon a desp'rate Bett*
> *Then plunges in the Southern Waves,*
> *Dipt over Head and Ears—in Debt.*[2]

This historical episode of speculative excess has a ring of disturbing familiarity. Get-rich-quick motivations; extravagant company claims; businesses that fail to make a profit and have not yet produced anything; investments based on vague prospects and exaggerated promises; and an unshakable, widespread belief that profits will rise forever in a new era of endless prosperity—these are the characteristics of all investment bubbles. The railroad mania of the nineteenth century, the property boom of the late 1980s, and now the information or knowledge revolution of the twenty-first century—these are all speculative bubbles, too.

Optimistic bias is the typical accompaniment to technological innovation. In his best-selling autobiography of his childhood in 1920s Blackburn, in the north of England, William Woodruff describes the moment that his Uncle Eric became the first person in the town to have electricity. Family, neighbors, and crowds of the curious flocked to his house to see it. After the lights had been switched on, somebody demanded a speech:

> Never stuck for words, a beaming uncle Eric began by saying that "eeelectricity" was going to change all our lives. There was no telling the wonders it would bring. With the help of "eeelectricity," things would buck up for everybody. None of us would have to work anymore. Electricity would do it for us. In the golden age of electricity that lay ahead, we'd all be rich. Strikes

and lock-outs, hunger and poverty were going to be things of the past. Progress would come if we all used our 'eads.[3]

One of the first studies of the South Sea bubble, *Extraordinary Popular Delusions and the Madness of Crowds,* concluded that

> in times of great commercial prosperity there has been a tendency to over-speculation on several occasions since then. The success of the one project generally produces others of a similar kind. Popular initiatives will always, in a trading nation, seize hold of such successes and drag a community too anxious for profits into an abyss from which extrication is difficult.[4]

THE KNOWLEDGE AND INFORMATION BUBBLE

All investment bubbles eventually burst—with dramatic and sometimes cataclysmic consequences. When we talk about the future of the knowledge society, we will, if we do not remember and learn from the fate of previous investment bubbles, be condemned to repeat their tragic history, as the philosopher George Santayana warned us.

In the late 1990s, the possibilities of the new knowledge society seemed limitless. The information society and knowledge economy appeared to represent a new age of optimism and opportunity. All indications pointed to a massive expansion in information and entertainment technology. By the early 1990s, for example, one in three Canadian adolescents had access to a personal computer at home.[5] By the end of the century, the proportion had increased to half.[6] In the second half of the 1990s, the advent of Netscape, then Microsoft's Internet Explorer, provided mass access to electronic communication and information gathering. From being an esoteric network of scholastic interchange among university researchers in the 1980s, e-mail turned into a mass-communication system in which people could connect from home with family, friends, and associates around the world.

By the late 1990s, the information investment bubble was expanding like a hot air balloon. Internet businesses were exchanged and appropriated for millions of dollars, even before they had traded for a single day. Technological innovations and services were increasing and diversifying at a phenomenal rate as inventions leapfrogged each other in a quest to create and capture the leading edge of consumer desire, and to outpace business competitors.

However, doubts began to creep in about whether this galloping consumption of new technology was really improving people's lives or relationships. Neil Postman contended that information technology gave us poor information, incorrect information, and far too much information altogether.[7] It did not give us any intellectual or moral guidance about which information we should select or how we should evaluate it all.

The reformed Internet addict Clifford Stoll complained that computers made us lose the ability to enter into spontaneous interaction with real people.[8] In England, mobile phones actually *increased* interaction within families—a sad commentary on how episodic strings of tiny interactions are replacing sustained family conversations and relationships. In a survey of female adolescents, the Guides (or Girl Scouts) Association of Britain discovered that teenage girls spent more time sending text messages to one another than engaging in face-to-face conversation with families and friends.[9] In airports and other public spaces, people with mobile-phone headset attachments walk around, talking aloud and alone like paranoid schizophrenics, oblivious to their immediate surroundings. Introspection is a disappearing art. An endless in-rush of e-mails and mobile messages makes us feel in demand, but it also demands quick responses that lead us to react rather than relate.

The knowledge society increasingly threatens to move us into a world that offers neither solitude nor community. Excessive use of computers and other technology is being linked with rising rates of childhood obesity and other disorders.[10] Walking or cycling to school is becoming an uncool anachronism.

The so-called knowledge society has immersed young people in a culture of "real virtuality"[11] where CDs, mobile phones, computers, video games and multichannel TV become their increasingly dominant reality. This world of digitized entertainment technology is one in which, in the words of a Bruce Springsteen' song, "There's 57 channels and there's nothing on!" The knowledge society in many ways is more of an entertainment society in which fleeting images, instant pleasure, and minimal thought have us "amusing ourselves to death."[12] Emotions are extracted from this time-starved world of shrinking relationships and reinvested in consumable things.[13] Advertising associates automobiles with passion and desire and mobile phones with inspiration and lust.

In the consumer-centered knowledge economy, choice for most people is inversely related to significance. Globalization has made the economic policies of developed nations look increasingly alike. Waging war against impoverished peoples arouses little dissent. Most people are left with a wealth of choice only in the colors for their cars, the options for their mobile phones, or the toppings on their pizza.[14] Much of the knowledge explosion in this sense is a gaseous one, where style prevails over substance, where most people have choice only of life's inessentials, where "all that is solid melts into air."[15]

Despite these warning signs of unease and excess, the knowledge economy at the turn of the century continued on its breathtaking upward curve. In the last years of the century, stock-market indices rose to dizzying all-time highs, largely driven by the continuing surge in technology stocks. Apart from fears of a Y2K computer catastrophe, most millennial talk was upbeat, not doom-ridden. President Clinton spoke optimistically about building a bridge to the twenty-first century, and when fireworks exploded triumphantly from city to city as the new millennium dawned across the globe, the future for the developed economies, at least, was brimming with hope.

As a Peter, Paul and Mary 1960s pop song proclaimed, however, "too much of nothing makes a man feel ill at ease." In the opening months of the new century, the knowledge-economy bubble began to burst. Its rhetoric had always been exaggerated—not just in sweeps of hyperbole, but also in distorted contrasts with the past. Advocates and analysts of the new knowledge economy typically describe and deride how the "old," industrial, rust-belt economy involved work that was heavy, dirty, and dull. The new information economy, meanwhile, is said to be built on work that is light (even "weightless"), clean, flexible, and constantly changing.[16]

This kind of "contrastive rhetoric"[17] persuades us that the changes we are making from old to new, heavy to light, and dirty to clean are ones of progress. Yet in the old industrial economy, not everyone was doing dirty work. Owners, managers, clerks, stenographers, and many shopkeepers did little or no heavy lifting. Similarly, trapped at the base of today's knowledge economy are millions of workers who flip burgers, flex their muscles in the security industry, and endure the machine shops and sweatshops of less-developed economies. Some researchers contend that it is these jobs, not the e-commerce occupations of "weightless" work, that have been expanding most rapidly in the knowledge economy.[18] It takes millions of uncelebrated under-laborers to support the "weightless" work of the privileged in the West.

The knowledge-economy bubble was punctured in the opening months of 2001. Internet businesses began to fade or fold—travel companies, booksellers, e-commerce of all kinds. Large electronics and communications companies such as Ericsson, Nokia, and Marconi—the icons of a prosperous information society—announced projected or actual losses and layoffs. Nortel, Canada's largest global communications company, saw its stock value fall by 90 percent in a few short months. The year 2000 was the first in history in which worldwide computer sales fell. Economic-growth forecasts were projected at below 1 percent per annum. The world was on the edge of a recession, and despite political statements of reassurance and successive cuts in interest rates, investors began to sense the end of an era. Eventually, inexorably, the stock market started to plummet, affecting not only investment tycoons and great speculators but also ordinary people's savings, pensions, confidence, and security. America's leading financial indicator, the Dow Jones Industrial Average, fell some 20 percent between the fall 2000 and fall 2001. The Nasdaq, the index of high-tech shares at the leading edge of the informational economy, lost 70 percent of its value.

Many people might have wished they had heeded Machiavelli's warning in *The Prince* (1532) that "it is a common defect in men, not to consider in good weather the possibility of a tempest."[19] The prosperity brought by the information era, like that of any era, was never going to be infinite. Those who believed or proselytized to the contrary were fakes or fools.

FROM INFORMATION TO INSECURITY

On September 11, 2001, around 8:00 A.M., thousands of eager investment analysts, successful stockbrokers, bankers, traders, security guards, and secretaries made their way on the New York subway, on the city's harbor ferries, and in its yellow cabs to southern Manhattan. The offices that awaited them filled 220 vast floors in the twin towers of the World Trade Center, where more than half the world's financial and market business was transacted. Routinely, unremarkably, the global economy was reopening for another day of business.

Two hundred miles up the eastern seaboard, in Boston, barely more than 100 passengers on two commercial airliners were boarding their flights to Los Angeles. The passengers included parents and children, people visiting their families, schoolteachers, successful executives in high-tech companies, and—mainly up front, in business class, next to the cockpit—ten fiercely determined hijackers. Shortly after takeoff, armed only with box cutters and bravado, the terrorists seized the controls of the two aircraft. In a swift and callously synchronized operation, they turned the planes south and headed them directly toward the city of New York.

At 8:45, as elevators were ascending, offices were filling, and breakfast meetings were in mid-flow, the first plane ploughed into the upper decks of the first World Trade Center tower. This sedate civilian aircraft had been transformed into a deadly killing machine. Just eighteen minutes later, with the instant eyes of CNN already broadcasting the scene to the world, the second plane tore the very heart out of the remaining tower. Across the globe, millions watched helplessly as television screens showed the towers buckle and implode—the twin icons of global enterprise and American self-regard reduced to rubble.

The pictures portraying the aftermath of this attack were apocalyptic. The charred facades of the seven remaining floors of the World Trade Center hung like twisted skeletons in architectural agony over the devastated remains that were quickly called Ground Zero, the name first given to the site of the atomic bomb dropped on Japan. Americans now recycled this grim phrase to describe the site of their own particular horror.

The scale of human catastrophe was colossal. Thousands of people perished in the New York carnage alone. One of them was a young man named Thomas More Brennan, after whom my chair at Boston College has been renamed. Those who survived lost scores of friends and colleagues. Companies had their entire operations obliterated. Of 1,000 staff members in a New York bond-trading company, for example, 700 lost their lives.[20]

Business was immediately paralyzed. The New York Stock Exchange closed for an entire week. When it did resume trading, the Dow Jones Industrial Average plummeted by 14 percent. For several days, the U.S. skies were empty of civilian traffic as all airports were closed, leaving passengers stranded from Asia to South America and outposts in the Arctic. Airline reservations later dropped by half, and major airlines announced immediate layoffs of more than 20 percent. National airlines with distinguished reputations ceased to exist. In the shadow of terrorism and in the face of intrusive security, travel has become an inconvenient burden and frequent-flyer points a heavily devalued currency. Economic globalization may not have been completely halted by the tragic events of September 11, but business slowed, confidence sagged, and the world was accelerated into its already impending recession.

Globalization and technology did not make the United States invulnerable to this terrible assault. In the aftermath of the attacks, analysts were critical of the FBI's and CIA's overconfidence in high-technology surveillance at the expense of more traditional forms of human undercover intelligence. Airlines and airports were condemned for having put security operations out to private contract—paying low-skill people minimum wage to perform a publicly vital job. The principles of the flexible economy catastrophically compromised public safety, placing airline clients and the nation's citizens in mortal danger.

September 11 was a day on which Americans realized that the borders of their oceans, their tools of technological surveillance, and their unsurpassed military might could not make their nation impregnable in the face of the globalization of terror. The United States was no longer only the originator of globalized markets, knowledge, and information. It had become the target of another kind of globalization that moved the world in a few short minutes from the optimistic age of information to an anxiety-ridden age of insecurity.

Organizational-change theorists usually describe the age we are in as one of uncertainty, complexity, or risk. These words highlight the ambiguities of globalization, flexible economies, and rapid change, warning people about the threats but urging them to embrace the opportunities. Unlike uncertainty, the idea of insecurity points less ambiguously to the disturbing human consequences of globalization.

In the age of insecurity, as L. Elliott and D. Atkinson call it,[21] people experience increasing job and pension insecurity, environmental degradation, the collapse of welfare safety nets, the erosion of supportive communities and relationships, and the growing threat of crime and violence to their physical and psychic safety. This affects people's basic capacity to trust others, to rely on their relationships, and to not spend their lives looking over their shoulders.[22] It creates a society of suspicious minds. John Vail argues that

> the rise in insecurity in contemporary society . . . has been immensely destructive of human potential and social justice. Insecurity damages individual lives, it destroys self worth and self-esteem, and it has generated intolerable levels of fear, anxiety, hopelessness and powerlessness.[23]

The pervasive insecurity that accompanies globalization amounts to more than issues of personal safety and national security[24]—locks on the doors, cameras in the shopping mall, walls around the community, and barriers to discourage immigrants. Governments in the global economy have had "the inclination to trade off a lot of security (economic, environmental and social as well as physical) in exchange for removing more and more constraints cramping the exercise of free choice."[25] The result has been displacement of support and protection away from governments onto individual citizens. This has created an unacceptable redistribution of risk and accompanying insecurity across the entire population.[26] Unlike uncertainty or complexity, widespread insecurity is not an unavoidable state of being. It is a political choice in the knowledge society. As Chapter 3 will show, this insecurity extends into the work and world of teaching itself.

FUNDAMENTALISM OR COSMOPOLITAN IDENTITY

It is important to understand what was behind the terrible violence of September 11, beyond sheer wickedness, hatred, and envy. In his disturbingly prophetic book *Jihad vs. McWorld,* Benjamin Barber argued that our future depended on a struggle between two opposed globalizing influences. Both of these were indifferent to civil liberties and undermined the democratic nation-state.[27] On the one hand, what he called McWorld pursued the "bloodless economics of profit" in which people's interests only as private consumers were explicitly addressed while their concerns as citizens, who were part of the public good, were thrown to one side.[28] On the other, the opposing force of Jihad pursued a "bloody politics of identity, . . . rooted in exclusion and hatred," in which the tribe was the arbiter of all truth.[29] The moguls and managers of McWorld, said Barber, painted its future as

> a busy portrait of onrushing economic, technological and ecological forces that demand uniformity and integration and that mesmerize people everywhere with fast music, fast computers and fast food—MTV, Macintosh or McDonald's—pressing nations into one homogeneous . . . McWorld tied together by communications, information, entertainment and commerce.[30]

However, Barber continued, McWorld is actually a kind of global theme park where standardized goods and services are delivered swiftly with choices of only optional extras. In McWorld,

> everything is for sale and someone else is always responsible and there are no common goals or public interests and . . . everyone is equal as long as they can afford the price of admission and are content to watch and consume.[31]

McWorld follows the logic and principles of a market that observes no higher moral order beyond itself. Not that markets are wrong or bad; we just should not expect too much of them. Markets are excellent at stimulating economic growth, innovation, and consumer choice. George Soros, the international philanthropist and financier, acknowledges the economic value of markets. Yet he also argues that "markets are amoral: they allow people to act in accordance with their interests—but they pass no moral judgments on the interests themselves." By leaving right and wrong out of the account, "markets allow people to pursue their interests without hindrance," he says. But despite the great economic benefits of this, "the untrammeled pursuit of self-interest does not necessarily serve the common interest" of the public good.[32]

Commerce can find ways to be moral but only when morality serves or does not threaten its interests. Do not expect automobile manufacturers to promote public transportation, warns Barber. Beer companies may promote moderation but draw the line at advocating abstinence. Pharmaceutical companies would not spontaneously slash their profit margins so that the tens of millions of Africans who are casualties of the AIDS/HIV pandemic could have access to the drugs that could save them. Corporations need not be made to feel too guilty about protecting their own interests. They are simply not designed to promote the public good. As John Kenneth Galbraith and numerous other economists have pointed out, it is the prime job of democratic governments, communities, and voluntary-sector organizations to do that.[33]

When the financial sector has created and driven the agendas of international policy organizations, it has done so less to serve the public interest and common good of all people in less-developed nations than to create open borders and markets for business advantage.[34] The reluctance of international banks to forgive debt in less-developed nations creates realities and emotions of exclusion among the people of those countries. The knowledge economy is widening the gap between developed and less-developed economies and between the rich and the poor within those countries.[35] Exclusion from the benefits of the knowledge economy by the prosperous West creates feelings of hopelessness, envy, resentment, anger, and hatred among the starving and the poor. These are the seedbeds in which withdrawal, opposition, resistance, and even terror start to grow. Alain Michel, the inspector-general of France's educational system, puts it this way:

> Globalization, because of the risks it brings of soulless standardization, can lead to fragmentation and a reduced sense of belonging to a wider community. The excesses of unbridled markets, in which prices and the market are more important than social or cultural relationships, are being met with a reaction of narrow nationalism, regionalism and parochialism.[36]

At the turn of the twenty-first century, those whom globalization had excluded began to vent their anger, demand their share, make their presence felt. They filled the streets of Seattle, Genoa, and Quebec City with chaos and disorder as they protested at the World Trade and Group of 7 (G7) summits. Refugees trudged across the Sahara and lined the shores of North Africa, pressing their black-skinned bodies against the affluent edge of Europe as they sought illegal passage. And in England, white working-class youths incited race riots in the old textile towns of the industrial northwest that had been left hopelessly behind by the "cool Britannia" of England's prosperous south.

The paradox of globalization, as I have called it, is that economic globalization and homogenization lead many of those who cannot share in its benefits to turn inward to culture, religion, and ethnicity as alternative sources of meaning and identity.[37] The extreme expression of this response is Jihad.

For Barber, Jihad is a second powerful force of globalization and the very antithesis of McWorld. *Jihad* is an Islamic term that refers to religious struggle on behalf of faith against the faithless. In its strongest political manifestation, argues Barber, "it means holy war on behalf of partisan identity that is metaphysically defined and fanatically defended."[38] Jihad arises from Islam but is not essential to or normal within it. Yet it gives focus and direction to those who struggle against what they regard as the culturally corrupting influences of Western market values, modernization, and moral degradation.[39] Jihad is a fundamentalist force, resting on what its subscribers believe to be given, incontrovertible truths that cannot be negotiated and discussed. Supporters of Jihad defend their fundamentalism in the fundamental way: by recourse to assertion and authority, not reason and debate.[40] Jihad shows intolerance toward other faiths and forms of life and expresses this in violence and hatefulness when its own form of life is threatened. It is a refuge for those without hope in this life. Through self-sacrifice, it provides hope and meaning for them in the life beyond and for the people in this one that they leave behind. Jihad seeks to be the nemesis of the knowledge society, attacking the lifestyles of others and destroying the learning of its own, especially its women.

In his chillingly prophetic conclusion to *The Rise of the Network Society*, Manuel Castells issued a disturbing diagnosis and a somber warning. The diagnosis:

> In the Information Age, the prevailing logic of dominant global networks is so pervasive and so penetrating that the only way out of their domination appears to be out of those networks, and to reconstruct meaning on the basis of an entirely distinct system of values and beliefs. . . . Religious fundamentalism does not reject technology but puts it at the service of God's law, to which all institutions and purposes must submit without possible bargaining.[41]

This was followed by a warning about how the world's excluded might set about excluding their excluders:

> Because the whole world is, and will increasingly be, intertwined in the basic structures of life, under the logic of the network society, opting out by people and countries will not be a peaceful withdrawal. It takes and will take the form of fundamentalist affirmation of an alternative set of values and principles of existence, under which no coexistence is possible with the evil system that so deeply damages people's lives. As I write, in the streets of Kabul, women are beaten for improper dress by the courageous warriors of the Taliban. This is not in accordance with the humanistic teachings of Islam. There is, however, an explosion of fundamentalist movements that take up the Qu'ran, the Bible or any holy text, to interpret it and use it as a banner of their despair and a weapon of their rage. *Fundamentalisms of different kinds and from different sources will represent the most daring, uncompromising challenge to one-sided domination of informational, global capitalism. Their potential access to weapons of mass extermination casts a giant shadow on the optimistic prospects of the information age.*[42]

The social theorist and political adviser Anthony Giddens points out that, in reacting to Western decadence, fundamentalism also rejects democratic reason, emotional democracy between women and men, and the principles of what he calls *cosmopolitan identity*. Writing before September 11, Giddens predicted that

> the battleground of the twenty-first century will pit fundamentalism against cosmopolitan tolerance. In a globalizing world, . . . we are all regularly in contact with others who think differently, and live differently from ourselves. Cosmopolitans welcome and embrace this cultural complexity. Fundamentalists find it disturbing and dangerous. Whether in the areas of religion, ethnic identity or nationalism, they take refuge in a renewed and purified tradition—and, quite often, violence.[43]

Note that the forces of Jihad extend beyond one religious base, and even beyond religion altogether, to any intolerant, violently articulated forms of cultural or national meaning and faith. Most fundamentalisms represent powerful forces of resistance to the culturally and spiritually flattening influences of McDonaldization and McWorld, as well as to democracy and cosmopolitan identity.[44] Nor are these forms of resistance confined any longer to corners of the world safely removed from the dominant centers of the West—to ethnic cleansing in Eastern Europe, tribal conflict in Africa, or suicide bombings in the Middle East. When the Pentagon was penetrated and the World Trade Center collapsed, globalization came home to America

armed not with weapons of mass destruction but with a bunch of box cutters and the supreme self-sacrifice of fanatically desperate men. America had
to start to take the rest of the world more seriously.

The point is not whether we are for or against globalization. Inwardness,
protectionism, and xenophobia are not only undesirable but also impracti-
cal in a world of extensive migration and instant communication that
respects no barriers of time or space. What is at issue are the kinds of globalization we support. Through its participation in the World Trade and G7
summits, for example, the United States has strongly supported and promoted *economic* globalization. At the same time, it refused to be a signatory
to the Kyoto Protocol on World Climate Change in March 2001. It will not
observe the principles of the International Criminal Court. It has largely
withheld military spending on overseas missions other than those that
directly protect U.S. interests. The United States has demonstrated little
recent commitment to environmental or humanitarian responsibility on a
global scale for its own sake. Canada did little better on the environment,
signing the Kyoto agreement only when it could wriggle out of its pollu-
tion-reduction targets by having its existing forests counted as environmental credits.

Globalization is clearly suffering from a vast morality deficit. Soros argues
that

> the lesson we have to learn from September 11 is that morality has to play a
> larger role in international affairs. The asymmetric threats that confront us
> arise out of the asymmetry . . . [of] globalization. We have global markets but
> we do not have a global society. And we cannot build a global society with-
> out taking account of moral considerations.[45]

Soros does not advocate abolishing international economic organizations.
Instead, he proposes creating equally strong global, social, and humanitarian ones—as in the Marshall Plan of social reconstruction after World War
II. He urges the United States to take an interest in the rest of the world not
just when its own interests are at stake. As President John F. Kennedy put
it, increased development aid is necessary "not to defeat communism, not
to win votes, but because it is right."[46] It is not just religious fundamentalists who need to develop stronger cosmopolitan identity; the nations who
are threatened by them need to do so, too.

In an open society and a safe free world, both kinds of global responsibility—economic and social—must be pursued by individuals, organizations, and governments. British Prime Minister Tony Blair's party-conference
address on October 1, 2001, reached for this high ground. Blair presented

globalization as a potential force for good in which Britain and the international community could become active in tackling international injustice, "breathe new life" into the Middle East peace process, heal the conflicts in Africa that were "a scar on the conscience of the world," combat world poverty, and address global climate change.[47] The events of September 11 show all too starkly that failure to promote the human as well as the economic side of globalization can carry a terrible price.

There are two possible responses to the globalization of terror and fear. One is to globalize counterterrorism, sending armed units far and wide to root out terrorists from every nook and cranny of the planet. This military outreach is paralleled by intensifying safety and security in the dominant nations—creating gated nations, fortress societies where people hide behind parapets of paranoia; excluding immigrants; enduring the endless surveillance of security cameras in playgrounds, parking lots, and shopping malls; restricting civil liberties and freedom of movement of those who exercise their right to protest; and subjecting people to relentless questioning and intrusive inspection wherever they travel. This paranoia spreads like a plague. In education, it makes us exaggerate school safety, exclude the disaffected, show zero tolerance for the slightest signs of violence, and create padded playgrounds, no-touch classrooms and a world where children wear helmets for everything. This overall response, driven by concerns for safety, security, retribution, and revenge, deals with the *consequences* of terrorism, violence, and disaffection. But it does not address the *conditions* that give rise to these things and offer them sanctuary.

An alternative response that will reduce the necessity for military reaction is for those who prosper most from the knowledge economy to share its bounty more evenly with poorer groups in their own society, and with less-developed nations beyond it. It is to create a cosmopolitan rather than conquering vision of a globalized knowledge society that is inclusive rather than exclusive in its logic. Globalization here is a matter not only of market opportunity but of moral responsibility to the less fortunate of our world. The dark clouds of September 11 may have a silver lining if they prompt many of us to think beyond how we act as consumers, to what we want as citizens, for others as well as ourselves. The challenge is to think again about how we should live our lives, and for what kind of life we should be educating young people. This second response refocuses our attention from revenge to relationships, from commerce to community, from private interest to public life. This is what teaching *beyond* the knowledge society must address: developing cosmopolitan identity and humanitarian responsibility at home as well as abroad.

COMMUNITY AND CHARACTER

In addition to offering a world of prosperity and choice, the new knowledge society brings with it great risks and adverse side effects. The knowledge society is a Trojan horse: It seems to bear gifts, but it brings trouble.

Robert Reich acknowledges these threats when he says that "the deepest anxieties of this prosperous age concern the erosion of our families, the fragmenting of our communities and the challenge of keeping our own integrity intact."[48] The rewards of the new economy, he warns, "are coming at the price of lives that are more frenzied, less secure, more economically divergent, more socially stratified."[49] How, he asks, do we find a balance between making a living, and living a life?[50]

Schools directed primarily toward the ends of the knowledge economy do not automatically serve the public good. Jill Blackmore warns that

> the other side of the knowledge society is the "high-risk society" which demands the resilience to deal with ambiguity, change and uncertainty. Education is thus not only about cognitive learning but also about developing a range of social and interpersonal capacities, including a sense of rights and responsibilities, the building of trust, identity and citizenship formation.[51]

The high-risk society of today is one of escalating danger—of terrorist destruction and environmental devastation on a grand scale.[52] These risks also extend to our personal lives, families, and communities. Overworked parents are so busy trying to stay out of poverty or keep up with their neighbors and competitors that they have little or no time for their children. Parents increasingly send their children to other carers, downsizing their own time commitments and emotional responsibilities as parents in the process.[53] In high-school systems driven by performance results at the expense of relationships, too many adolescents find themselves disengaged from learning and alienated from the knowledge society. The spate of high-school shootings in North America represents not so much an inability to enforce gun control as a failure of high schools to provide *all* students with a sense of belonging and community. Although the United Kingdom, with its relentless drive to raise standards, now sits high in international league tables of literacy achievement among 15-year-olds, it is one of the worst-performing countries in terms of differences in achievement between those from wealthier and poorer social backgrounds. In too many nations, the drive to increase excellence has come at the price of educational and social exclusion.[54]

The sociologist Richard Sennett contends that one of the greatest threats of the new knowledge society is to the fundamental nature of human character. In his provocative book *The Corrosion of Character,* Sennett looks at how

> character particularly focuses upon the long term aspect of our emotional experience. Character is expressed by loyalty and mutual commitment, or through the pursuit of long-term goals, or by the practice of delayed gratification for a future end.[55]

Character is built on what Keith Oatley calls long-term emotions such as love and loyalty, rather than on short-term emotions of infatuation or transient joy.[56] As Michael Ignatieff puts it, "intimacy requires permanence."[57] Sennett himself asks, anxiously,

> How do we decide what is of lasting value in ourselves in a society which is impatient, which focuses on the immediate moment? How can long term goals be pursued in an economy devoted to the short-term? How can mutual loyalties and commitments be sustained in institutions which are constantly breaking apart or continually being redesigned? These are the questions about character posed by the new, flexible capitalism.[58]

Sennett illustrates this argument with a graphic case study. In 1972, while writing *The Hidden Injuries of Class,* a powerful analysis of working-class life in Boston, Sennett interviewed and came to know an office-building janitor named Enrico.[59] He epitomized the old industrial economy. Although he had been a teacher in Greece, Enrico found that the only work for which he was qualified in the United States was laboring. The work was mundane and menial, but it gave Enrico a sense of security and predictability in his life. Enrico and his wife saved steadily for years until they could purchase their own home. He measured his progress in life by each repair and renovation he made to it. He knew when he would retire and the money he would retire on.

This modest life gave Enrico a measure of respect, but by age 36, he had given up his own dreams and was investing his greatest hopes in his son, Rico, and his education. Many years later, Sennett met Rico, by accident, in an airport lounge. Rico seemed the perfect emblem of the knowledge economy. He had an expensive briefcase, fancy jewelry, designer clothes. He looked and was prosperous and successful as a technology analyst and was married to an equally successful corporate accountant.

Rico believed in taking risks and being open to change. He and his wife had already changed jobs and homes several times. They worked hard but stayed connected by the Internet to former work associates elsewhere. Here was a family that was and wanted to be everything the new, flexible knowledge economy asked of it—prosperous, successful, hard-working, independent, flexible, and open to change. But in all this, says Sennett, something was being lost: character.

Rico and his wife had to work frantically to keep up, stay successful, remain in the game. Insecurity, the next downsizing or market dip, was their ever-present adversary. So their work consumed their time, their emotional energy. There was no time for community and not much more for family. "We get home at seven, do dinner, try to find an hour for the kids' homework, and then deal with our own paperwork. . . . [I]t's like I don't know who my kids are," Rico complains.[60]

Rico wants to set an example to his son and daughter of resolution and purpose,

> but his deepest worry is that he cannot offer the substance of his work life as an example to his children of how they should conduct themselves ethically. The qualities of good work are not the qualities of good character.[61]

Rico tries to teach his children loyalty and commitment, but they see none of it in their father's work and life. "You can't imagine how stupid I feel when I talk to my kids about commitment," Rico says. "It's an abstract virtue to them: they don't see it anywhere."[62] Similarly, teamwork practiced at home simply means endless discussion with the children, where issues are talked to death and the parents never dare say "No."

The problem for this flexible family and others like it in today's knowledge economy is:

> How can they protect family relations from succumbing to the short-term behavior, the meeting mind-set and above all the weakness of loyalty and commitment which mark the modern workplace?[63]

How, in other words, can they escape from what Christopher Lasch called the culture of narcissism, which arises from a work culture of self-promotion, change, and flexibility; that favors cleverness over wisdom and the quick and the nimble over the steady and the just; where children become lifestyle role models for their parents rather than parents being moral exemplars for their youngsters?[64]

In "The Rights Revolution," his radio-broadcast Massey lectures, the Canadian intellectual Michael Ignatieff argues that the knowledge economy and the investment it requires is overturning existing forms of life and work.

These convulsions make it difficult for families to maintain continuities of care. If wage pressure and time pressure deplete the emotional reserves of family life, children are less likely to learn the values on which the larger society depends. Children who do not learn how to trust and how to love turn into selfish and aggressive adults. The result ... is a brutal and uncaring social order.[65]

The destabilizing effects of work in the industrial economy were ones of scarcity, necessitating long working hours and strong dispositions of scrimping and saving. In the knowledge economy, the destabilizing effects are often ones of abundance. As Ignatieff puts it, "[A]bundance changes the moral economy of a society by favoring values of consumption over saving."[66]

In today's knowledge society, secure and steady saving for the future is increasingly replaced by personal gambling in worldwide investment.[67] When I was a child, the "insurance man" called every Thursday evening at our home, collecting the few shillings my mother and father saved for a policy that would pay for their funerals and give them a small bonus if they lived to retirement. Now, popular guides to personal financial planning sneer at saving as the old-fashioned refuge of the unadventurous and present stock-market investments as the only viable options.

Financial insecurity is paralleled by a collapse of community. In place of vanishing community we are offered commercialized simulations of it. Manufactured smiles are the selling point of the service industry, where people insist that you "have a nice day" only because it profits their company.[68] Instead of paying attention to one another, financially rich but time-poor people pay for attention to themselves, purchasing the simulated intimacy of coaches, counselors, therapists, party planners, and personal trainers.[69] No wonder that, when a Californian woman casually refers to consulting her therapist in the movie *Crocodile Dundee,* Paul Hogan's exasperated and earthy retort is, "Haven't you got any mates?"

In the knowledge society, corporate loyalty is being replaced by temporary commitments between employers and employees that last only as long as their bargains benefit them both.[70] Employers invest heavily in developing the skills of their young talent, only to see them leave for better deals elsewhere. Downsizing and contracting out reduce costs but kill culture and commitment with job insecurity. In their analysis of the effects of the knowledge economy on social progress in Britain and North America, Phillip Brown and Hugh Lauder show that too much flexibility in knowledge-economy organizations fragments relationships, corrodes the foundations of trust and commitment, and destroys the understanding and informal learning that is passed on through institutional memory.[71]

Trust and loyalty are also in retreat in communities, as, in the evocative title of Robert Putnam's book, most people are left *Bowling Alone*.[72] The result of all this is a pervasive corrosion of character, of the long-term sentiments and moral virtues that hold people together in families, communities, and corporate life.

One of the places where this corrosion of character is particularly evident is in the rise of self-managing work teams and teamwork in general. Teams are valuable when they are underpinned by relationships and driven by shared moral purpose. But unlike groups or communities that endure over time, through thick and thin, when teams exist by themselves they become "a group of people assembled to perform a specific immediate task rather than to dwell together as a village."[73] In closely bonded groups, people test one another, patrol their ethics, question one another's judgments, and enjoy exploring differences. But the short-term task-team, Sennett argues "takes us into that domain of demeaning superficiality which besets the modern workplace,"[74] where "shared superficiality keeps people together by avoiding difficult, divisive, personal questions."[75] The team decides, then dissolves, as each task requires. There is no long-term commitment here.

> In a turnstile world, the masks of cooperativeness are among the only possessions workers will carry with them from task to task, firm to firm. . . . [P]eople who fail to develop quickly the masks of cooperativeness . . . will wind up pumping gas.[76]

In the knowledge economy, even Daniel Goleman's emotional intelligence is a poisoned chalice. According to Stephen Fineman, emotional intelligence "commodifies" human emotions, turning them into marketable products. "The popularization of emotional intelligence," he says, "presents emotion in a form that can be contained and 'sold' in the corporate world."[77] Goleman, he says, tends to discuss emotions that are easy and acceptable to manage (anxiety, sadness, or optimism, for example) but ignores inconvenient emotions such as disgust (the basic emotion of racism) or envy (the prime emotion behind competitiveness) that hold out fewer prospects for creating a feel-good factor. Only emotional selves that are marketable and manageable get corporate attention in the knowledge economy. Creating healthy communities and a strong civil society beyond the knowledge economy requires even deeper understanding of emotions than the idea of emotional intelligence allows.

For all these reasons, a strong system of public education is not only integral to a prosperous knowledge economy; it is also vital for protecting and strengthening democracy in the way it builds community and develops character.[78] Now more than ever, teachers should not just be catalysts of the knowledge economy. They are also essential counterpoints to it, building and preserving the public, communal democracy that parallels the knowledge society and is also imperiled by it.

CULTIVATING SOCIAL CAPITAL

Teachers who teach beyond the knowledge society develop not only intellectual capital in their students but also social capital: the ability to form networks, forge relationships, and contribute to as well as draw on the human resources of the community and wider society. Francis Fukuyama defines social capital as "a set of informal values or norms shared among members of a group that permits cooperation among them" and that establishes a basis for trust.[79] Drawing on the work of James Coleman, who was responsible for bringing the concept of social capital into broad use,[80] Fukuyama describes how the norms that produce the social capital that underpins cooperation include truth-telling, meeting obligations, and reciprocity. In modern societies, the challenge is to expand the radius of trust beyond the immediate family. For Fukuyama, social capital "is critical for the creation of a healthy civil society, that is, the realm of groups and associates that fall between the family and the state."[81] He contends that, "[w]ithout social capital, ""there would be no civil society, and . . . without civil society there would be no democracy."[82]

Social capital depends on social learning—much of it informal. Children who move schools a lot or who live in urban neighborhoods where the jobs and businesses have disappeared find it hard to gain access to or develop social capital.[83] Isolation and polarization within society destroy social capital and limit the educational opportunities and learning capacities of young people. Social capital supports learning, feeds it, finds an outlet and a purpose for it. If teachers, schools and communities do not cultivate social capital, students generate their own in inverted and perverted ways—in the subcultures of the smoking pit, the washrooms, and other dark corners of the peer group where friendship consolidates failure and economic opportunity is denied through shared social and educational exclusion. Social capital is foundational to prosperity and democracy. Developing it is educationally essential.

EDUCATING FOR DEMOCRACY

In the developed Anglophone world, humanitarianism, democracy, and public life have largely disappeared from governments' education-reform agendas. Instead, there has been too exclusive a focus on academic results, examination and test scores, international competitiveness, league tables of performance, and narrowing achievement gaps—with little thought or attention being given to what counts as the substance of children's achievement. Achievement has been everything, and democracy has been left to fend for itself.

Like a marriage, democracy cannot be sustained through indifference or neglect. It must be tended to, cared for, defended and reviewed everyday. The world's post-totalitarian nations have understood this all too well. People in Spain, Portugal, South Africa, the former communist nations of Eastern and Central Europe, and most of South America remember vividly what it is like not to have democracy.

Almost every older educator I have met in countries such as Chile and Argentina was tortured, went into exile, or "disappeared" for months or years under these nations' former totalitarian regimes. Teachers are always among the first casualties of democracy's demise. These people's, and their nation's, memories of life without democracy have energized and articulated their educational goals and missions, imbuing them with strong elements of democracy and humanitarianism.

At the turn of this century, for example, South Africans' concern with the struggle for a democratic curriculum led them to embrace a broad outcome-driven approach with integrated elements that promoted social justice and performance goals that sought to generate high skills, full employment, and a strong labor movement.[84] South Africa's National Curriculum statement boldly attempts

> to ensure a broad, high level of education for all. It strives to produce a life long learner who is confident and independent, literate, numerate and multi-skilled. Compassion, respect for the environment and ability to participate in the society as a critical and active citizen should characterize the learning produced by this curriculum.[85]

The vision of the teacher behind these goals is not of someone who merely delivers other people's curriculum; it is of someone who "is socially and politically critical and responsible, professionally competent and in touch with contemporary developments." It is of a teacher as a true intellectual who engages with the world as well as instructs in the classroom, and who grasps the connection between the two.

Against these trends, global agendas concerned with measurable standards and targets, performance results, accountability data, basic-skills emphases, and a push for privatization are increasingly colonizing the educational-reform practices and priorities of less-developed countries.[86] But post-totalitarian nations still cling to parallel values of humanitarianism and citizenship, albeit in a weakened way. Thus, while Portugal's Program for the Development of Education for 2000–2006 emphasizes initial training, employability, and the goal to "guide and promote the development of the Knowledge Society," it also advocates "promoting a culture of initiative, responsibility and citizenship."[87]

In the international arena, organizations such as the United Nations Educational, Scientific, and Cultural Organization (UNESCO) keep the democratic discourse in education alive. UNESCO's report *Learning: The Treasure Within* identified four essential pillars of learning.[88] Two are the prime pillars of the knowledge economy: *learning to know,* and *learning to do* (to apply knowledge). The other two pillars are just as important. *Learning to be* focuses on developing a strong sense of personal responsibility for the attainment of common goals.[89] In a world that is falling apart in the face of economic globalization, the most important pillar of all, perhaps, is *learning to live together.* This emphasizes democracy, community, and cosmopolitan identity by

> developing an understanding of others and their history, traditions and spiritual values and, on this basis, creating a new spirit which, guided by recognition of our growing interdependence and a common analysis of the rules and challenges of the future, would induce people to implement common projects or to manage the inevitable conflicts in an intelligent or peaceful way.[90]

The powerful nations of the G7, which dominate the global knowledge economy, have much to learn about educational and moral priorities from their economically less-favored peers. The teacher's role as a vital socializing agent in preparing the generations of the future must never be underestimated or overlooked.[91] If we do not make democracy and humanitarian goals central to the mission of public-education reform, they will be overrun by the unrestrained market.

The Scottish philosopher and economist Adam Smith is best remembered for claiming, in *Wealth of Nations,* that the "hidden hand" of economic self-interest would ultimately serve the common good.[92] But Smith was by no means a free-marketeer, in money or morality. Among many memorable words in his *Theory of Moral Sentiments* are those stating: "The wise and virtuous man is at all times willing that his own private interest should be sacrificed to the public interest of his own particular order of society."[93] It is people's emotional capacity for sympathy, said Smith, that makes it possible to pursue the public good.

If we teach only for the knowledge society and those who prosper from it, we will create no sympathy or empathy for those who do not succeed and develop no feelings of responsibility for their future. We will have no way to listen to their voices or include them in the democratic process. As we feather our own nests with consumer comforts, we will also incarcerate more and more of the excluded in prisons for adults or special schools for disruptive children. We will close our eyes to the untouchables of the world and show concern about less-favored nations only when our own interests are threatened. This is an unfair and unjust world for the excluded and a dismally fearful world for the rest. Charles Handy acerbically comments:

> I find it hard to feel sorry for this particular "anxious elite". Instead of involving themselves with their neighbors, the rich choose to pay taxes to the state, demanding of governments that they clear the streets of crime and improve the schools without giving them enough money to do it, while tucking their own wealth away in international hidey-holes, isolating themselves in their guarded compounds from other people's problems.[94]

Teachers and others, therefore, must think about how to teach not only *for* the knowledge society but also *beyond* it, so we address other compelling human values and educational purposes in addition to those that make a profit—purposes concerned with character, community, democracy, and cosmopolitan identity. We must think beyond public education as providing value for money to ensuring that it also promotes values for good.

TEACHING BEYOND THE KNOWLEDGE SOCIETY

How well or poorly are teachers and schools teaching beyond the knowledge society? Recent patterns of educational reform in England and the United States begin to provide an answer. An appraisal of how England's educational reforms fared under Tony Blair's first period of Labor government found much to commend in its first wave of initiatives.[95] Raised standards, a commitment to narrowing the achievement gaps between advantaged and disadvantaged students, relaxation of government intervention when schools were doing well, celebration of successful schools and teachers, a range of initiatives promoting professional development, and the establishment of a National College for School Leadership, as well as a self-regulating professional body for teachers (the General Teaching Council)—all these developments indicated decisive support for professional learning and organizational flexibility as a platform for continuous improvement.[96] These are hallmark knowledge-economy initiatives.

Yet in all these initiatives, critics complained, something was also crucially missing: values. In government policy, operational issues eclipsed ethical and emotional ones. As Michael Fielding put it, England's reforms, despite their achievements to date, have provided no place for values, no sense of how people should live among and care for others or how they should conduct their own lives. The reforms, he said, seemed to have

> no place for either the language or the experience of joy, of spontaneity, of life lived in ways that are vibrant and fulfilling rather than watchfully earnest, focussed and productive of economic activity.[97]

What the reform culture still needed was "an aspiring human narrative," at the heart of which would be a belief in educating individuals as people in and through community.

In the United States, Jeannie Oakes and her colleagues undertook a sobering review of the failure (or short-lived success) of a range of liberal and democratically inspired educational reforms.[98] The late 1980s and 1990s, they showed, had seen several initiatives make early headway. Among them was the Carnegie Corporation's bold effort to reform the middle years of schooling.[99] This initiative established high-profile commissions at national and regional levels (which included President-to-be Bill Clinton), to implement changes that were known to be successful with young, diverse, and at-risk adolescents. The changes included smaller schools or mini-schools, mixed-ability teaching (de-tracking), interdisciplinary teaching based on a core of academic knowledge, and extensive professional involvement and development for teachers and leaders.

Through sixteen vividly described case studies, Oakes and her colleagues showed the great power of these reforms to boost all students' learning in their observations of examples of striking success and impact. But all too often, it was hard to spread the success beyond a few schools or teachers and still harder to sustain it over time. Reform failed when elite parents insisted on gifted and honors programs' being retained to keep their children apart from and ahead of the rest; when caring and respectful relationships with poor parents and students were replaced by more hierarchical deliveries of bureaucratic "services" to them; when interdisciplinary teaching trivialized learning for disadvantaged students instead of elevating it to higher levels; and when competing state- or district-reform imperatives such as standardized testing or the introduction of a specialized, content-driven curriculum, directly contradicted all the emphases of the innovative effort. A few courageous and inspiring educators were able to hold out against these contrary tides, but in the main positive change that directly addressed social justice and values issues in the classroom did not spread or last.

The reason for the failure, Oakes and her colleagues found, is that those who implemented the changes, like the leading change theorists whose advice they followed, treated change as a technical, neutral process of pressure and support that was emptied of all controversy and values. It was the failure to address such values and controversies head-on in the process of change; to tackle issues of race, color, and injustice; to challenge deep-seated beliefs about the incapacity of children in poor or minority families; and to resist political cowardice and tendencies to compromise in the face of elite parents' pressure that ultimately undermined the reforms. What Oakes and her colleagues' work shows is that values, social justice, and caring have to be central to professional development among teachers, to community development among parents, and to the agenda of large-scale policy-making if change is to make schools better for all students and foster the public good.[100]

Teaching beyond the knowledge society therefore means serving as a courageous counterpoint for it in order to foster the values of community, democracy, humanitarianism, and cosmopolitan identity. Without these, there is little hope of sustained security for any of us. By being counterpoints for the knowledge society, the role of the teacher is to

- Promote social and emotional learning, commitment, and character;
- Learn to relate differently to others, replacing strings of interactions with enduring bonds and relationships;
- Develop cosmopolitan identity;
- Commit to continuous professional and personal development;
- Work and learn in collaborative groups;
- Forge relationships with parents and communities;
- Build emotional understanding;
- Preserve continuity and security; and
- Establish basic trust in people.

Teaching today must include dedication to building character, community, humanitarianism, and democracy in young people; to help them think and act above and beyond the seductions and demands of the knowledge economy.

Tom Sergiovanni talks about the importance of developing not just school effectiveness and high performance but also what he calls *school character.* Schools with character, he says, have "unique cultures."

> They know who they are, have developed a common understanding of their purposes, and have faith in their ability to celebrate their uniqueness as a powerful way to achieve their goal. A school displays character when the purposes, hopes and needs of its individual members are taken seriously by its culture at the same time that these members are committed to the common good.[101]

Schools with character recognize that teaching is not only a cognitive and intellectual practice but also a social and emotional one. Good teachers fully understand that successful teaching and learning occur when teachers have caring relationships with their students and when their students are emotionally engaged with their learning. Policymakers, administrators, educational researchers, and others who shape the nature of teaching, however, tend to neglect the emotions, play down their importance, leave them to take care of themselves. Performance standards, targets, checklists of competencies—these are their priorities. By putting exclusive or excessive emphasis on them, those who shape teaching often not only neglect but also actively undermine the emotional dimension of educating. They turn learning into a clinical and disengaging race toward targets or fill teachers' time with technical tasks so no time is left for creativity, imagination, and relationships—for all those things that fuel the passion to teach.

Teaching and learning, however, are *always* social and emotional practices, by design or neglect. Students are excited or bored, involved or excluded. Charles Darwin showed that even the most seemingly singular cognitive activity of reflection is itself an emotion because it relies on an affective state of quiet concentration.[102] Emotions are therefore not only important as a context for learning (as in setting an effective classroom climate, or establishing safe schools); they are integral to learning and teaching themselves—as part of the learning process and as social and moral goals and consequences of it. Sympathy is the emotional foundation of democracy. Efforts to teach beyond the knowledge society must recognize, incorporate, and attend to this social and emotional dimension of teachers' work.

One of the first implications of reintroducing a more overt emotional emphasis into teaching is the importance of teachers' establishing emotional bonds with and among their students—building enduring relation-ships in which children (and their parents) are known and feel known by the teacher. One of the most common causes of high-school dropout is students' feelings that no adult really knows or cares for them.[103] England is trying to solve a massive block in performance as children move from primary school to secondary school by making improvements to the curriculum.[104] But the curriculum is not the main problem. Kathryn Riley and her colleagues' research shows that students who do badly in the early years of high school experience incredible fragmentation in their lives—between different parents and families and constantly changing homes. They are denied social capital. The school then compounds this fragmentation by subjecting students to a multitude of subject teachers, by repeatedly excluding them from class or school because of behavior problems, and by exposing them to an endless parade of substitute teachers and "casualized" teachers who make up the staff of many urban schools.[105] Tragically, it is the students with the most fragmented lives who get the most fragmented experience of secondary schooling and who are prevented from developing social capital.

The educational answer to the angst of early adolescence is mainly to be found not in more curriculum but in stronger community. Especially at this point in young people's education, improving achievement, especially among those most at risk, is not secured by concentrating on achievement alone. At a time that adolescents are assailed by so many other influences in their lives, focusing their minds exclusively on achievement is futile. Achieving at learning also demands intellectual and emotional engagement with schooling and all the relationships it contains.[106]

Innovative and highly successful Grade 7 and 8 teachers my colleagues and I studied put the establishment of the emotional bonds of engagement at the core of everything they did. Teachers involved children in their own assessment, included students in parent–teacher meetings, advised and mentored students individually, extended their lesson periods to strengthen classroom relationships, and "looped," or followed, their students from one grade to the next.[107]

Our research on the emotions of teaching, however, reveals that high-school teachers often treat students' emotions as negative things that intrude into the classroom from outside, for which they then have to make allowances. High-school teachers tend not to see it as their responsibility to develop their students' emotions in a positive way as an integral part of learning. Instead of being built on relationships, therefore, high-school classrooms are often reduced to strings of loosely connected interactions.[108]

Relentless drives for increased, measurable achievement and batteries of subject-based standards exacerbate these tendencies.

In elementary schools, caring has traditionally been a stronger priority for teachers. Typically, it is one of the most salient qualities of people's most memorable teachers. Albert Camus, for example, wrote in *The First Man* that during his poor childhood in Algeria, his teacher was a man whose method "consisted of strict control on behavior while at the same time making his teaching lively and entertaining, which would win out even over the flies."[109]

This kind of caring has a rather paternalistic quality about it, though, that is not enough any more. When today's learners are more diverse and demanding, caring must become less controlling; more responsive to students' varied cultures; more inclusive of their ideas, perceptions, and learning requirements; and more ready to involve and not just compensate for the families and communities from which students come. The curriculum must be flexible enough to allow for these accommodations. If students are to become democratic adults, they must experience democracy in their learning choices and in their contribution to school policies and school missions.[110] Care must become more than charity or control. It must become a relationship in which those who are cared for (students or parents) have agency, dignity, and a voice. This is the social and emotional mandate for teachers in a profession that strives to reach beyond the knowledge economy.

Caring begins with people you know, people you can see. Sympathy starts with people around us. In a globalized world, though, caring also stretches far beyond our immediate face-to-face relationships. Arlie Hochschild argues that in today's complex and interconnected world, we are all connected in chains of caring or uncaring to people in communities and continents far beyond our own.[111] These chains of caring or uncaring are expressed in what we buy (and the labor conditions that produce it), in the money and time we donate to other people and causes, and in our attitudes toward other cultures. Teaching beyond the knowledge society means developing a cosmopolitan identity that can build chains of caring for those who are out of sight but should never be out of mind. There are many ways to do this, including environmental and global education, community-service programs in the curriculum, student and teacher exchanges with other countries, paired relationships and resource-sharing between schools in rich and poor communities, and so on.

This moral mandate involves teachers' paying attention not only to their continuous professional *learning* but also to their own personal and professional *development*. Professional development involves more than learning knowledge and skills. It is through professional and personal development that teachers build character, maturity, and other virtues in themselves and others, making their schools into moral communities. Professional development amounts to more than a slick, self-managed portfolio of certificates and achievements accumulated as individual credits, like frequent-flyer points. Collecting course credits does little more than put "bums on seats." It rarely reaches people's souls. Professional development, rather, is a personal path toward greater professional integrity and human growth.

Teachers who are personally and professionally developed have evolved a strong sense of themselves as teachers and as people. Their ego boundaries, their senses of identity, are secure enough for them not to feel flooded, invaded, or overwhelmingly vulnerable when they are challenged by, evaluated by, or asked to work with other adults. Well-developed teachers display as much self-confidence and openness in their professional relationships with adults as they do with children.[112] They are at ease in their own skin. Reaching this stage of maturity is a matter of personal growth, not of formal learning—and still less of in-service training on government or district priorities. It is the product of shrewd selection, varied experience, good leadership, and effective mentoring. All these things are being threatened by the pressures of rapid demographic turnover in the teaching profession. This suggests a need for initiatives to keep older teachers engaged and motivated so they will be eager to support their younger colleagues part time or voluntarily after they have retired. Dragooning teachers into early retirement in climates of recrimination and bitterness removes these essential sources of wisdom and memory from the profession. Professional-development priorities must pay attention to these vital processes of informal learning and personal growth. Professional learning and professional development *both* matter in the knowledge-society school.

Teaching beyond the knowledge society therefore means developing new and better relationships with other adults as well as with children.[113] There is more to this than learning to work in short-term cooperative teams that disband when the pressure is off and the learning task is done—as often occurs in the context of large-scale, top-down reform.[114] Teaching beyond the knowledge economy also calls for teachers to work in long-term collaborative groups together; committing to and challenging one another as a caring professional community that is secure enough to withstand the discomfort that disagreement creates. A humane knowledge society needs teams and groups. Teaching in the knowledge society means constructing a profession where teachers can experience and become effective at both forms of working with their colleagues.

If teachers are to serve as strong counterpoints for the excesses of the knowledge society, their schools must be not only dynamic learning organizations in a flexible economy but also caring, moral organizations in a public democracy. Nowhere is this more true than in teachers' relationships with parents and communities. Being true partners in children's learning entails more than being recipients of workshops and other kinds of learning as described in the previous chapter. Teachers also have much to learn from parents and communities—about the children whom parents mostly know best, and about the unseen strength and wisdom that is possessed in even the most apparently deprived communities. Learning from parents and communities requires building caring, trusting, respectful, and reciprocal relationships in which parents are more than the targets of government services and teachers' intervention. They are vigorous participants in improving their children's opportunities. This may mean moving into the parents' space and away from the school, a space that may have intimidated the parents when they were students themselves. Holding parent–teacher nights and school celebrations in a community center or a high-profile professional sports club is just one way to achieve this.

Developing mature, caring, and respectful relationships with children and adults also calls for more than the learnable skill sets of emotional intelligence. It draws on what N. Denzin calls *emotional understanding*—the ability to recognize what others feel as they feel it.[115] Accurate emotional understanding depends primarily on establishing relationships with people so we know how to "read," "interpret," and respond to the subtleties of their emotional responses. Absence of these relationships creates *emotional misunderstanding* in which teachers misinterpret slender cues about students, parents, or others and, as a result, misconstrue and respond inappropriately to others' emotional states—believing they are interested when they are bored, hyperactive when they are enthusiastic, or angry when they are embarrassed. An overcrowded curriculum and school structures that fragment teachers' contacts with students, parents, and one another impede emotional understanding. Emotional intelligence comes down to questions of individual, learned skill. Emotional understanding is a matter of enduring relationships and the organizational conditions that make them possible. Without these conditions, students, parents, and colleagues are really not known and are easily reduced to stereotypes.

Strong relationships often prosper and grow from change, but they are ultimately rooted in experiences of fundamental security. Alongside being forces of change, risk, and endless improvement, teachers who are counterpoints for the knowledge society must help to preserve the continuity and basic trusting relationships that are the very core of risk-taking, and community-building among students and adults alike. Valuing many different kinds of excellence among teachers, celebrating real achievements, cherishing and capitalizing on the school's collective memory through mentoring and other measures, making all members of the school feel part of and knowledgeable about the "big picture" of the school's development, and taking leadership succession seriously so there is continuity between one principal and the next—these are just some of the ways to create the security that is a platform for risk. Exotic travel can be enjoyed only when there is a home to return to. Endless change, like endless travel, is like eternal exile, the tragic destiny of homeless minds. The line between being committed to change and addicted to it is a very fine one. It is important that principals and teachers stay on the right side of it.

In fast-changing, flexible organizations, teachers certainly need to trust processes of teamwork with many different colleagues (some of whom they may not know well). But somewhere, sometimes in their workplace, they have to trust particular people, too—leaders, close colleagues, supportive parents on whom they know they can rely. This basic trust that is first established in childhood and extended through close personal and family relationships is essential to making other, more flexible kinds of process trust possible. People with basic trust are less likely to feel unnecessarily suspicious, envious of, or betrayed by colleagues in their schools.[116] Balancing change with continuity, professional trust in the process with personal trust in people, is an important professional priority in a humane knowledge society. Teachers who are personally supported by their leaders and their colleagues are less likely to have suspicious minds.

We live in a lopsided world of growing intolerance, individualism, exclusion, and insecurity. Being a teacher who is a counterpoint for the knowledge society therefore means being concerned with character as well as performance; social and emotional as well as cognitive learning; personal and professional development as well as professional learning; group life as well as teamwork; caring as well as cognition; and preserving continuity and security alongside promoting risk and change. It means developing social capital, laying the emotional foundations of democracy, and creating the kernels of cosmopolitan identity. Teaching beyond the knowledge economy means being in a reinvented profession that does not just deliver value but that is driven by values. In short, teaching beyond the knowledge economy cultivates

- Character
- Community
- Security
- Inclusiveness
- Integrity
- Cosmopolitan identity
- Continuity and collective memory
- Sympathy
- Democracy
- Personal and professional maturity

Teaching in the knowledge economy requires levels of skills and judgment far beyond those involved in standardized test scores and simply delivering someone else's prescribed curriculum. It requires qualities of personal and intellectual maturity that take years to develop. Teaching in the knowledge society cannot be a refuge for second-choice careers, a low-level system of technical delivery, or, as some policymakers are saying, an exhausting job that should be handled mainly by the young and energetic before they move on to something else. Teaching in the knowledge society, rather, should be a career of first choice, a job for grown-up intellectuals, a long-term commitment, a social mission, a job for life. Anything less leaves our sights far below the knowledge-society horizon—and teaching should never be about settling for less.

NOTES

1. This discussion of the South Sea bubble is largely drawn from MacKay, C., *Extraordinary Popular Delusions and the Madness of Crowds,* London, Crown Publishers, 1841. The quote is from chapter 3, published on the Internet: <http://www. litrix.com/madraven/madne003.htm>.

2. Swift, J., "The bubble," in H. Williams (ed.), *The Poems of Jonathan Swift* (vol. I), London, Oxford University Press, 1937, p. 251.

3. Woodruff, W., *The Road to Nab End,* London, Abacus, 2002, pp. 30–31.

4. MacKay, *op. cit.,* note 1, chap. 4.

5. Lowe, G., "Computer literacy," *Canadian Social Trends* 19, 13–14.

6. Statistics Canada. Available on-line at: <http://www.statcan.ca/cgi-bin/comments>.

7. Postman, N., *Technopoly: The Surrender of Culture to Technology,* New York, Alfred A. Knopf, 1992.

8. Stoll, C., *Silicon Snakeoil,* New York, Doubleday, 1995, p. 58.

9. Guide Association, *Girls and Citizenship,* London, Guide Association, 2001.

10. These include repetitive-stress and eye disorders caused by the repeated use of a mouse, keyboard, and screen.

11. Castells, M., *The Rise of the Network Society,* Oxford, Blackwell, 1996.

12. Postman, N., *Amusing Ourselves to Death: Public Discourse in the Age of Show Business,* New York, Penguin Books, 1985.

13. Mestrovic, S. G., *Postemotional Society,* London, Sage, 1997. Some countries in Mediterranean Europe, such as Spain and Portugal, hold out against this trend. There, most cards do not have a prescripted verse but are blank—the assumption being that people can express their own feelings well enough without corporations having to do this for them.

14. Barber, B. R., *Jihad vs. McWorld,* New York, Times Books, 1995.

15. Berman, M. *All That Is Solid Melts into Air: The Experience of Modernity,* New York, Viking Penguin Books, 1988. The original phrase belonged to Karl Marx and Friedrich Engels.

16. Examples include Reich, R., *The Work of Nations: Preparing Ourselves for 21st Century Capitalism,* New York, Alfred A. Knopf, 1991; Leadbeater, C., *The Weightless Society: Living in the New Economy Bubble,* New York and London, Texere, 2000; Drucker, P., *Post-capitalist Society,* New York, HarperCollins, 1993.

17. Hargreaves, A., "Contrastive rhetoric and extremist talk: Teachers, hegemony and the educationist context," in L. Barton & S. Walker (eds.), *Schools, Teachers and Teaching,* New York and Philadelphia, Falmer Press, 1981.

18. Brown, P. & Lauder, H., *Capitalism and Social Progress: The Future of Society in a Global Economy,* Basingstoke, Hampshire, and New York, Palgrave, 2001.

19. Machiavelli, N., *The Prince* (trans. G. Bull), London, Penguin Books, 1999 (1532), p. 88.

20. These passages were written just two weeks after the World Trade Center and Pentagon disasters and drew their information from a range of high-quality newspapers of the day.

21. Elliott, L. & Atkinson, D., *The Age of Insecurity,* London and New York, Verso, 1999.

22. Fukuyama, F., *Trust: The Social Virtues and the Creation of Prosperity,* London, Hamish Hamilton, 1995; Giddens, A., *Modernity and Self-Identity,* Cambridge, Polity Press, 1990; Kramer, R. M. & Tyler, T. R., *Trust in Organizations: Frontiers of Theory and Research,* London, Sage, 1996; Reina, D. S. & Reina, M. L., *Trust and Betrayal in the Workplace,* San Francisco, Berrett-Koehler Publishers, 1999.

23. Vail, J., "Insecure times," in J. Vail, J. Wheelock & M. Hill (eds.), *Insecure Times: Living in Insecurity in Contemporary Society,* New York, Routledge, 1999, pp. 3–4.

24. Bauman, Z., *Globalization: The Human Consequences,* Oxford, Basil Blackwell, 1998.

25. Ibid., p. 116.

26. Elliott & Atkinson, *op. cit.,* note 21.

27. Barber, *op. cit.,* note 14.

28. Ibid., pp. 6–7.

29. Ibid., p. 6.

30. Ibid., p. 4.

31. Ibid., p. 136.

32. Soros, G., *George Soros on Globalization,* New York, Perseus Books, 2002.

33. Galbraith, J., *The Affluent Society,* Boston, Houghton Mifflin, 1984; Handy, C. B., *The Hungry Spirit: Beyond Capitalism: A Quest for Purpose in the Modern World,* New York, Broaday Books, 1998.

34. Barber, *op. cit.,* note 14; Castells, *op. cit.,* note 11.

35. Castells, M., *End of Millennium,* Oxford, Blackwell, 1998.

36. Michel, A., "Schools for an emerging new world," in Organization for Economic Cooperation and Development (OECD), *Schooling for Tomorrow: What Schools for the Future?* (pp. 217–230, quoted from p. 219), Paris, OECD, 2001.

37. See Hargreaves, A., *Changing Teachers, Changing Times: Teachers' Work and Culture in the Postmodern Age,* London, Cassell and New York, Teachers College Press, 1994, chap. 4. See also Ignatieff, M., *Blood and Belonging,* London, Chatto & Windus, 1993.

38. Barber, *op. cit.,* note 14, p. 9.

39. Ibid., p. 209.

40. Giddens, A., *The Consequences of Modernity,* Stanford, CA, Stanford University Press, 1990.

41. Castells, *op. cit.,* note 35, p. 354.

42. Ibid., p. 355; emphasis added.

43. Giddens, A., *Runaway World: How Globalization Is Reshaping Our Lives,* London, Profile Books, 2000, pp. 4–5.

44. Ritzer, G., *The McDonaldization Thesis: Explorations and Extensions,* Thousand Oaks, CA, Sage Publications, 1998.

45. Soros (2002), *op. cit.,* note 32, p. 165.

46. Steele, J., "Last of the old style liberals," *Guardian Saturday Review,* 2002, pp. 6–7.

47. As reported in *The Independent* (newspaper), October 2, 2001.

48. Reich, R., *The Future of Success,* New York, Alfred A. Knopf, 2001, p. 8.

49. Ibid.

50. Ibid., p. 6.

51. Blackmore, J., "A critique of neoliberal market policies in education," *Journal of Educational Change* 1(4), 2000, 381–387.

52. Giddens, *op. cit.,* note 40; Beck, U., *Risk Society: Towards a New Modernity* (trans. M. Ritter), London, Sage, 1992.

53. Hochschild, A., *The Timebind,* New York, Metropolitan Books, 1997.

54. OECD, *Knowledge and Skills for Life: First Results from the Program for International Student Assessment,* Paris, OECD, 2001.

55. Sennett, R., *The Corrosion of Character,* New York and London, W. W. Norton, 1998, p. 10.

56. Oatley, K. & Jenkins, J., *Understanding Emotions,* Cambridge, MA, Blackwell, 1996.

57. Ignatieff, M., *The Rights Revolution,* Toronto, Anansi Press, 2000, p. 90.

58. Sennett, *op. cit.,* note 55, p. 57.

59. Sennett, R. & Cobb, J. *The Hidden Injuries of Class,* New York, Alfred A. Knopf, 1973. In this earlier book, Enrico is called Rica.

60. Sennett, *op. cit.,* note 55, p. 21.

61. Ibid.

62. Ibid., p. 25.

63. Ibid., p. 28.

64. Lasch, C., *The Culture of Narcissism: American Life in an Age of Diminishing Expectations,* New York, W. W. Norton, 1979.

65. Ignatieff, *op. cit.,* note 57, p. 91.

66. Ibid.

67. Harvey, D., *The Condition of Postmodernity,* Oxford, Blackwell, 1989.

68. Mestrovic, *op. cit.,* note 13; Fineman, S. (ed.), *Emotion in Organizations* (2nd ed.), London, Sage Publications, 2000.

69. Reich, *op. cit.,* note 48.

70. Leinberger, P. & Tucker, B., *The New Individualists: The Generation after the Organization Man,* New York, HarperCollins, 1991.

71. Brown & Lauder, *op. cit.,* note 18.

72. Putnam, R. D., *Bowling Alone: The Collapse and Revival of American Community,* New York, Simon & Schuster, 2000.

73. Sennett, *op. cit.,* note 55, p. 110.

74. Ibid., p. 106.

75. Ibid., p. 108.

76. Ibid., p. 112.

77. Fineman, S., "Commodifying the emotionally intelligent," in Fineman, *op. cit.,* note 68. Goleman's work in this area was discussed in chapter 1.

78. I make this argument more fully in Hargreaves, A. & Fullan, M., *What's Worth Fighting for out There?* Toronto, Elementary Teachers Federation of Ontario; New York, Teachers College Press; Buckingham, Open University Press, 1998.

79. Fukuyama, *op. cit.,* note 22, p. 16.

80. Coleman, J., "Social capital in the creation of human capital," *American Journal of Sociology* 94 (supplement), 1988, 595–620.

81. Fukuyama, *op. cit.,* note 22, p. 16.

82. Ibid., p. 18.

83. Coleman, J. & Hoffer, T., *Public and Private schools: The Impact of Communities,* New York, Basic Books, 1987.

84. Fleisch, B., *Managing Educational Change: The State and School Reform in the New South Africa,* Johannesburg, Heinemann Publishers, 2002.

85. South Africa Department of Education, *Draft Rural National Curriculum Statement for Grades K–9 (Schools),* Pretoria, Department of Education, 2001.

86. Ibid., p. 7.

87. Ministerio da Educaçào, "PRODEP III: Objectivos estratégicos" (on-line), 2002. Available at: <http://www.prodep.min-edu.pt/menu/2.htm>.

88. Delors, J., *Learning: The Treasure Within,* Geneva, UNESCO, 1996.

89. Ibid., p. 29.

90. Ibid., p. 20.

91. Tedesco, J. C., *The New Educational Pact: Education, Competitiveness and Citizenship in Modern Society,* Paris, International Bureau of Education, UNESCO, 1997.

92. Smith, A., *An Inquiry into the Nature and Causes of the Wealth of Nations,* London, W. Strahan & T. Cadell, 1796.

93. Smith, A., *The Theory of Moral Sentiments* (12th ed.), Glasgow, R. Chapman, 1809, p. 321.

94. Handy, C., *The Elephant and the Flea,* London, Hutchinson, 2001, pp. 148–149.

95. Fielding, M. (ed.), *Taking Education Really Seriously: Four Years' Hard Labor,* New York, Routledge/Falmer Press, 2001.

96. Barber, M., "High expectations and standards for all, no matter what: Creating a world class education service in England," in Fielding, *op. cit.,* note 95.

97. Fielding, *op. cit.,* note 95, 9.

98. Oakes, J., Quartz, K. H., Ryan, S. & Lipton, M., *Becoming Good American Schools: The Struggle for Civic Virtue in Education Reform,* San Francisco, Jossey-Bass, 2000.

99. Task Force on the Education of Young Adolescents, *Turning Points: Preparing American Youth for the 21st Century,* New York, Carnegie Council on Adolescent Development, 1989.

100. See also Talbert, J., "Professionalism and politics in high school teaching reform," *Journal of Educational Change* 3(3), 2002.

101. Sergiovanni, T., *The Lifeworld of Leadership: Creating Culture, Community, and Personal Meaning in Our Schools,* San Francisco, Jossey-Bass, 2000, p. 18.

102. Darwin, C., *The Expression of the Emotions in Man and Animals, 1872,* Chicago, University of Chicago Press, 1965.

103. I discuss this evidence and develop the argument more fully in Hargreaves, A., Earl, L. & Ryan, J., *Schooling for Change: Reinventing Education for Early Adolescents,* Philadelphia, Falmer Press, 1996.

104. Recent government reform policies in U.K. education are summarized in Department for Education and Skills, *Achieving Success,* London, Her Majesty's Stationery Office (HMSO), 2001.

105. Riley, K. & Rustique Forrester, E., with Fuller, M., Rowles, D., Latch, R. & Docking, J., *Successful Practices with Disaffected Students,* London, Paul Chapman, in press.

106. Vibert, A. B., Portelli, J. P., Shields, C. & Larocque, L., "Critical practice in elementary schools: Voice, community, and a curriculum of life," *Journal of Educational Change* 3(2), 2002, 93–116.

107. Hargreaves, A., Earl, L., Moore, S. & Manning, S., *Learning to Change: Teaching beyond Subjects and Standards,* San Francisco, Jossey-Bass/Wiley, 2001.

108. Hargreaves, A., Beatty, B., Lasky, S., Schmidt, M. & James-Wilson, S., *The Emotions of Teaching,* San Francisco, Jossey-Bass, forthcoming.

109. Camus, A., *The First Man,* Harmondsworth, Penguin Books, 1994.

110. Levin, B., "Putting students at the centre in education reform," *Journal of Educational Change* 1(2), 2000, 155–172.

111. Hochschild, A., "Global care chains and emotional surplus value," in W. Hutton & A. Giddens (eds.), *On the Edge: Living with Global Capitalism* (pp. 130–146), London, Jonathan Cape, 2000.

112. Fuller, F., "Concerns of teachers: A developmental characterization," *American Educational Research Journal* 6, 1969, 207–226.

113. Saltzberger-Wittenberg, I., Henry, G. & Osborne, E., *The Emotional Experience of Learning and Teaching,* London, Routledge & Kegan Paul, 1983.

114. Helsby, G., *Changing Teachers' Work: The Reform of Secondary Schooling,* Milton Keynes, Open University Press, 1999.

115. Denzin, N., *On Understanding Emotion,* San Francisco, Jossey-Bass, 1984.

116. One of the best accounts of trust in teaching is Troman, G., "Teachers' stress in the low trust society," *British Journal of Sociology of Education* 21(3), 2000, 331–353.

3

TEACHING DESPITE
THE KNOWLEDGE SOCIETY, PART I
The End of Ingenuity

(with Michael Baker and Martha Foote)

THE COST OF THE KNOWLEDGE SOCIETY

Teaching for the knowledge society and teaching beyond it need not be incompatible. It is easy to stick to one side of the paradox or the other; to educate young people either for the economy or for citizenship and community. Yet these polarized positions do young people few favors. Teaching only for the knowledge society prepares students and societies for economic prosperity, but it limits people's relations to instrumental, economic ones; it confines group interactions to the "turnstile world" of transient teamwork; and it channels people's passions and desires toward the retail therapy of shopping and entertainment and away from interactions with one another.

Teaching exclusively beyond the knowledge society cultivates caring, develops character, and builds cosmopolitan identity. But if people are unprepared for the knowledge economy, they will be excluded from it—lacking the basic necessities that enable communities to survive and succeed in the first place.

Reconciling the economic and social goals of education, preparing people for making a living and living a life, has proved historically difficult, leading to endless swings of the policy pendulum. Teachers and others must now dedicate themselves to bringing together these two missions of teaching for the knowledge society and beyond it, making it the pinnacle of their professional purpose. For, as Professor A. H. Halsey of Oxford University puts it:

> [T]here is no necessary logic in global capitalism, no good reason why nation states cannot pursue both economic growth and social fairness, both prosperity and progress, both entrepreneurship and security.[1]

72

Yet as teachers try to reach for the skies in education, too many have found themselves shackled to the base concerns and uninspiring bottom lines that policymakers and the public impose upon them. These teachers' working reality has not been an energizing one of expert judgement, invigorating learning and strong professional community. It has been a dispiriting world of micromanagement, standardization, and professional compliance in which demands have increased, resources have been scarce, and public trust has been wanting. Although policymakers should be the wind beneath teachers' wings, they have more usually been an albatross around their necks.

This is not an accident or an unhappy coincidence. It is a direct consequence of the knowledge economy itself—or of how many governments have responded to it. Teachers and schools that should be the catalysts of change in the knowledge society are too often its casualties—of the weakening welfare safety net; of students' disrupted families being "squeezed between the millstones of two precarious incomes";[2] of reduced expenditure for and commitment to the public good. Rolling back the state, privatizing everything that moves, and applying abstract performance standards to hold the resulting fragments together is the ruthless result of market fundamentalism. It is not a smart way to build human capacity for a successful knowledge economy.

MARKET FUNDAMENTALISM

In the late twentieth century, the economic and public policy of many nations was dominated by the ideology of market fundamentalism.[3] Governments believed that the public interest was best served by the accumulated effects of freeing people to pursue their private interests. The state was regarded as a nuisance or a "nanny," undermining individual initiative and people's capacity to take responsibility for their own future. Competition from the private sector against the public sector and competition within the public domain were viewed as the best means to improve quality and raise standards. Where choice and competition could not bring about improvement, intervention and force would ensure the regulation of minimum standards among the rest.

The results in public education made themselves felt in cost-cutting and downsizing (with declining resources and deteriorating work conditions for teachers), in the growth of charter schools and schools of choice, and in tax incentives or campaigns to disparage the public system that encouraged parents to shift their investments into private education. Market fundamentalism also brought about moves to measure and compare achievement by the results of performance standards, to increase educational testing, and to impose zero tolerance and exclusion policies on those who spoiled public schools for the rest. Market fundamentalists, in other words, tried to build a flexible, free-market economy by making a quasi-market of the reduced yet still highly regulated public sector.[4]

In this shortsighted view of the knowledge society's needs, teachers have had to teach despite the knowledge economy's public-sector shortages and stringencies. More and more nations are now grasping the nature and importance of the knowledge economy and its implications for taking a more generous stance toward public education. They are moving beyond market fundamentalism to reinvest in public education, to foster more creativity and flexibility in schools, and to treat teachers with renewed respect as the frontline knowledge workers of the new economy. But even here, as we will see in chapters 6 and 7, stubborn residues of market fundamentalism remain in command and control styles of policy, and in the maintenance of extensive testing systems that enforce political will.

Not all the legacies of market fundamentalism are negative. Choice has challenged the self-servingness and complacency of many educational bureaucracies. Performance contracts have exposed incompetence in system cultures that used to hide their weaknesses and keep their problems to themselves.[5] Yet downsizing, standardization, deteriorating work conditions, and disparagement of educational professionals have undermined the development of a creative knowledge economy and a civilized knowledge society. Because these trends persist in many parts of teachers' world, it is important to document their effects and learn some lessons from them. An analogy will help.

EDUCATION OFF THE RAILS

In December 2000, our family rented a cottage in the north of England to see our relatives and spend Christmas together. Our son was arriving from Japan and had to take a connecting train from London to the north. The journey normally takes about four hours. Unfortunately, he arrived in the midst of a near-paralysis of Britain's rail network. The country's railways had been subjected to more than 500 daily speed restrictions. More than 50 percent of trains were running late. Britain's trains were crawling through the countryside, and our son's four-hour journey turned into a ten-hour marathon.

The restrictions were the immediate consequence of three major rail accidents that followed in rapid succession in 1997, 1999, and 2000, leading to forty-two deaths and grim media images of a national rail system turned into twisted metal. The crippling restrictions that followed were not just a consequence of necessary caution to ensure further safety. In *Broken Rails,* an investigative analysis of Britain's rail disasters, Christian Wolmar shows that the restrictions and the accidents preceding them were largely the result of two factors: privatization of the railways and an over-reliance on performance standards as the way to ensure quality.[6]

When Britain's railways were privatized, a company called Railtrack was established to manage the rail infrastructure, including the track itself. Separate private rail companies were then also created on a regional basis to run the trains on the system. Engineering, maintenance, and repairs, once part of an integrated system along with track and services, were now contracted out to private tender. Contracting out was supposed to keep costs down in a more flexible system while performance standards and targets were set to try to ensure safety and quality of service.

This effort to run a public service on private lines had calamitous consequences. First, standards of repair and inspection suffered:

> Railtrack and its contractors had to reduce costs by 3 per cent per annum in order to retain the same level of profits. Instead of teams of four or six people, which would allow the vital look-outs at the front and back [for oncoming trains], the [work] gang [now] consisted of just two men. This meant they could not venture onto the gap between each set of lines or the gap between the up and down lines.[7]

Because of the gap, a lot of deteriorating track, such as the one in Britain's last disaster at Hatfield, went unobserved. Profit prevailed over safety.

Second, the performance system rewarded quick fixes rather than long-lasting improvement. One way in which the performance of repair crews was measured and rewarded was by determining whether the trains ran better or faster as a result of their work. A rail track has three components: the metal rail, the ties that hold the rails together, and the ballast of stones that supports the whole structure. Repair contractors quickly found that replacing the rails led to the quickest improvements in trains' speed, so they just repaired the rails rather than also attending to the ties and the ballast that supported them over time. This performance culture rewarded quick-fix maintenance rather than long-term sustainability of safety and improvement. Any system—industrial or educational—that does not attend to sustainable improvement is a system waiting for disasters to happen.

Third, privatization, downsizing, and contracting out swept away middle-level cultures of engineers who knew the rail system and its people. It also eliminated local cultures of signal workers, crews, and station personnel who knew the trains, the track, and one another. Collective memory disappeared.[8] Contractors who roamed the country for work had little or no local knowledge of the problems they were fixing. The flexible economy of private contracts eradicated deep-seated cultures of engineering wisdom and expertise. In high-risk environments, people without experiential wisdom are unable to make effective judgments and can become overly cautious, even paranoid, in their actions. Hence, the endless restrictions and the paralysis of the railways at the end of the year 2000, when wise experts would have seen that far fewer restrictions were necessary.

Like the privatization of U.S. airport security, the privatization and fragmentation of Britain's railways imperiled people's safety. Amtrak in the United States seems to be headed in a similar direction. The privatization of Britain's railways created an unacceptable redistribution of insecurity and risk from government institutions to private individuals. It prioritized quick-fix maintenance over sustainable renewal. Because of the loss of cultures of local and national expertise, it also created a paranoid backlash about baseline competences and minimum standards. All of this added up to a fourth factor: a loss of learning, of ability and willingness to improve throughout the entire system. As one of the railway company's directors of operations and safety said:

> The organization [of Railtrack] does not look very often at some of the big picture issues. They tend to be reactive to incidents and single problem-solving processes . . . and sometimes not taking a broad risk based approach to the management of safety, which I do not think is helpful to long term improvement. . . . They do not seem to be a learning organization.[9]

Sounds familiar, doesn't it, this cost-cutting that leads to dangerous shortcuts; performance standards that push people into quick fixes rather than sustainable improvement; the loss of people with experience, wisdom, and judgment from the heart of an organization's culture? In a low-trust system, high on standards but weak on discretionary judgment, comes an associated overemphasis on bottom lines, basic competence, and zero tolerance— anything that will protect the weak and the witless from future liability. As Ivor Goodson pointed out, these are features not only of Britain's railways but also of other public organizations that have been subjected to the principles of the flexible, private economy.[10] Public education is among them.

Its excessive concentration on minimum standards and short-term performance targets in a context of low-cost investment and proliferating choice is pushing public education off the rails. When governments and organizations try to stimulate a more flexible economy through principles of market fundamentalism in the form of downsizing, flexible workforces, flattened management, and blanket performance standards, expenditure is withdrawn from public education to free up the economy instead of investment in education and knowledge being used to fuel it.

The global economy is hungry for flexible resources, for the free and expanded flow of investment capital and for a movement of resources from the coffers of the state to the pockets of the people. To pay down national debts and liberate the power of personal investment, governments driven by market fundamentalism have made repeated cutbacks in public expenditure. Public education is one of the most expensive and vulnerable items on the list. In country after country, educational-spending levels fell for many years. Consultant, supervisory, and staff-development support positions and all the cultures of wisdom and experience that they embodied were cut back, with outsourcing of any remainder. Teachers' salaries were held down. Paid positions of teacher leadership were reduced. Workloads continue to increase. Teachers became trapped in a world of doing more for less.[11]

Especially in the inner cities of the United States and the housing projects in many parts of Europe, levels of investment and support for public education have fallen to or remained at desperately low levels—one of the patently obvious but less-remarked-on reasons for the highly publicized epidemics of school failure. In the 1990s, the State of California, for example, spent more on its prisons than its schools.[12] Finding qualified teachers and leaders who are prepared to work in urban schools has been an increasingly widespread problem in the United States, Britain, and elsewhere.[13] In the United States, the educational interest and investment shown by corporate and philanthropic foundations such as Annenberg, Carnegie, Rockefeller, MacArthur, Gates, and others has demonstrated the optimistic potential of reforms that invest in the creativity and capacity of teachers and leaders—but only in selected schools and districts that have the traditions of grant-writing that enable them to gain access to these scarce pools of money. Scaling up what is learned from these reforms to the more generally underfunded urban system remains frustratingly beyond reach, as does sustaining the improvements that have been made after the foundation money has run out.

Confronted with demands for better results in public schools but voters' unwillingness to pay higher taxes for them, and faced with the political realities of underfunded, low-capacity urban systems that often have had to rely on poorly qualified and badly paid teachers, some senior officials have taken drastic measures. Standardized tests and texts have been at the center of them. Since the late 1980s, centrally prescribed curricula, with detailed and pressing performance targets, aligned assessments, and high stakes accountability, have defined a "new orthodoxy" of educational reform worldwide, providing standardized solutions at low cost for a voting public keen on accountability.[14]

More recently, standardized practices have also focused on a limited number of tightly defined instructional priorities such as literacy and mathematics. Teachers are required to meet these priorities in closely prescribed, carefully scripted, and precisely timed formats. Intensive training in these "scientifically proven"[15] teaching strategies is then applied to large numbers of a system's teachers, with the accompanying involvement of their principals.[16] Credible claims have been made that these strategies can lead to dramatic gains in students' achievement as well as narrowed achievement gaps between students from wealthy and poor families.[17] Yet it is questionable whether the win or the short-term way of achieving it will prove to be worth the long-term cost.[18] Strong intervention strategies with prescribed programs, intense training, and follow-up coaching may yield the quickest improvements in the poorest, low-capacity schools and their communities, but they can also reinforce cultures of dependency among teachers who, like karaoke singers, learn only to follow the bouncing ball of the script. Instead of attacking the economic causes of low investment and low capacity in poor communities, these measures run the risk of dealing largely with their effects and of recycling cultures of low capacity and strong dependency among the teaching force as they do so.[19]

Quests to narrow achievement gaps typically do not question the kinds of achievement at stake. Evidence is mounting that gaps in achievement defined in relatively simple basic skills *can* be narrowed in the short term among younger children by harder work and extra practice, but gaps in achievement of more sophisticated "knowledge-society" kinds that can be sustained in the long run, especially among older students, cannot. It has been much easier to raise basic literacy and mathematics achievements through micromanaged intervention in the early years of schooling than to raise standards at the high-school level.[20] Reformers have yet to address what is needed to develop the sophisticated forms of learning that constitute achievement at these higher levels.

In their late conversion to the power and necessity of large-scale educational reform, some of those change theorists who once said, "You cannot mandate what matters to effective practice,"[21] now seem to believe the opposite.[22] Yet all they may actually have demonstrated is that you can mandate what does not matter so much—that you can get teachers to mimic their trainers or crank out the scripted performances of the karaoke curriculum (which may disappear once the pressure in the short term is off and the focus shifts) but not to foster deep and complex teaching and learning for the knowledge society in the long run.

Linda McNeil has shown how Texas's heralded standardized-test movement has undone the success that schools were sometimes able to achieve with minority students by eliminating the creative pedagogy and integrated curriculum change that allowed teachers to engage with their students' styles of learning and their distinctive cultural concerns.[23] Nel Noddings goes further and predicts that once the coercive measures of standardization and pervasive testing fail to deliver sustainable improvements in learning standards for all children and at all levels, the entire public-school system will be declared a failure and put out to private tender.[24]

None of this helps teachers prepare young people, least of all poor young people, with the educational and economic ingenuity they need to succeed in the knowledge economy. Nor does it develop the relationships, experiences and social capital that will prepare them to contribute to public life beyond the knowledge economy. Instead of care, there has been coercion; instead of professionalism, there has been prescription; instead of deep learning, there has been surface performance. This is not what a creative and civilizing knowledge society needs.

Teachers are therefore trapped in an infernal triangle of competing pressures and expectations in the knowledge society. They struggle to reach an apex of professional achievement in being both catalysts for a successful knowledge economy and effective counterpoints for some of its more socially disruptive effects. As they do so, they are continually dragged down by market-fundamentalist reactions to the costs of that same knowledge economy—in restricted support for public education, in unending micromanagement by coercive bureaucracies, and in disparaging discourses of blame and shame that stain teachers' character. Instead of being catalysts of and counterpoints for the knowledge society, too many teachers have become casualties who must:

- Coach children to memorize standardized learning;
- Learn to teach as they are told;
- Undergo in-service training on government priorities;
- Work harder and learn alone;

- Treat parents as consumers and complainers;
- Perform emotional labor;
- Respond to imposed change with fearful compliance;
- Trust no one.

Instead of promoting deep learning and students' emotional engagement with their learning and with one another, teachers, as casualties of the knowledge society, find themselves increasingly preoccupied with coaching children for standardized tests. Socrates said that the unexamined life is not worth living. For teachers, it is the overexamined life that is the problem. Instead of learning continuously to teach differently and better and to relate more effectively with students and others as a foundation for that learning, teachers are increasingly pressured to teach as they are told. Research in best classroom practice is imposed on them rather than offered as a source of professional reflection and adaptation to their own classroom circumstances. Teaching and learning are not intelligently informed by evidence; they are driven by the imperatives of results. Rather than experiencing continuous professional learning and development, teachers are subjected to mandated (and usually inadequate) in-service training on government or district priorities. Teachers who crave support and learning from their colleagues in teams and in groups find that limited resources, increased demands, and mandated priorities condemn them to a time-starved life of corrosive individualism where they work, learn, and respond to change alone. And the partnerships and relationships with parents that are so essential in supporting students' learning are either reduced to market transactions where schools treat parents as consumers or to defensive reactions that characterize parents as interfering complainers.

Under intensive and insensitively imposed change, teachers also find their emotional worlds turned upside down. Instead of using their emotional intelligence to be more effective with their students, or having the time to invest in the relationships that build emotional understanding with those around them, teachers have to engage in what Arlie Hochschild calls "emotional labor."[25] This takes place when people manufacture or mask their emotions to align with the ways of feeling that are expected and approved of in their profession. The emotional labor required of workers varies from one occupation to another. Funeral directors must be solicitous. Debt collectors need to sound irritated. Nurses have to care at a distance. In teaching, optimism, enthusiasm, and a caring disposition are called for every day. Emotional labor—making an effort to feel and express the "right" emotions that your job requires—can be a great professional virtue, a labor of love. Nursing and teaching would be nothing without it. But under certain con-

	Catalysts Teaching For	Counterpoints Teaching Beyond	Casualties Teaching Despite
Learning as	Deep cognitive	Social and emotional	Standardized performance
Professional	Learning	Development	Training
Colleagues as	Teams	Groups	Individuals
Parents as	Learners	Partners	Consumers and complainers
Emotional	Intelligence	Understanding	Labor
Tone of	Change and risk	Continuity and security	Fear and insecurity
Trust in	Processes	People	No one

FIGURE 3.1. Teaching in the Knowledge Society

ditions, the effects of emotional labor can be perverse. This happens when people have to use their emotional labor to fulfill other people's purposes, not their own, or when the conditions of their work make emotional labor unachievable. Teaching standardized knowledge to raise test scores, or being so overwhelmed with extraneous tasks that there is no time for classroom and collegial relationships, turns emotional labor into a draining process that increases stress, saps motivation, and depletes morale. It is hard to remain authentically optimistic and enthusiastic when you are overloaded, have no time to care for students properly, are constantly criticized by governments, get little opportunity to work with colleagues, and must grapple with change alone.[26]

In this kind of climate, instead of taking risks and committing to continuous improvement on a solid platform of secure and trusting relationships, teachers wait in fear of the next capricious reform initiative, suffer unending performance anxiety in the face of constant evaluation and inspection, and feel neither trusting of nor trusted by their superiors. Being a teacher is like being Fox Mulder in the television show "*X-Files*": You learn to trust no one. The knowledge economy thrives on risk and depends on trust. Low trust and insecurity are its enemies. This reality of teaching as a casualty of the knowledge society, rather than as a catalyst for or counterpoint to it, is summarized in Figure 3.1.

STANDARDIZED POLICIES

The effects of large-scale standardized reform on teachers in the knowledge society are evident across the world.[27] This chapter and the next focus on two clear examples of standardized reforms and their consequences for the knowledge society, in New York State and Ontario, Canada. Each of these settings underwent major movements toward standards-based reform in the years leading up to and at the turn of the new millennium. The policies were large-scale, high-stakes, and inescapable, and they have had sweeping effects on their systems' teachers.

In both cases, the rightful pursuit of higher standards has degenerated into a counterproductive obsession with soulless standardization. Our evidence will show that teachers are being robbed of the flexibility and creativity that is essential in the knowledge economy. Downsizing and standardization have corroded collaboration, depleted teacher leadership, and reduced teachers' investment in their professional learning, destroying the collective intelligence that is vital for knowledge-based organizations. Standardization is irrelevant to or drains the energy of high-performing schools at the top as it increases the exclusion of schools and students at the bottom, who find the standards dispiritingly beyond their grasp. Increased exclusion further depletes the pool of talent and collective intelligence on which economic prosperity depends. In the face of relentless standardization, we will see, an exhausted and demoralized teaching force turns to resignation and early retirement, creating massive problems of recruitment and retention in this knowledge-based profession.

These two chapters show that the obsession with soulless standardization is anathema to educational and economic regeneration in the knowledge economy. Chapter 5 looks at how far an outstanding knowledge-society school is able to navigate and maintain its own distinctive course through these storms of standardization.

With teams of colleagues in two projects, I have investigated the impact of standardized reforms on teachers in three New York State high schools and nine Ontario secondary schools. In one of these projects, co-directed with Ivor Goodson and funded by the Spencer Foundation, we took a retrospective look at teachers' experiences of educational change over the past 30 years in eight secondary schools (three in New York; five in Ontario).[28] We conducted more than 200 interviews with teachers who had worked in the schools in the 1970s and 1980s, as well as with those who were dealing with educational change at the very end of the 1990s and beyond. Our data consist of extensive and sometimes repeated interviews with these three cohorts of teachers, further interviews with present and past school leaders, ongoing observations in the schools, and collection of extensive archival information from the schools and their districts. The interviews were transcribed and analyzed in depth and were used to compile extensive case studies on each school according to a common format and set of themes developed by the project team. These case studies then provided the foundation for a cross-case analysis of key factors that affected the sustainability of educational change over time.

Three of the project schools were in an urban school district that we call the Bradford school district in lower New York State. They were a "magnet" school (Barrett); a small alternative high school that has provided flexible individualized programs for students who have chosen an education outside the mainstream (Durant); and a regular high school that has to cope with increasing poverty and other challenges in its student population (Sheldon).

Like many cities in the United States, Bradford saw a dramatic shift in its population in the last two decades of the twentieth century. "White flight" to the suburbs left a core of poor families—mainly minorities, particularly African American—in the urban core. According to Bradford district statistics, in 1985, 40 percent of Bradford students lived in poverty; that proportion had risen to 69 percent in just five short years. By 1989, the district's student population was 62 percent African American and 18 percent Hispanic.

Partly in response to these demographic shifts, the Bradford school district set about creating "magnet" schools in 1981. Magnet schools were created federally in the mid-1970s to encourage voluntary desegregation. Under the Reagan and Bush administrations, magnet schools were given the additional purpose of promoting market competition and school choice.[29] The initiative continued under President Clinton, maintaining an unusual combination of emphases on desegregation and academic excellence.

The Barrett magnet school was created from a school that was once known for student violence, low attendance, high levels of poverty, and poor academic performance. With an infusion of $1 million in federal resources, Barrett was able to become selective and attract middle-class families who sought safe and academically challenging experiences for their children, as well as motivated teachers and administrators who were drawn to the school's mission. Barrett quickly became the shining star of the district, and in a few short years it was being rated among the best 150 schools in the United States and one of the top ten in the state.

Magnets repel as well as attract, however. Other schools felt Barrett's gain as their loss. Sheldon High School was one of those. From being a large comprehensive high school with a strong academic reputation in the early 1960s,

Sheldon saw desegregation bring more diversity into its building (from 10 percent non-white in 1966 to 25 percent in 1970). Maintaining its traditional emphasis alongside a tightening of discipline did not avert race riots in the early 1970s, and many white families took flight to the suburbs or the private sector. Sheldon continued to hold a reasonable reputation for almost a decade, though, until the magnet initiative drew away its academically and artistically strongest students (what some teachers described as the second white flight). At the same time, the closure of a neighboring poor African American high school with serious problems of discipline and violence led to the transfer of a large percentage of its students and a number of its staff to Sheldon. With this transfer pulling poorer students in and the magnet initiative drawing some of the highest performers away, combined with the continued socioeconomic decline of the urban core, 50 percent of Sheldon's students by 1989 were living in poverty, rising to a staggering 70 percent 10 years later. Not surprisingly, Sheldon now has the ironic label of being the district's "special education magnet."

With federal funds for new magnet initiatives fading, and in an effort to spur improvement of schools through competition, the Bradford district in 1988 introduced open enrollment and schools of choice from Grade 9. In an effort to create greater equity across schools, it also regulated the distribution of students' choices according to quartile grade categories. In the 1990s, the effects of the inclusion of special education also brought a wider range of students and teachers into the district's regular schools. The diluting effect this began to exert on Barrett's standing led it to introduce the prestigious International Baccalaureate as a way to try to arrest the school's incipient decline in status.

The Bradford district's adoption of standards-based reform—a movement that emerged in the United States in the 1980s—was a process of encroachment, not an act of eruption. In the late 1980s, the state mandated competency tests in five subjects (it had previously mandated three). The number was increased to six in 1990 and accompanied by an extension of required credits for graduates from 20.5 in 1986 to 23.5 for entering students in 1991. After a period of parallel experimentation with portfolios and other forms of "authentic assessment" in the early 1990s (when the district mandated portfolio assessment for English teachers, for example), the second half of the 1990s heralded more rigorous enforcement of a new testing regime tied to the state's new high standards. Students' graduation was made dependent on passing demanding tests in five assessed subjects.

The specific, extremely demanding, and escalating requirements of standards-based reform in Bradford are that students who entered Grade 9 in

1998 will have to pass four out of five examinations with a minimum score of 55 to graduate. Students entering a year later must pass all five examinations at the same standard. For students entering Grade 9 in 2000, the standard is increased to 65 in three of the exams, and this score is applied to all five subjects for Grade 9 entrants in 2001. Math and science course requirements have also been increased to three years, from two. These assessments are very high-stakes, with schools and districts across the state being ranked by their test scores, then given highly public "report cards" to accompany them.

As a result of a 1997 amendment to the U.S. Individuals with Disabilities in Education Act, the district requires that special-education students be included in the testing that is linked to graduation requirements. Initially, special-education students will be required to take more basic "competency" exams in five subjects that will confer a lower-status diploma. Eventually, however, it is planned that even special-education students will graduate only if they pass all five of the main exams.

All these changes are occurring with a teaching force that is experiencing mixed working conditions. A landmark agreement between the district and the unions in 1987 significantly raised teachers' salaries by 40 percent in exchange for their commitment to a number of reforms and responsibilities. In the same period, however, department heads were replaced by administrators of larger units. Meanwhile, Bradford's teaching force, like others elsewhere, has continued to age: Thirty percent are expected to retire in the first five years of this century.

STANDARDIZED PRACTICES

In practice, these changes have significantly affected teachers and their capacity to prepare children for the knowledge society and beyond it. The effects are especially evident in relation to curriculum and teaching practices, exclusion of marginalized students, and teachers' work and relationships.

Curriculum and Teaching

One of the most evident effects of standards-based reform on teachers in the Bradford school district has been on the scope and flexibility of the curriculum. These effects were felt particularly strongly in the Durant alternative school, which prided itself on its commitment to adjusting the curriculum to students and to the things that motivate them to achieve. As long ago as the mid-1980s, when curriculum demands began to escalate,

> more credit requirements were placed upon them [students], then we had to create a more rigid academic program. . . . We still had flexibility, but it got to a point where a lot of the time [that we used to have] to allow kids to grow and explore was pulled off the table.

By the late 1990s, the competency tests and exam requirements had forced teachers to reduce the range of options they could offer students, to narrow the range of curriculum choices, and to restrict opportunities for multidisciplinary initiatives. In addition, the requirements for one- or two-year-long periods of preparation in an increased number of tested core courses eliminated the possibilities of teaching students in mixed-age groups.

The demand of covering the required and intensified curriculum, of keeping up appearances and producing "anything that looks good for PR" (Barrett), and of having to prepare students for tests, was that "so much emphasis [is] put on the amount of material you're supposed to cover that [all] you're really doing is a skim job—a question of quality versus quantity" (Sheldon). Understandably, Durant teachers were the most indignant about having to deliver more "direct instruction," where they had to emphasize "things that they [the students] don't choose to learn about." What was lost in their teaching and in students' learning were all the things most prized in a knowledge economy—creativity, spontaneity, deep understanding, critical thinking, and the development of multiple forms of collective intelligence.

One teacher described how afternoon classes that had always been flexible and "based on what the kids were interested in" were now "geared toward" the state tests and "more teacher-directed." In the past, the teacher explained, "I would teach based on making sure kids understood things." Now all that mattered was "getting through the curriculum" and preparing for the tests, which the teacher characterized as "very frustrating." Another teacher who had once taught highly engaging classes on Native American history, ethics, and Vietnam—prime ways to develop cosmopolitan identity—had been "reduced to U.S. History I and II [and] World History I and II."

Other teachers described the effects of the high-stakes tests on their practice in graphic terms, as in the following teacher's description of a class that

> was based on literature and the Teacher's Curriculum Institute, which is all based on Howard Gardner's theories about how people learn,

the multiple intelligences and cooperative learning. . . . After a week
or so, a couple of kids said, "Are you going to teach like this the rest
of the year?" I was using overheads, giving class notes, and I just sort
of stopped. I said, "Unfortunately, I'm probably going to have to
because [of] what is happening. . . . I've seen the tests and I've seen
the sample . . . and it's content, content, content. There's no way that
I could allow you to go and sit for this exam knowing that I have not
used the book that the district has given us." And they're basically
saying, "You use this book." The kids can get ready for the [state
tests]. Comparing that book to [the Teacher's Curriculum Institute's
material] is just a world of difference. The reading level is much
more difficult, it's much more content-driven, a lot more dates,
vocabulary, identification rather than probing, thinking, critical
thinking questions. . . . And I said, "Kids, I'm not any happier than
you are about this, but I could not live with myself knowing that
I did not teach you in a way that would prepare you to jump through
that hoop." I couldn't do it personally or professionally.

At Barrett, a number of teachers complained that they had to "teach to the
test," making students "too test conscious" by "focusing on passing the
exam." "From September to January," an administrator explained, "[teach-
ers] teach at a certain pace so that by January they have covered [the re-
quired] numbers of units in order for the kids to pass the midterm in January." As one special-education teacher at Barrett noted, some of the most
damaging effects are on the school's best teachers:

> I see the state government saying more and more students will tap
> dance this way. I think we are losing something in the process.
> I think it is good to raise your level of expectation and certainly for
> some teachers. Kids maybe are mastering more material because
> expectations have been raised overall. But I see it kind of taking away
> from some of the good teachers who are now spending an inordinate
> amount of time teaching students a rhetoric that they have to follow
> to perform, rather than being able to really spend time teaching them
> to enjoy the learning process, to read and really get into what you are
> reading and maybe take off and read something related, taking it
> apart and looking at it because it is an interest that the students have.
> But the interests of the students do not seem to be focussed any-
> where. You are told what needs to be done and what students need
> to do to master a test.

Diversity and Division

Not all teachers dislike standards-based reform. At the Barrett magnet school, the majority of teachers spoke in support of the standards because of their affirmation of Barrett's tradition of high-performance expectations. "I am not sure that it is a reform for us," said one teacher, who approved of having as many students as possible take the exams because it set high expectations for them. "The teacher's job is to make sure the students meet the standards," ventured another. An English teacher pointed to a wider standards context:

> I have done some things with America's Choice schools and with the National Center on Education and the Economy, and those things are just incredibly standards-based and seem really relevant to the things that we expect in this state and this district. So I think there is this kind of synthesis of national, state, and local requirements or goals that make sense to me.

Many of the teachers in this high-status, high-performing magnet school felt secure with their academic standards and therefore comfortable with standards-based reform. The reform's prime purpose and value, they felt, rested in providing some direction for their less effective colleagues elsewhere. "I really think that the new state exam might wake up a lot of people and make teachers do the job that they should have been doing for years," said one teacher. Others adopted similarly self-righteous tones:

> I think the new comprehensive exam in one way is a good idea because it keeps a high standard of learning in the school and throughout the state. Now the district wants to have a central midterm exam that everyone is giving at the same time. We saw as we were making it up that some people were not quite as rigorous maybe as the other schools. So I think you can see it is kind of easy to lower the bar. And as your population is getting more diverse in their abilities, you could just let things start to slide: "Oh, well, if kids are not going to do well at this level, then we will keep lowering it." So I think is it good, that it keeps standards high.

> I think the whole standards-based curriculum idea has really come to the fore in the 18 years that I have been here. And I think that good teachers probably always have been aiming for those same goals, but I think it is a way of kind of shoring up things for people who maybe

were unsure and were not quite clear on how to come up with a program that leads everybody to this kind of place and this is where everybody needs to be at the end of the program. So I am pretty comfortable with that.

At the other pole at Barrett are the school's special-education and English as a Second Language (ESL) teachers. They are highly critical of the impact of standards-based reform on students with language or learning difficulties:

> The fact that every kid in this state has to take Regents biology is a travesty and a tragedy because there are some kids who will not be able to pass and deserve a high-school diploma. A high-school diploma does not mean that you know what a nucleus is, or what it can do, or is that important to that kid. To say to me that a special-education kid needs to know what a restriction enzyme is is a sin and . . . an abomination.

> This talk about all the kids having state comprehensive diplomas is unrealistic. The more they say they want the kids to come to a certain level, bottom line, somebody is lowering the bar overall or else a lot of kids are going to be set up for failure. Not all these kids are going to reach this particular level they have set. Especially for some of the special-education kids, there is no way they are ever going to get a real diploma if they have to hit the same level as everyone else.

> The comprehensive English exam in 11th Grade is a two-session exam, three hours each session. Our kids, . . . many of them have extended time to complete tests. So they now sit for a three-hour exam, only it's probably going to take them four and a half. . . . We now have made kids sit for nine hours to fail an exam because very, very few will pass it. And then as a reward they get to take a competency test.

Teachers in the high-poverty, high-minority Sheldon school echoed these sentiments (although, interestingly, teachers at the Durant "alternative" school, whose clientele used to be more white and middle class, did not). Sheldon's teachers resonated with Noddings's critique that standards-based reform ultimately will implode because large numbers of challenged students will fail unless the standards are self-defeatingly lowered to accommodate them.[30]

I understand trying to raise the bar and get everybody to work at a higher level, but when you have more than half of your classes failing, raising the bar doesn't seem like it's really helping these kids. So I think this latest reform of trying to get everybody into an academic program maybe is sort of shortsighted, in a way. I don't think everyone is going to be able to meet that.

The superintendent decided three years ago, all the kids are going to be in an academic program. That's bullshit. I'm sorry, but that's bullshit. In my fifth- and sixth-period class, you ought to come in here and watch them someday, you'll see. These kids are no more academic track than I am an astronaut. These kids are coming in here with a reading level of three and four grades down from what it should be. They can't write worth a damn. You're telling me these are academic-program kids?

In summary, standards-based reform produced a divided response among these New York State teachers. Academically oriented teachers of successful middle-class students approved of or found it relatively easy to accommodate standards that they felt they already met. Somewhat piously, perhaps, they also conceded that imposing the standards may be necessary to raise the performance of colleagues elsewhere who were less excellent than themselves. Teachers in the high-poverty, high-minority schools and in the special-education and ESL sections of the more exclusive ones, though, despaired about the ways in which standards-based reform would simply inscribe failure more deeply into their disadvantaged students' souls. These responses point to disturbing and damaging, non-inclusive consequences of standards-based reform, where seemingly common and neutral standards that actually favor middle-class students exclude and further marginalize the rest. This is no way to build community, create inclusiveness, and educate young people beyond the knowledge society, or to develop and draw on the collective intelligence and pools of talent that are needed for the knowledge economy.

TEACHERS' WORK AND RELATIONSHIPS

The micromanagement of standards-based reform had deleterious effects on teachers' teaching, on teachers' students, and on teachers' relationships to their work and with one another. Some spoke of stress, burnout, loss of enjoyment and motivation, and withdrawal from the job as a whole. Two teachers at Barrett put it this way:

> Sometimes I think people feel like they are being chased by state reg-ulations, board examinations, state regulations for graduation, and state regulations for special-education students. There just seems to be so much focus on meeting standards set from the outside that I don't think we get to spend as much time thinking about what we're going to be doing in the classroom and enjoying it. I don't see the same level of enjoyment in teaching that I did once, just because it's become so much more stressful. And I'm seeing it in other teachers. I'm seeing the stress level of the paperwork that's required. . . . It takes away from your investment in kids and your investment in your classroom and your investment in what's going on a day-to-day basis because you're so preoccupied with all this other stuff that has to be taken care of. I see that as . . . a real negative.

> Do I sound like I am getting burned out? I am. I am. I am getting very, very burned out. And I am going to retire early because of it. I have visions of maybe doing some volunteer tutoring. If I go in, it [will be] to work with a specific kid who has a specific problem, and I will try to help see that kid does not have a problem anymore by the time I leave . . . definitely where I do not have the state capitol determining how the day is going to go on a day-to-day basis.

At the Durant alternative school, some staff coped by separating their life from work. "I am putting in less time because of decreasing morale. I some-times fall into a 'What's the use?' frame of mind," said one teacher. On weekends, "I'm outta here; see you on Monday," said another. A third, who had accepted a district retirement package said,

> I'm still excited about teaching. I'm still excited about learning. I'm still excited about the kids. But I can't deal with the system. [It] has absolutely torn me apart and I'm tired of fighting it.[31]

Teachers were worn down by the loss of creativity and spontaneity in their work and wounded by the theft of their autonomy. They talked about valu-ing the ability to "call their own shots" and be imaginative in their class-rooms. They felt that it was a "damn shame" that "that sense of autonomy, that ability to create your own curriculum with high standards, has to be thrown out of place by something that is artificial," a teacher said. "You're selling your soul to the devil." A colleague also bemoaned the "taking away of professional judgment and autonomy as a teacher." Everything this teacher had learned and done before now seemed to be regarded as worthless.

> I spent years learning how to teach, learning why kids learn, how they learn, what I can do to help that happen. And suddenly the state says, "No, none of that means anything. None of that means anything at all. We're going to tell you what to teach." Essentially, tell you how to teach.

Standards-based reform also affected teachers' relationships with others, particularly their colleagues. It corroded their capacity to collaborate. The director of Durant complained, "Sixty to 70 percent of my day is spent fighting the [state tests, which] prevents me from spending time with students and staff." There was less time to meet together or mentor new staff members. Teachers' priorities were displaced to the goals of test performance and away from high-quality learning in the classroom and with their colleagues.

The evidence of our New York State schools suggests, therefore, that in teachers' eyes standards-based reform is preparing students neither for the knowledge economy nor for character and community beyond it. In general, teachers are being treated and developed not as highly skilled, high-capacity knowledge workers, but as compliant and closely monitored producers of standardized performances. Whereas teachers in more privileged settings can accommodate standards-based reforms relatively easily, and sometimes even regard such reforms as a source of affirmation, other teachers feel that students who are poor, who have learning difficulties, or who are learning English as a second language experience standardization as a stigma that merely confirms their failure through public spectacles of exclusionary shame.

New York State reveals much about how the substance of standards-based reform has affected the lives of teachers and students in schools—not just in this case but in many others like it. Particularly for teachers with long professional memories, the substance of standards-based reform in New York has created an overexamined professional life that erodes autonomy, restricts creativity, removes flexibility, and constrains teachers' capacity to exercise their professional judgment. As we will see in the closing chapter, the deep and pervasive sense of professional disillusionment among teachers that these patterns create is at the heart of an impending demographic disaster: The vast majority of the existing teaching force will retire in the first decade of the twenty-first century, and nobody will want to step up to replace them when all that awaits them is micromanaged careers of teaching to the test. There will be no knowledge society without teachers who are high-skilled knowledge workers. This is an unavoidable economic and demographic reality that all standards-based reformers ultimately will have to confront.

The substance of standards-based reform also inhibits and threatens to annihilate innovative practices in non-standard subjects and non-standard schools. Subjects such as music, which often fall outside the framework of paper-and-pencil standards, find themselves increasingly marginalized within the standardized school curriculum, even though they may have had their own strict standards for decades. Or if these subjects are included within the standards, their content is ironically narrowed and trivialized so it can easily be captured in written form—lowering the very standards that intervention is meant to enhance.[32] Innovative and alternative schools such as Durant find it hard to maintain their distinctiveness in the face of agendas of standardization. Even more striking examples of this will be given in the following chapters. Innovation and ingenuity are essential to the knowledge economy, but judging by our evidence, standards-based reform in New York State may be eradicating them.

Last, by insisting on full inclusion of all students within a standardized system of inert, reproducible, content-driven knowledge, standardized reform excludes the so-called "included" or special students even more by subjecting them to inappropriate criteria for achievement, denying them graduation, and putting their failings in the public spotlight. J. Falk and B. Drayton have noted the same phenomenon in their research on the impact of high-stakes testing in Massachusetts.[33] By insisting on absolute inclusion, standardization actually increases exclusion. This does little to develop collective intelligence for the knowledge society or build character and community beyond it.

NOTES

1. Halsey, A. H., "Foreword," in P. Brown & H. Lauder, *Capitalism and Social Progress: The Future of Society in a Global Economy*, Basingstoke, Palgrave, 2001, p. xii.

2. Ignatieff, M., *The Rights Revolution*, Toronto, Anansi Press, 2000, p. 90.

3. On quasi-markets in education, see Whitty, G., Power, S. & Halpin, D. *Devolution and Choice in Education: The School, State, the Market*, Buckingham, Open University Press, 1998.

4. The different economic strategies that can be taken in a knowledge economy, including those that amount to market fundamentalism, are discussed in Brown & Lauder, *op. cit.*, note 1.

5. These arguments are developed in chapter 6.

6. Wolmar, C., *Broken Rails: How Privatization Wrecked Britain's Railways*, London, Aurum Press, 2001. The remaining material in this section draws largely on Wolmar's book.

7. Ibid., pp. 158–159.

8. See Goodson, I., *The Personality of Change*, Paper presented at the invitational conference on Social Geographies of Educational Change (funded by the Spencer Foundation), Barcelona, Spain, March 2001.

9. Alison Foster, director of operations and safety of Great Western Trains, as quoted in Wolmar, *op. cit.*, note 6, p. 144.

10. Goodson, *op. cit.*, note 8.

11. The best summary of the evidence from a range of countries can be found in Whitty, Power & Halpin, *op. cit.*, note 3.

12. Castells, M., *End of Millennium*, Oxford, Blackwell, 1998.

13. Darling-Hammond, L., *Doing What Matters Most: Investing in Quality Teaching*, New York, National Commission on Teaching and America's Future, 1997.

14. I develop a more detailed discussion of the "new orthodoxy" of educational change in Hargreaves, A., Earl, L., Moore, S. & Manning, S., *Learning to Change: Teaching beyond Subjects and Standards*, San Francisco, Jossey-Bass/Wiley, 2001.

15. The best known of these is Slavin, R. E., *Every Child, Every School: Success for All*, Newbury Park, CA, Corwin Press, 1996, on which England's large-scale National Literacy Project partly draws.

16. Elmore, D. & Burney, D., *Investing in Teacher Learning: Staff Development and Instructional Improvement in Community School District #2, New York City*, New York, National Commission on Teaching and America's Future, 1997; Hill, P. W. & Crévola, C., "The role of standards in educational reform for the 21st century," in D. Marsh (ed.), *Preparing Our Schools for the 21st Century*, Alexandria, VA, Association for Supervision and Curriculum Development, 1999.

17. Fullan, M., *Leading in a culture of change*, San Francisco, Jossey-Bass/Wiley, 2001.

18. Ibid.

19. The idea of the karaoke curriculum is described in Hargreaves, Earl, Moore & Manning, *op. cit.*, note 14.

20. Department for Education and Skills, *Achieving Success*, London, Her Majesty's Stationery Office (HMSO), 2001.

21. The phrase is originally in Berman, P. & McLaughlin, M., *Federal Programs Supporting Educational Change: Factors Affecting Implementation and Continuation* (vol. 7), Santa Monica, CA, RAND Corporation, 1977.

22. Fullan, M., "The return of large-scale reform," *Journal of Educational Change* 1(1), 2000, 5–28.

23. McNeil, L., *Contradictions of School Reform: Educational Costs of Standardization*, New York, Routledge, 2000.

24. Noddings, N., "Care and coercion in school reform," *Journal of Educational Change* 2(1), 2001, 35–43. See also Boyd, W. L., "The 'R's of school reform' and the politics of reforming or placing public schools," *Journal of Educational Change* 1(3), 2000, 225–252. I will return to these arguments in the final chapter.

25. Hochschild, A. R., *The Managed Heart: The Commercialization of Human Feeling*, Berkeley, University of California Press, 1983.

26. For more extended discussion of the role of emotional labor in teaching, see Blackmore, J., "Doing 'emotional labour' in the education market place: Stories from the field of women in management," *Discourse: Studies in the Cultural Politics of Education* 17(3), 1996, 337–349; Hargreaves, Earl, Moore & Manning, *op. cit.*, note 14.

27. For summaries, see Whitty, Power & Halpin, *op. cit.*, note 3; Hargreaves, Earl, Moore & Manning, *op. cit.*, note 14.

28. Hargreaves, A., & Goodson, I., *Change over Time? A Report of Educational Change over 30 Years in Eight U.S. and Canadian Secondary Schools* (final project report to the Spencer Foundation), Chicago, in press.

29. Henig, J. R., *Rethinking School Choice: Limits of the Market Metaphor*, Princeton, NJ, Princeton University Press, 1994.

30. Noddings, *op. cit.*, note 24, pp. 35–43.

31. This teacher returned in 1996 and was speaking not about the most recent tests but about the earlier competence tests and credit requirements.

32. Siskin, L. S., *Outside the Core: Tested and Untested Subjects in High-Stakes Accountability Systems*, Paper presented at the American Educational Research Association annual conference, Seattle, 2001.

33. Falk, J. & Drayton, B., *High Stakes Testing and the Inquiry Based Classroom: Complementary or Colliding Visions of Reform?* Paper presented at the American Educational Research Association annual conference, Seattle, 2001.

4

TEACHING DESPITE
THE KNOWLEDGE SOCIETY, PART II
The Loss of Integrity

(with Shawn Moore and Dean Fink)

INTRODUCTION

The province of Ontario in Canada provides a second example of the implications of market fundamentalism and standardization for knowledge-society objectives. The province was a relative latecomer to market fundamentalism, when its oxymoronically named "Progressive Conservative" government was elected in 1995, partly on a platform of fundamental school reform. The government initiated sweeping budget cuts to the public service, including education, while creating a 30 percent tax cut for the affluent. Newspaper reports revealed that a portion of the salary of the deputy minister of education (the government's seniormost bureaucrat) was directly linked to the budget-reduction targets she had to meet. The seeming insincerity of the government's claim to be motivated by the improvement of quality in education was revealed when the education minister was caught on videotape saying that bringing about educational reform necessitated having to "invent a crisis." More tellingly, still, he proclaimed in the same video that "you can't change if you are improving,"[1] suggesting the intention of the market fundamentalists to "manufacture" a crisis that their own intervention could be seen to resolve.[2]

What followed was the most intensive and extensive period of reform ever seen in the province. In the last five years of the twentieth century, more legislation was passed on educational change than in all the province's preceding history.[3] Educational financing was drastically restructured; government grants to school districts were severely cut; and the discretion of districts to manage their own finances or raise their own revenue was heavily restricted.[4] The results of these and other budget-saving measures on teachers' working conditions and responsibilities were dramatic. They included increased hours of teacher time in the classroom; accompanying decreases in scheduled planning and preparation time; substantial reductions in the number of paid teacher-leadership (head of department and assistant head) positions; and extensive cutbacks in counseling, special-education, and teacher-librarian staff. These measures were accompanied by a set of curriculum and assessment reforms of remarkable pace and scope that included centralization of curriculum design and development into the Ministry of Education, with increased standardization across the public system; compression of the high-school curriculum from five to four years and rapid introduction of a comprehensive new curriculum; tracking (streaming) of the high-school program into applied and academic routes;[5] imposition of Grade 10 literacy testing, which all students had to pass to graduate, to be followed by Grade 9 testing in mathematics; introduction of new report cards, along with computerized systems of reporting; a new Teacher Advisory Program in which all students in Grades 7–11 were to be assigned a teacher adviser by 2001; and a range of regulations enforcing school dress codes, zero tolerance for school violence, and automatic suspension of students by teachers without the need for administrative approval.

One effect of these cumulative policy changes was to generate a negotiated agreement between the government and the secondary-school teachers' union in 1998 in which enhanced and accelerated early-retirement packages were offered to the aging teaching sector. Demoralization with reforms and their consequences increased the number of staff taking early-retirement options, which led to a large turnover of teachers and administrators in the schools.

With my colleagues, I have worked with nine high schools over a five-year period as they have responded to these external reform initiatives. Five of these schools are part of the *Change Over Time?* project discussed in chapter 3. Two of those schools were also included with four others in a second project, *Networks for Change,* that was co-directed with Paul Shaw and developed in partnership with one of Canada's largest school districts. This second project was designed to assist six high schools in this urban and suburban district to develop improvement efforts and implement the government's Secondary School Reform (SSR) policies in ways that were consistent with the school's own improvement goals. The project culminated in the fifth and final year with a survey of the school staffs' responses to and perceptions of the reform agenda and their efforts to implement it.[6]

The survey comprised 55 closed items eliciting teachers' responses to government reforms and their impact on themselves and their schools along a four-point scale.[7] The final part of the survey included an open-ended section, inviting teachers to comment on any other issues concerning the implementation of government reforms and to add further remarks that they regarded as important. The survey instrument was administered at all school staff meetings within a one-week period in May 2001. A total of 480 surveys were completed and returned, yielding a 60 percent response rate. Despite teachers' repeated protests about shortage of time in their work, half of them responded to, and many wrote copiously in, the open-ended section, eager to make their voices heard.[8]

This chapter draws on the survey results, as well as on staff-focus-group responses to the raw data, which we invited them to help us interpret collaboratively in June 2001. It also draws on data collected during monthly meetings with the schools' administrators, where they discussed the impact of SSR on their schools and their responses to it.

Among the nine Ontario schools with which we worked, the five that were part of the *Change over Time?* study were Lord Byron, one of Canada's most innovative secondary schools; Blue Mountain, a high-tech institution that is self-consciously run as a learning organization and that is the focus of Chapter 5; Eastside, a school with a long tradition of technical and commercial education; Talisman Park, a traditional academic high school beginning to encounter an increase in cultural diversity; and Stewart Heights, a school that has shifted from being in an enclosed, largely middle-class, culturally homogeneous village to being at the heart of a rapidly expanding center of cultural diversity.

Talisman Park and Stewart Heights were also included, along with four other schools, in the *Networks for Change* project. The other four were North Ridge, an established traditional high school serving a mainly middle-class population, with two new vice-principals who possessed strong expertise in curriculum and assessment; Wayvern, one of the few high schools in Ontario that begins at Grade 7 rather than Grade 9 and that has a large-population of English as a Second Language (ESL) students; Dale Park, recently formed through the merger of two schools on the residentially least desirable periphery of the city; and Mountain View, one of the district's few vocational schools that educates culturally diverse students, most with special needs, from all over the region.

THE END OF INGENUITY

How did teachers in these schools react to an agenda of standardized reform within the context of market fundamentalism and a shrinking state in which money was moved from the public to the private sector to free up the economy? How did they fare in the struggle to teach creatively for, and beyond, the knowledge economy in these conditions of market fundamentalism? The analysis in this chapter looks at the substance of the reform in the areas of curriculum and assessment change, then at the implementation process, the tone of change, and the alterations in working conditions that accompanied these substantive changes.

Curriculum and Assessment

Teachers in the six schools in the *Networks for Change* project were not uniformly opposed to the substance of contemporary curriculum change.[9] Many valued the quality the curriculum offered and improvements it made to students' learning, and others felt able to incorporate its demands into their practice without too much difficulty. Subject by subject, much of the content of the new curriculum embodied and expressed the standards and creativity needed in a knowledge economy. Between 40 percent and 60 percent of teachers in our survey felt that they understood the new academic curriculum; that it was appropriate to their students; that it engaged students from different cultural backgrounds; and that it had led teachers to use a wider variety of assignments and did not diminish the range of their teaching strategies. Fully 60 percent of the teachers had no wish to return to the previous interdisciplinary Grade 9 curriculum. In open-ended responses, teachers acknowledged that "many of the changes are excellent"; that they had "no difficulty with the reforms . . . [with] the clarity and consistency for students; the fairness of the assessment principles." The reforms had "much good." The new curriculum was "not bad," and for some teachers it was even "a major improvement."[10]

There was also guarded approval for the substance of some of the changes in classroom and curriculum assessments (see Table 2, Appendix). Almost two-thirds of teachers in our survey said that they understood the new assessment methods, and one-third supported the assessment policy overall. Teachers were more evenly split on whether they used a wider range of assessment strategies and on whether they involved students more in the new assessments. Support for the new assessments was far from unequivocal, however. For instance, about four-fifths of teachers did not feel that their communication with students had improved or that they had become more confident about assessment as a result of the new policies. Yet many teachers welcomed the classroom-assessment changes, and one even described them as "excellent."

The substance of many curriculum- and classroom-assessment changes in Ontario and elsewhere provides promising starting points for future improvement. The curriculum standards and content had been written by some of the finest teachers in the province, who, subject by subject, injected quality and creativity into the materials they produced in ways that encouraged and demanded deep learning from students. The content of these curriculum- and classroom-assessment changes therefore contains some potential for building a creative knowledge economy.

The opposite was true for teachers' responses to systemwide testing. Some of the most widespread teacher criticisms were reserved for the Grade 10 literacy test (Table 3, Appendix). This was based not on a sample of students across schools and districts, but on a census of every student in the province. To enable reliable comparisons to be drawn, year by year, test items were shrouded in the strictest secrecy, and teachers were unable to learn how their students had performed on particular items. Yet according to the schools' principals, teachers spent many weeks preparing students for the tests based on sample items released by the assessment agency. Teachers' responses overwhelmingly indicated that the test was seen as having little value for improving teaching and learning. Just one in five teachers felt that the test promoted their students' improvement. Meanwhile, nine of every ten teachers believed that the test neither motivated students to learn nor enhanced their own confidence as teachers. Only 23 percent of teachers supported the new testing policies, and only 24 percent felt the policies made them more accountable. More than two-thirds of the teachers claimed that their classroom-assessment strategies were consistent with the literacy test, and just over half felt they had successfully integrated the skills required for the test into their classroom teaching. But even though their teaching was more aligned with the tests, 46 percent of teachers felt that the new testing policies had reduced their range of classroom strategies. In their open-ended responses, teachers criticized the poor feedback the test provided to students about their own performance, and one teacher was outraged that the testing agency had lost his son's test script.

On this evidence, systemwide testing conducted on a census rather than sample basis does not help, and in some ways actively hinders, teachers in supporting their students to learn in a knowledge society. It reduces the range of teachers' teaching, stunts many teachers' creativity, and does not help them help their students' learn. After many years of experience, England is now in the process of reducing rather than increasing its systemwide testing. It would be wise to consider slimming it down elsewhere.

Diversity and Division

As shown in chapter 3, standardized curriculum and assessment reforms often pose the greatest problems for students who are decidedly "nonstandard"—such as students with language and learning difficulties. There were clear signs of this in the Ontario survey data (Table 4, Appendix). Whereas 50 percent of teachers felt that the academic (higher-track) curriculum was appropriate for their students, only 28 percent of teachers regarded the new curriculum as being appropriate for their "applied" (lower-track) students, and 80 percent did not feel that the test helped them identify the learning needs of students who scored below provincewide norms. Some teachers were concerned that the new curriculum was "too difficult for the majority" of students, including three teachers at the increasingly multicultural Stewart Heights school, who complained about the curriculum's "unrealistic expectations." Indeed, only 26 percent of teachers in the survey felt that the curriculum expectations were realistic for their students.

Almost four-fifths of the surveyed teachers were concerned that their lower-ability students were especially anxious about how well they would perform in the literacy test. Only one-fifth of teachers believed that the test helped them identify the learning needs of students who scored below the norm. But it was at the vocational school Mountain View, with its high concentrations of special-needs, culturally diverse students, that the most vociferous objections to standardized reforms were raised (Table 5, Appendix).

None of the teachers who filled out the survey at Mountain View felt that the new academic-curriculum expectations were appropriate for their students or that the Grade 10 literacy test had enhanced their confidence as teachers. Just one in ten teachers or fewer supported the new student-testing policy or felt that the new assessment, reporting, and testing strategies had improved their communication with students, improved the feedback that teachers gave to students, motivated their students to learn, or enhanced their own confidence about assessment. The vast majority of Mountain View's teachers (86%) felt that the new applied curriculum was inappropriate to their distinctive student population, and 71 percent of the respondents favored returning to the more flexible and inclusive Grade 9 curriculum, compared with 38 percent in the remaining schools. On several other key measures, Mountain View teachers scored higher than the general school sample by 10 percent or more. These included how far Mountain View teachers did not support the new assessment policy (81% versus 66%) and whether lower-ability students were anxious about the Grade 10 literacy tests (88% versus 76%).

Of the 30 open-ended survey responses that mentioned the inappropriateness of the new curriculum for certain students, 17 (more than half) came from Mountain View teachers. Teachers at Mountain View were vociferous about the curriculum's complete inapplicability to their students and its impossibly unrealistic expectations for students with severe reading problems or genuine learning disabilities (including two of the teachers' own children). They berated the government for setting these students up for failure, for treating vocational and special-needs students and schools as if they did not exist, and for denying the right to graduate to students who already had to endure too many setbacks in their lives. Teachers also despaired about the emotional consequences of the reforms that made their students feel discouraged, "hopeless," even "traumatized." The moving quotes from Mountain View's teachers that follow give a sense of their indignant reactions to the inflexible and insensitive application of standardized tests to students who are most in need.

> Literacy test requirements are politically motivated for the benefit of politicians and not for the benefit of kids. Should a child be denied a high school diploma because he or she fails one test? Special-ed kids have been given a raw deal because of this requirement and I speak of it as a parent of a learning disabled kid and as a teacher of special-ed kids.

> Vocational students do not exist in the eyes of the Ministry of Education or the provincial government. This in spite of the fact that industry continues to cry out for . . . skilled workers.

> The literacy test is useless and detrimental. My son, dyslexic, failed, and all Mountain View students failed the test. Learning-disabled students should be exempt from the test and still get their diploma. How will the government handle the fact that students like my son will get 30 credits and not get his diploma because of the literacy test? Unconstitutional! He has the right to get a diploma in spite of the bogus literacy test.

Too much to assess—not realistic—doesn't give students a real report on progress. Doesn't apply to students with special needs. [The government] doesn't acknowledge that special-needs children are a valuable part of society.

Special-ed students have been "psychologically traumatized" by failing the Grade 10 test and have learned nothing except that their disability has rendered them hopeless in the academic mainstream. I'd sue if I were a parent.

In a focus group of teachers from the participating schools that worked with the research team to examine the meaning and implications of the survey results, one Mountain View teacher spoke with a heavy heart about the damage the Grade 10 literacy test inflicted on the school's students:

In a regular academic school you . . . have the students who are going to be successful, who are going to earn their diploma. Our students are identified as being three grades behind their age appropriateness. . . . They are being told they cannot receive their diploma . . . if they do not pass this literacy test. . . . The reality of it is that we were delighted we had 18 kids who have passed. . . . That's 18 out of 140 Grade 10s that might . . . and hear the word "*might*" . . . earn a diploma. How do you keep a school motivated? How do you keep those students motivated if you cannot offer them something else? . . . We need to find these students something that will give them an alternative to the regular high-school diploma, whether it's a workplace diploma that identifies that they may not be able to pass the literacy test but they have skills, they do good work, and they work hard. They're decent people who need to have a future. . . . The Grade 10 [test] is absolutely inappropriate for them. It does not motivate them. It (de)motivates them . . . because they're anxiety-ridden over not passing it. How are these students going to feel? They're being bashed every day with not being successful in the literacy test, being told they're stupid—and that's the word they use to describe themselves . . . special-needs students, learning disabled students, culturally diverse students.

Other Mountain View teachers, like the special-education and alternative-school teachers in New York State, made a plea for exemptions, for locally developed curriculum that would enable teachers to address their students' distinctive needs and help them experience achievement and success in their

lives. Instead, political promoters of soulless standardization are taking society's most marginalized students—its poor, minorities, and refugees; those
with extensive learning disabilities; and recent immigrants whose native language is not English—and holding them hostage to the agenda of an influential middle-class electorate that is anxious for and insecure about its children's future in an unstable knowledge economy and that has fallen easy prey
to politically fomented moral panics about falling standards and failing schools.
When the full battery of standardized tests is aimed at students and teachers
in public education, it is usually the poorest, the weakest, and the most marginalized who are the first to fall in its line of fire. In other words, systemwide
standardized testing that takes a census of everyone not only restricts creativity; it also increases educational and social exclusion, limits society's pool
of collective intelligence, and sows the seeds of future adult resentment.

The Tyranny of Time

It is now a staple truth of educational-change knowledge and wisdom that
successful and sustainable change requires time for teachers to understand
it and integrate it into their practice. Similarly, for change to be successful
and sustainable it needs a prudent focus on a manageable number of key
priorities rather than scattered attempts to change everything. It must also
be supported by sufficient resources, high-quality learning materials, and
adequate professional development.[11] Despite the Ontario government's
access to world-class advice on change implementation,[12] almost everything that is known about successful change management was absent in the
speed with which the Ontario government rushed through its reform
agenda, the scope of the issues that the reforms addressed, and the quality
and levels of support that were provided to (or withheld from) teachers
responsible for implementing them.

Almost all teachers (91%) in our secondary-school survey indicated that
they were experiencing severe time constraints as a result of the changes.[13]
In their open-ended responses, teachers repeatedly protested that the reforms
amounted to being "too many changes, too fast"; "too much, too quickly";
"just so much, so soon"; "too vast and just overwhelming."

Time is perennially a problem for teachers, and few teachers will ever con-
cede they have enough in their workday. The work of teaching is demanding: It is never over, and there is always more to be done.[14] Moreover, any
change makes demands on people's existing commitments and calls for
patience and perseverance in understanding what the change requires, in

working clumsily and less than competently through the change's first faltering steps, and in learning how to integrate the changes into existing routines so they become an effortless aspect of the new approach to the job.[15] These time demands apply to all people and all organizations. Teachers are no different.

Advocates of the fast-paced knowledge economy might want to go further and argue that organizations are necessarily chaotic and demanding for everyone nowadays. They might even say that instead of complaining about feeling overwhelmed and nostalgic about what they have lost, teachers should be more forward-looking. They should thrive on the chaos and go with the flow. This, after all, is what the knowledge society is all about. Life today is fast for everyone. We are all working harder. Perhaps teachers should just stop whining, think out of the box, deal with the reality of change, or do something else.

The problem is that schools and educational-policy systems are behaving nothing like fast-paced, flexible knowledge organizations. Rather than thriving on the power of chaos, too many teachers must endure the manufactured chaos of politicians' power. Instead of creating dynamic learning organizations, educational-policy systems such as Ontario's have been cutting costs to create starved public institutions.

The teachers we studied had to deal with three time-related reforms:

- A barrage of simultaneously imposed and inescapable changes—a newly imposed set of curriculum and assessment requirements that arrived late, in fragments, almost as teachers were walking up the stairs to their classes; high-stakes tests in literacy, then mathematics, that took several weeks out of the teachers' curriculum to prepare the students; the introduction of a new advisory and career-planning program for students that would involve all teachers; and the management of a new, unwieldy, and technologically faulty report-card system.
- Loss of existing preparation and planning time (including what is needed to understand and implement the reforms) because of the legislated requirement that teachers teach for seven rather than six periods out of eight each day, and loss of professional-development days due to further government economies (and with it, loss of time to understand and deal with the change).
- Disappearance of support from the drastically reduced number of department heads (whose administrative time had also been taken from them), and from guidance and special-education teachers whose numbers had been cut by a third or more.

In the face of this remarkable increase in pressure, combined with a decimation in systems of support, teacher after teacher complained of feeling "overwhelmed," "overloaded" by "last-minute" changes, and "hurried implementation" that came in "multiple demands" and "all at once." A teacher at North Ridge outlined just what was required of teachers:

> Quite simply, [there is] too much too fast! Added workload, demoralization of teachers made getting the PD time to design the course work very difficult. Teachers had to:
>
>   (1) read/understand new documents
>   (2) do a gap analysis (of the difference between existing practice and reform requirements)
>   (3) collaborate with department members
>   (4) design new curriculum materials and assessments to ensure skills in place
>   (5) try to find new resources
>   (6) use new reporting methods.

A new teacher at Lord Byron complained that

> it was very difficult for me to not have had the entire thing. I had unit one and five from my new Grade 9 curriculum. So I was trying to set things up in the summer, but I only had two units out of it and I just received two weeks ago the entire, full thing, but we're already halfway through the semester.

A department head at Talisman Park who approved of many of the substantive changes in curriculum and assessment felt the tyranny of time personally in terms of his own capacity to implement the changes effectively:

> Having to teach an extra half course has significantly reduced my prep time and has increased my workload. In addition to this, I feel that I do not have time to prep adequately or thoroughly. The Teacher Advisory Program has also taken a great deal of time. No time to learn the new curriculum! Due to my leadership position at the school, I have received much training regarding Secondary School Reform. However, these sessions have been during after-school hours (many hours). I am confident and knowledgeable about the new curriculum because of this training, but what about my colleagues? They have received little training and have been faced with

implementing a very challenging curriculum. Teachers have not been given any time to absorb, learn, and plan how all this info can be transferred into the classroom. . . . The new curriculum is not bad and shouldn't disappear. The implementation, however, has been overwhelming. Lack of time and technology has grossly affected teacher acceptance as well as student performance.

A teacher at the Eastside school described how all the time pressures converged in ways that made it virtually impossible to implement change effectively:

We have fewer Professional Development days to allow for retraining and sharing of ideas among staff. We don't even have time to think about the imposed changes, let alone manage them. Since supervision and teaching time have increased, and with decreases in funding, we have teachers doing more, and less time accessible for planning and professional development.

In the case of assessment, for instance, there was "not enough time to plan for . . . the implementation of the new types of evaluation," "to share assessment ideas with other teachers," "to work on appropriate assessment methods," or "to update . . . assessment" in general. The new electronic report card (E-teacher) came in for particularly virulent criticism because of its technical inadequacy and rushed implementation (Table 6, Appendix).

As one teacher at Stewart Heights noted, all of the change was emotionally draining and ground down teachers' competence and creativity:

When we don't have enough time in between these reforms to experience our success and change things to make them better, it becomes so exhausting. We just barely finish one thing and feel good at it and [then we] rip it apart and do something else!

Loss of Learning

When teachers have their time stolen from them, one of the most precious things they lose is the time to learn and to think. Knowledge-driven organizations depend on effective brainpower—on understanding, reflection, ingenuity, and creativity. Standardized reforms have taken away teachers' time to think, and their imposed, prescriptive requirements have replaced creativity with compliance. An overexamined professional life is producing an unexamined, unreflective one.

This was most obvious in the inadequate professional development and training that was provided to support the implementation of SSR. More than 80 percent of surveyed teachers felt that professional development on curriculum change had not been adequate (Table 7, Appendix). The ineffectiveness and inappropriateness of professional development that would assist teachers in implementing the changes was one of the most frequently mentioned themes, after problems of time, in teachers' open-ended responses: It was mentioned by 48 respondents. These teachers described professional development and the loss of professional-development days as a "huge issue." In the area of assessment, for instance, they complained that there was just no time "to plan, collaborate, or learn."

People who cannot learn, who are prevented from learning, are a loss to their organizations and to their organizations' capacity to improve over time. They are not an asset to the knowledge society. Deep professional learning involves more than workshops of in-service training in government priorities (scarce though these also were). At the very least, implementing change effectively requires time to understand, learn about, and reflect on what the change involves and requires. Even for the best teachers, changing successfully is hard intellectual work.[16] Yet many teachers in the open-ended survey responses were frustrated that there was "no time for reflection to decide upon what worked well, what to change," no "time to reflect and plan," "lack of time to understand the curriculum . . . to digest and create new materials," absence of "clear understanding of all these changes," and generally no time to "learn new curriculum," "to think/plan/evaluate," "to learn how to implement."

Learning to teach better, to be a continuously improving professional, involves more than implementing other people's ideas and agendas compliantly. Good teachers must also be good learners, but the government's SSR agenda made it hard for them to be so. Teachers were so preoccupied with implementing imposed reforms that they could find no time to discuss or develop their subject with their colleagues; no time or energy to catch up with their own professional reading and development; and no opportunity to "grow personally" in their profession. They regretted and resented "not being able to recharge the battery, to have ownership of my professional development, not what someone else thinks I should be doing." To one teacher at North Ridge, intensified, imposed reforms were a travesty to the teaching profession because the pace of change "negate[d] the creative muse-based nature of the profession." An exasperated teacher at Stewart Heights summed up how performance-driven reforms ruined teachers' abilities to be effective learners and knowledge workers:

> The primary motivation of the government has been to increase productivity at the expense of creativity. I do not have time for professional development, or for casual reading related to my interests in education. I would love to read more about performance-based assessment, technology, multiple intelligences, etc., but with a single extra class, I spend too much time marking. I also do not have the time to fit the curriculum to the needs of my students (on an individual, personal basis). What a waste of my intelligence, creativity, and leadership potential!

You do not get students to learn well by making their teachers learn badly or by making it difficult for them to learn at all. In the schools with which we worked, the reform process had made a mockery of teachers' professional learning by reducing formal professional development time, by creating conditions that gave teachers no time to understand or reflect on what was asked of them, and by replacing intellectual creativity with fearful compliance.

The Demise of Professional Community

One of the most powerful resources that people in almost any organization have for learning and improving is one another. Knowledge economies depend on collective intelligence and social capital, including ways of sharing and developing knowledge among fellow professionals. Sharing ideas and expertise, providing moral support when dealing with new and difficult challenges, discussing complex individual cases together—this is the essence of strong collegiality and the basis of effective professional communities. Strong professional communities in teaching are not only emotionally rewarding for teachers; they are also directly responsible for improving standards of student learning and achievement results.[17] They are key components of knowledge-based organizations.

Teaching has a long tradition of isolation. This has kept standards down, and teachers have sometimes been blamed for clinging to it.[18] In Ontario, though, many school districts, often working in partnership with universities, made great strides in the 1980s and early 1990s to develop more collegial cultures of shared planning, reflection, coaching, and mentoring in schools, where teachers worked and learned more closely together on behalf of their students.[19] In the data from our two studies, many teachers criticized SSR because it took away the benefits and traditions of collegiality and professional community that they had learned to value over the previous decade.

Elsewhere, it has been suggested that imposed, large-scale reform can increase collegial planning and interaction as teachers work in teams to understand and implement the new curriculum.[20] However, these forms of contrived collegiality seem to be ephemeral, disappearing once the immediate crisis of implementation has passed.[21] These patterns of temporarily increased collegiality seem to occur in systems where cultures of teaching immediately before the reform are strongly individualistic and where the collegiality that results from legislated change amounts to a net gain. This was not the case in the schools we studied at the time of SSR, where legislated change was responsible for a dramatic loss of highly valued collegiality and professional community among many teachers (Table 7, Appendix).

Only a third of the teachers surveyed felt there was more collaboration with colleagues around student learning as a result of SSR. Seventy percent of teachers felt less involved in school decision-making; just 23 percent perceived that communications with departmental colleagues had improved because of the reforms; and fewer than one in six felt that reform measures had led to improved communications with colleagues across departments. After several years of starting to think "out of the box" as educators and to move beyond the traditional "egg-crate" structure of the classroom-based school,[22] reform put these teachers back in the box, nailing them into classroom coffins of deadened professional learning, with 85 percent of teachers believing that reform had led to reduced involvement for them outside the classroom.

In the open-ended survey responses, reduced opportunities for professional collaboration was the sixth most frequently mentioned item of concern (37 responses).[23] Most responses referred to how the pace of reform, reduction of support, increases in teachers' work responsibilities, and loss of scheduled time away from the classroom had brought about "no time for collaboration," "no time for communication with colleagues," and fewer opportunities to "share and implement," "work together," "consult," "discuss best practices," "conference with other individuals who are teaching similar courses," and "prepare and implement the curriculum and assessment changes with each other."

The extra teaching load had taken away teachers' "time and energy for real and meaningful collaboration necessary to implementation" and made it almost impossible to work with colleagues "to do the job properly." Teachers complained about being "too tired and too busy to communicate with colleagues." In the words of a North Ridge respondent:

> The greatest challenge to effective implementation is the lack of individual time and collaborative time to work on the preparation of new programs. . . . No time release, no assistant heads, and the responsibility of teaching 6.67 classes out of 8 [make it] impossible to do a thorough, thoughtful job of implementation. . . . At the end of the day, people just want to go home to do their own lesson plans and marking.

It was exceedingly difficult for teachers to find time to work with colleagues within their departments to discuss common subject matter. More than this, a number of teachers complained about how the reforms had actively created "departmental competitiveness," making it "difficult to get departments together to try to attain the same goals" and leaving teachers feeling "isolated by department."

At Stewart Heights, one teacher described how

> more and more people would eat in little cubbyholes and be working and eating at the same time . . . By the time I left [in 1998], there were a lot of teachers that I might not know their names . . . some of the new teachers I saw at staff meetings and didn't really know who they were or what they did.

Eastside's refurbished staff room was more reminiscent of beautiful but empty pictures in a furniture-store catalogue than the hub of a thriving professional community. The pressures of reform ensured that the school and its teachers remained as balkanized by department as they had been in the 1970s.

> We have a lovely staff room where people can congregate and share, but you never see more than four or five in there, and usually it's empty. So where are the teachers? In their offices, planning and marking, often by themselves, to keep caught up.

> I feel like I'm on my own. I use my lunch hour to mark and work with students. I use my prep period to prep for the next day's class to talk to my student teacher. I have to make myself leave my office

or classroom to talk to my colleagues. I only see them when I pick up my mail in the morning or on the way out the door at the end of the day.

At Lord Byron, which prided itself on its tradition of innovation and teacher collegiality, staff meetings were no longer occasions for professional learning. They were mainly conduits for procedural announcements. At most staff meetings, the principals' explanations of the latest ministry or district pronouncements made up more than half of the agenda. Although staff were usually consulted to some degree, there was no time for them to make decisions. As a result, an undercurrent was present among some staff members that "sometimes decisions are already made, and yet we have the meeting on things and then find out it was fruitless, essentially a waste of time." One teacher reflected that, compared with 10 years earlier, "the rules are at the top, and now we're being told what to do. It's no longer a . . . democratic decision-making situation. I think it's a function of the times—perhaps efficiency. Money probably has a lot to do with it."

The school's administrators acknowledged that pressures of time and mandated reform meant that they had to be more directive and less collegial. For example, the district required all schools to implement the new electronic reporting system immediately, even though the technology was flawed. As relatively new leaders, the principal and vice-principal were in no position to refuse. In addition, a number of staff members were reluctant to embrace the government's new approaches to assessment. To achieve staff compliance in a very short time frame, both of the female administrators felt forced to function in ways that conflicted with their preferred leadership styles. As the principal stated:

> What we have had to impose upon them is that you will become knowledgeable in computer areas, you will work on an electronic marks-manager, and you will change your assessment and evaluation. If you're having trouble with this, we're here to help you. Assessment and evaluation—we've come in and said, "You will change," and we have taken responsibility of that with a steering committee of staff. We ask the staff to come forward and bimonthly at the staff meetings, we talk about various things that they should be changing in their assessment and evaluation practices. So that is laid on.

One of the most traditional schools in our study is Talisman Park. Some of its older staff long for a lost golden age of traditional academic standards, a reform agenda that encouraged local curriculum change in academic subject disciplines, and the purpose of educating children in a high-status, high-achieving and culturally homogeneous community. Under its previous principal and before the full onslaught of SSR, these staff members had begun to work much more collegially to develop a school-improvement agenda that was being tackled across departments and to reach out to its more culturally diverse community. The deluge of directives from SSR, however, along with a new principal who construed his role as one of devising a minimalist response to its demands to protect his staff, led Talisman Park's teachers to turn aside from improvement, away from the community, and apart from one another.

> Now no one will join any committees if they can possibly avoid it. There's still a School Success Committee, but I never hear of them meeting. . . . They met once a month regularly, and then the subcommittees would always meet. No one will join anything. . . . I've been part of the staff now and we have trouble getting staff out for even social occasions. We have students' commencement coming up, which was postponed. . . . No one wanted to run the commencement, even though there had been two people assigned to running it. They reneged on those responsibilities. [The principal] had to come up with two other people.

One staff member confessed to standing by while a new teacher who had been assigned the task of organizing commencement made a mess of it because no senior colleagues were prepared to intervene and assist her. Meanwhile, a "coffee circle" of embittered, older staff who met before school each morning focused much of its energy on anticipating and complaining about government policies.

Schooling for the knowledge economy and for democratic community each depend on teachers' being able to work and learn in strong professional communities. In the schools in our study, however, the educational-reform agenda not only failed to strengthen professional learning communities in schools. It actively undermined them. The tyranny of time and the imposition of unwanted political will in educational reforms have weakened the rich collegial traditions at Lord Byron, turned Talisman Park into an embittered distortion of its lost traditional self, and reversed the systemwide progress that had been made in changing teachers from a profession of isolated individuals into a community of engaged colleagues. When the knowledge society came knocking on the doors of these schools, the government sent it packing.

The Corrosion of Competence and Creativity

Any self-respecting professional finds it hard to admit he or she might be becoming less effective. There is no pride to be had in being poor at one's job and only guilt and shame in knowingly neglecting or failing to care for one's clients.

In the survey's open-ended response section, 43 teachers confessed that the quality of their teaching had diminished, that there was less time to mark students' work properly, that their role had narrowed and their world had shrunk to deal only with the immediate pressures of the classroom, that they were losing confidence and competence, and that the creativity of their job had gone. Given people's reluctance to admit to failing, these are almost certainly underestimates. Many teachers wrote in distressing terms about "not doing the job well," "not doing an effective job," having a "lack of time to do a thorough job," showing "limited productivity," and not having the "quality time to make a positive impact on students." They confessed to being "less effective in instruction," complained about having "less time for individuals" and "no time for contact with students" or "to help students in difficulty," and they deeply "resent[ed] being made to feel incompetent" and to having "feelings of inadequacy" because of the government's reform process. As one teacher said, "For me, to keep my high standards in class with less time . . . on-calls, no time to prepare, has been a great source of anxiety." A teacher at North Ridge who supported much of the substance of the reforms poignantly declared:

> The challenge also is to lower my standards of perfection and excellence. I can't work the way I have in the past. I can't do the job the way I used to—making time for students, being involved in the life of the school as much as I used to be, being creative with my lessons, supporting my colleagues, keeping up with professional reading. It's just not happening to my satisfaction. It's a frustration, not to be able to meet my professional goals in these areas. Meeting my own high expectations used to provide me with a great deal of job satisfaction. At times it is a pressure and a frustration to know that I must take shortcuts. I don't always feel that I can do my best work. Reforms are depleting teacher passion in the current implementation conditions.

Teachers wrote about having to "teach to the test instead of being creative" and feeling "forced to leave out interesting exercises" in the rush to get curriculum covered. One teacher said that she "used to love being creative; now I'm too busy to try." Another wrote despairingly about how "creativity and

enthusiasm have become hopelessness and depression, and a lethargic outlook has evolved."

An experienced teacher at Lord Byron who had a long memory of three
decades of teacher-generated innovation and improvement within the school
put it this way:

> The creativity is gone. In the past, people were very creative in many
> types of programs and courses. I think part and parcel of that was the
> ministry allowed you to do that, but also the school encouraged the
> type of creativity. . . . [N]ow it's much more dictated that this is the
> program that you're going to have. There's less flexibility with courses;
> you don't have the wide diversity of options available for people, and
> people are more in tune with the ministry. . . . [T]herefore, that cre-
> ativity part has been taken away from them. . . . The focus much
> more is on ministry directives, and that's what we have to do.

Standardization is making school systems less like rich, biologically diverse
rain forests of cross-fertilizing influence that can achieve sustainable improvement over time[24] than like regimented coniferous plantations whose hyper-
efficient ugliness is exceeded only by their limited capacity for mutual influence and their lack of contribution to wider environmental sustainability. The
evidence of our research about the impact of educational reform in Ontario
and New York State is that standardized reform seems to be destroying diversity and seriously endangering the lives and futures of the weakest members
of the school system—the poor, the marginalized, those who are learning
through a new language, and those with special educational needs.

Along with the elimination of diversity, standardized reforms are also
bringing an end to creativity and ingenuity in education. As so many teachers said, in one way or another, "the creativity has gone." Schools bereft of
creativity and a profession that has lost its ingenuity are unable to create
and maintain a strong knowledge economy and to help young people deal
with uncertainty, work flexibly, and develop their own dispositions of creativity and ingenuity. Standardized reform has, in these cases, become the
antithesis of an emerging knowledge society.

THE ABSENCE OF INTEGRITY

In addition to bringing an end to ingenuity, standardized reform has consistently undermined teachers' trust in the integrity of governments and
administrators in terms of their moral sincerity about introducing changes

that will benefit all students. It has also threatened teachers' professional integrity in terms of having to prepare their students to fulfill educational purposes that they find increasingly hard to justify.

The Tone of Change

To be fair, teachers rarely like imposed, top-down change of any kind. Interestingly, though, fewer than 10 teachers in the open-ended responses of our survey reported aversion to imposed change in general. Rather, most attributed the negative effects of change to the offensive tone and morally questionable intent of government manipulation.

The tone of educational change is cast on it by governments, the media, corporate institutions, and other groups through the language they use to describe the nature of the problem to which change is the solution. The tone of change can be urgent yet also professionally respectful. Under Ontario's Progressive Conservatives, the tone of change was very different.

In their open-ended survey responses, 33 teachers spontaneously referred to and complained about the government's tone. Many were "tired of being bashed," "vilified," and "constantly criticized" by a "vindictive" and "arrogant" government and by a government leader (formerly and briefly a physical-education teacher of allegedly undistinguished reputation) who, some teachers felt, had a "vendetta" against the profession. Teachers regretted that the government had taken an "adversarial position" that not only demonstrated a "lack of proper respectful communication" and "desire for partnership" but was constantly characterized by "inflammatory statements out of the blue."

Teachers felt "demeaned" and "degraded" by the government's "negative propaganda" and its "deliberate and destructive attacks" on their professionalism. They felt "unfairly criticized," and were "sick and tired of being asked to justify [their] existence"; of "too many assumptions that teachers are not and have never been professionals"; of "constant government put-downs" that teachers were "poisoning young minds"; of government mandates to "slander and deprofessionalize" teachers as a whole. In light of all this, one teacher wondered whether the government was "determined to make teaching unattractive as a career option."

The Emotions of Imposed Change

Imposed and negatively intoned change had emotional effects on teachers' motivation and morale. Forty-five teachers reported motivation and morale problems in the open-ended survey responses, the fourth most commonly cited issue after time, implementation, and professional development. We scanned all open-ended responses for emotion or emotion-related language and identified 54 uses of emotional discourse by teachers—every instance being ultimately negative. Exactly half of these referred to loss of purpose or personal investment in the work of teaching or to frustration at not being able to achieve valued purposes because of conditions and demands created by the government.

Teaching is not only an intellectual or cognitive practice of conveying knowledge or developing skills among students. As I argued in Chapter 2, teaching is also and always an emotional practice of engagement with learning, relationships with students and adults, and attachment to the purposes and the work that teaching achieves. Teaching is either a positive emotional practice by design that motivates teachers to perform at their best with those around them, or it is a negative emotional practice by neglect where teachers disengage from their teaching and lose quality in the classroom as a result.

Loss of purpose or inability to achieve purposes because they are obstructed, unwieldy, or unclear is one of the most common causes of negative emotion.[25] Several teachers wrote heartrendingly about loss of love, joy, passion, and soul in their work because of the impact of government reforms. A teacher at North Ridge who was "tired of being bashed" and had reluctantly decided to give up her middle-level leadership position and retire early confided:

> I love teaching, and I go home everyday feeling good about my relations with my classes, feeling energized by my students, believing that I am helping them to improve and develop their skills and looking forward to what we [my classes and I] will do next, but I am tired of being "bashed" by the [government] premier. So I have relinquished my headship for next year and will take retirement on or before my date, even if that occurs within a semester. That is something I never thought I would even contemplate, let alone plan to do. That says something. You have no idea of the feeling of betrayal I experience—and I know I'm not alone.

A colleague at Talisman Park felt like leaving the profession because her own purposes and the purposes of public education were being stolen. She described her reactions in the emotional language of frustration and demoralization (literally—loss of purpose):

> The abundance of change, the lack of time, and the constant criticism of teachers fueled by the government, and now some of the

community, is demoralizing and frustrating. I am seriously considering leaving the profession. I will question accepting future leadership
opportunities. I'm not bitter but quite sad for the future of public
education. The needs of teachers and students are not being met.

A teacher at Stewart Heights echoed these depressing sentiments

I'm a good teacher. I love teaching, and I really enjoy working with
teenagers. But right now I am so depressed about the politics surrounding teaching that I sometimes don't know how I will go on.
If these reforms do this to someone who used to be active, healthy,
and optimistic, what are they doing to someone with reservations
about teaching? What will happen to the future of education in this
province? I feel so helpless about the whole situation, and I'm tired
of having to defend the quality of public education to the public.

Some teachers were still able to love aspects of teaching when they were
with their students in the classroom. But for others, the experience of lov-
ing and liking the job was already fading into the past tense.

Since the Secondary School Reform, I do not have enough time to do
my job, which I loved, properly. I liked teaching but not so much any
more. Too much time spent on non-teaching activities—i.e., putting
marks (final) into the computers. Not enough time to discuss history.
Contacts with students? There is no time for it!

Teachers found much of the process of SSR "soul destroying." They were
"distressed to see so much discouragement among students and staff." They
spoke about demoralization, alienation, disillusionment, and even prosti-
tution of themselves as professionals in the service of ends they regarded
as morally indefensible.

In the face of endless public criticism against which they had no opportunity to speak in their own defense, teachers used the language of shame,
humiliation, and abuse to describe how they felt: "wounded," "violated,"
"degraded," "abused," "beaten down," "victimized," "browbeaten,"
"bashed," "belittled," "ramrodded," given a "hammering," "forced," and
having their "hands tied." Teachers were critical of "top-down" change in
earlier studies that I conducted of emotional responses to educational
change, but no discourse of abuse was evident in their remarks before the
impact of SSR.[26]

In his work on the sociology of shame, Thomas Scheff argues that the emotion of shame breaks the basic social bond among people, creating a distance that makes their pursuit of common purposes and shared goals impossible.[27] Along with the emotional experiences of demoralization and loss of purpose, political shaming of teachers not only broke the social bond between teachers and their government, it also broke the bonds between teachers and the public, their job, and their professional selves.

The effects of shaming and demoralization and the sheer exhaustion wrought by the unsustainable pace of reform reached into teachers' health and their experiences of stress.[28] Teaching became more "difficult and stressful and far less enjoyable." Teachers reported feeling "highly stressed and unappreciated." Three wrote about specific, clinical health consequences: "Never before have I heard so much 'alternative career' and 'How can I get sick leave?' talk." Another talked about the "increased absenteeism on staff as people are truly stressed out." One confessed that "stress-related medications and needed time for doctor visits should be calculated, since my costs alone are costing the system tremendously—and I am an eternal optimist!"

Retirement and Resignation

The most devastating emotional effects on teachers that tore apart their bonds with their work and their profession were on teachers' intentions to leave the profession early. In the open-ended survey responses, ten teachers announced that they intended to retire early under conditions of considerable disillusionment and disappointment about a mission that had vanished and a job that was losing its meaning. One teacher had "firmly decided to leave teaching" solely because of SSR. Others "considered leaving ... because of [the] consistent negative attitude of government" or thought about moving to a teaching job elsewhere. Despairingly, they related how they could "only think of the day when I can retire or find a new vocation," or would be "leaving the teaching profession as quickly as I can," or simply "look[ed] forward to retirement."

In our quantitative survey results, only 14 percent of teachers indicated that their commitment to their career as a teacher was deeper since the introduction of SSR. A mere 10 percent felt that their professional self-image had improved with SSR, and just 14 percent believed that the balance between their work and personal life had improved since the onset of reform (Table 8, Appendix). Eighty-five percent of teachers said that they had become more hesitant about seeking a leadership position since SSR. Startlingly, in a sample in which only 28 percent of teachers were older than 50, 73 percent of the total sample stated that the effects of SSR had motivated them to seek early retirement.

Not everyone would be appalled by this news. Market fundamentalists might rejoice at the rush to early retirement, believing that the teachers who would be leaving are old, expensive, and in the way. Good riddance to bad rubbish, they might say. Politicians might welcome an end to expensive salary bills. Others could quote the research on teachers' careers showing that many classroom teachers in their later careers are unwilling to commit to profound changes because they have seen waves of change fail in the past, are losing energy as their bodies begin to weaken, have growing commitments elsewhere in their lives that demand increasing attention from them, and feel that the remaining years they have left are best dedicated to their students in their own classroom, not the school or the system as a whole.[29] Creating a wave of retirements does the system a favor, not a disservice, these people might argue.

However, not all aging teachers become tired, cynical, and resistant to change. Whether they do so depends as much on the qualities of the school or system as an organization as on the natural aging process. With the right organization and leadership, many teachers become renewed in later career by embracing new opportunities, mentoring younger colleagues, and so on.[30] More years do not always mean greater weariness in teaching. Retiring too many teachers too fast also removes essential sources of mentoring and professional learning from the system at a time that large numbers of raw recruits are simultaneously replacing these older colleagues. Further, even if some teachers should be nudged into early retirement, there are less morally and emotionally offensive ways to go about it. The urgency of change can never justify the absence of moral integrity.

Disturbingly, though, young teachers as well as old ones in our survey were declaring the sad intention to abandon their profession. After cataloguing the lack of funds, supplies, technology, professional development, and time to participate in extracurricular activities, one teacher said, "As a young teacher I am disheartened by this environment, and I will move on professionally to the private sector. There is no joy in teaching—only a paper trail of grief." Another said that, "as a young teacher," she would "leave for a better work environment if the current situation does not end." A colleague at the same school similarly said, "I am a relatively young teacher but am seriously considering another profession or part-time teaching. It's a shame, because I love to teach." The saddest comment of all came from a teacher at North Ridge.

As a relatively new teacher, I am seriously concerned about the future of education in this province both for students and as a profession. I never thought that I would regret my current career path, but I do and wish I had done something else with my three degrees [B.A., B.Ed., M.A.]. There is no joy in being told that you are a no-good, freeloading fat cat for six years running. I surely wouldn't wish this profession on my children or other family members. I love working with children but not with this government. How can you encourage and attract good [newcomers] in a time of shortage with a government like the one currently in power? I would retire tomorrow if I could, but Hallowe'en 2026 will not be here soon enough! Eight years ago, I never thought that I would think that way. Unfortunately, I am jaded, tired, and disillusioned with what this profession has to offer. I wish I had written the LSAT [Law Degree Qualifying Test] in '92, because it was easier to get into law school than teacher's college. This is a worst-case scenario that I had no vision of in 1992.

She was not the only teacher to say she would not counsel her own children to join the profession. Seventy-eight percent of the sample overall said that, since the start of SSR, they would be less likely to advise their own children to go into teaching.

One of the most serious crises and challenges facing the public-school system and the teaching profession is the mass exodus from teaching related to the demographic turnover of teachers in the profession. This great historical movement of demographic retirement and turnover is in part a natural consequence of the aging Baby Boom generation having lived and worked through its professional lifecycle. If outstanding and highly qualified recruits can be attracted to replace the wave of those who leave, then this defining moment can be an immense opportunity for professional renewal. Yet a disturbing finding of our work is that it is not only older teachers who are becoming disillusioned with the profession; younger teachers are, too. Nor are older teachers advising young adults to fill their shoes, for the professional shoes of teaching have been treading narrowing paths unimaginatively designed by others.

In these conditions, the teaching profession will find it harder and harder to attract high-quality candidates with intellect and ingenuity, especially when other occupations with less regulation and more incentive are competing for their talent. Problems of professional and moral integrity may also limit the supply of candidates who feel called to the work of teaching. For when teachers in our study, young and old, signaled that they intended to leave the profession, they did so less as a result of depleted energy than of lost professional integrity, where an honorable teaching mission was being usurped by economic imperatives and political power. The standardized reforms of Ontario education offer only disincentives and discouragement to those who see their work as being about teaching beyond the knowledge economy and about creating values for good. The social mission is being squeezed out of teaching.

The Credibility Deficit

One of the factors that affects the success or acceptance of any communication is the credibility of its source. Even governments that are operationally inept have a chance of seeing their reforms succeed if they are regarded as well intentioned, educationally sincere, or, at least, not motivated by malice. When politicians are caught inadvertently proclaiming the necessity of inventing a crisis in education; when it is discovered that salaries of senior bureaucrats are linked to budget-reduction targets; and when a government's political leadership is seen to be making repeated derogatory attacks on teachers and their unions, the credibility of reforms and reformers reaches rock bottom.

In the open-ended section of the teacher survey, 43 respondents raised questions of mistrust and betrayal concerning the government's professed motives in relation to educational reform.[31] Reform for these teachers had not been about raising standards; it was only about cutting costs. The government's focus had been on "saving money, not education." Its market fundamentalism was starkly transparent. As a teacher at Talisman Park put it:

> The pretense that these new measures are intended to improve quality rather than just reduce costs is becoming very evident and will be clear to all within the next year or two when the damage is more visible.

Many saw the government's reforms as attempts to increase the free flow of resources from the public to the private sector and to advance a "corporate imperative." Several teachers saw the reforms as amounting to a deliberate attempt at "destroying public education" and attacking democratic, public life itself. To one teacher, the government and its allies were "malicious masters who seem bent on destroying the very system—perhaps to benefit privateers—that made the greatest economic boom in Canada's [and] Ontario's history possible." Other teachers referred to the strong belief that the government agenda involves a major upheaval in the political, social structure of democratic principles [fought for and nurtured by the "common people"] in education.

What is the end of education? If it is to produce . . . cogs for the corporate environment of the twenty-first century, then Secondary School Reform is a smashing success. There is nothing like an unintellectual, soulless horde of graduates to whet the appetites of multinationals looking for "skilled" labor. However, if the purpose of education is to create intelligent, soulful, caring, and perceptive human beings, Secondary School Reform is a disastrous milestone on the road to a dumbed-down society.

I think the government has done what it set out to do. Many parents are choosing private education. The public system will become second-rate without money and vocal or involved parents.

The changes have been too vast and overwhelming to be done in an effective way. It is as though someone wishes to demonstrate how broken the system is by not providing the time and development to be successful.

These statements might be dismissed as the unsupported assertions and unwarranted speculations of teachers engaging in conjectures far beyond their experience and expertise. They could be regarded as little more than litanies of retaliatory blaming—and, indeed, some of the emotional stimulus provoking them may be exactly of that order. However, there is also a considerable body of research on the origins and effects of this market-fundamentalist reform pattern in other parts of the world that supports the teachers' critical remarks.[32] More important still, the remarks signify what is personally believed and subjectively true for these teachers, disclosing a failure of government to win the trust of the teaching profession about the motives and morality of educational change. In these teachers' eyes, standardized educational reform that is combined with efforts to worsen teachers' working conditions—and that is embalmed in discourses of failure and shame—ultimately precipitates a decline in commitment to public education and to the overall public good. To paraphrase the revelatory words of Ontario's former education minister, it succeeds in being able to change something by putting an end to its improvement. This is a failure of ingenuity and integrity alike.

Our data from teachers in a range of Ontario high schools suggest that the province's educational reforms at the turn of the twenty-first century have modeled neither ingenuity nor integrity. They do not prepare young people to make a living in the knowledge economy or to live a life beyond it; nor will they make it possible to recruit, retain, and renew the required number of high-quality "knowledge workers" in teaching who will create the next generations of the knowledge society. Standards-based reform is a Trojan horse. It conceals danger within its gift. Standardization is just a dead horse, and it is time to stop flogging it.

NOTES

1. For more discussion of these policy developments and their implications for senior administrators in the system, see Lafleur, C., *The Time of Our Lives: Learning from the Time Experiences of Teachers and Administrators during a Period of Educational Reform,* unpublished Ph.D. diss., Ontario Institute for Studies in Education, University of Toronto (OISE-UT), 2001, pp. 3–4.

2. Berliner, D. & Biddle, B., *The Manufactured Crisis: Myth, Fraud and the Attack on America's Public Schools,* Reading, MA, Addison-Wesley, 1995.

3. Gidney, R. D., *From Hope to Harris: The Reshaping of Ontario's Schools,* Toronto, University of Toronto Press, 1999.

4. Lawton, S. & Bedard, G., "The struggle for power and control: Shifting policy-making models and the Harris agenda for education in Ontario," *Canadian Public Administration* 43(3), 2000, 241–269.

5. The program had been legislatively de-tracked (de-streamed) under the previous government.

6. Hargreaves, A., Shaw, P., Fink, D., Giles, C. & Moore, S., *Secondary School Reform: The Experiences and Interpretations of Teachers and Administrators in Six Ontario Secondary Schools* (final report), Toronto, Ontario Ministry of Education and Training/OISE-UT/Peel Board of Education, 2002.

7. The full survey results are listed in the Appendix. Subcomponents of the results follow within the text of this chapter.

8. The survey was not designed as a provincewide random sample and cannot be generalized to the whole teacher population through tests of statistical significance. Instead, the survey was developed collaboratively with staff and administrators in the six schools, partly to identify the schools' own needs in terms of support for implementing the government's reforms. The survey was piloted through staff discussion and responses within small groups in each school and underwent several revisions as a result. Although this sample is not random, six schools in one large school district constitutes a substantial grouping. Given that the schools benefited from the project team's assistance and support in dealing with change, including important monthly meetings of dialogue, reflection, and support among the schools' administrators, it is likely that unsympathetic responses to reform would be even stronger in other schools and districts within the province.

One further advantage of collecting data in six schools with which we developed long-term working relationships is that we were able to collect strong contextual data on each school, including a set of detailed case studies that we completed in 1998.

9. See Table 1, Appendix, for detailed results.

10. Importantly, though, more than half of the responses that were favorably disposed toward the new curriculum came from middle-level leadership heads, whose positions of responsibility typically incline them to be more favorably disposed to external reforms.

11. Fullan, M. & Stiegelbauer, S., *The New Meaning of Educational Change,* New York, Teachers College Press, 1991; Miles, M. B. & Huberman, A. M., *Innovation up Close: How School Improvement Works,* New York, Plenum Press, 1984; Anderson, S. & Stiegelbauer, S., "Institutionalization and renewal in a restructured secondary school," *School Organization* 14(3), 1994, 279–293.

12. For a time, Michael Fullan was co-chair of the government's implementation advisory committee.

13. See the general table in Table 9, Appendix, for the responses to the question on time.

14. Hargreaves, A., *Changing Teachers, Changing Times: Teachers' Work Culture in the Postmodern Age,* London, Cassell and New York, Teachers College Press, 1994.

15. Louis, K. S. & Miles, M. B., *Improving the Urban High School: The What and How,* New York, Teachers College Press, 1990.

16. On the intellectual and emotional work of change, see Hargreaves, A., Earl, L., Moore, S. & Manning, S., *Learning to Change: Teaching beyond Subjects and Standards,* San Francisco, Jossey-Bass/Wiley, 2001.

17. I discuss this literature in detail in chapters 5 and 6. But see especially Newmann, F. & Wehlage, G., *Successful School Restructuring,* Madison, WI, Center on Organization and Restructuring of Schools, 1995; Rosenholtz, S., *Teachers' Workplace,* New York, Longman, 1989.

18. Hargreaves, D., "The occupational culture of teaching," in P. Woods (ed.), *Teacher Strategies,* London, Croom Helm, 1982; Rosenholtz, *op. cit.,* note 17.

19. These developments are documented in Fullan, M. & Hargreaves, A., *What's Worth Fighting For? Working Together for Your School,* Toronto, Elementary Teachers Federation of Ontario; New York, Teachers College Press; Buckingham, Open University Press, 1996); Fullan, M., *Change Forces: The Sequel,* London and Philadelphia, Falmer/Routledge Press, 1999; Leithwood, K., Jantzi, D. & Steinbach, R., *Changing Leadership for Changing Times,* Buckingham, Open University Press, 1999; Stoll, L. & Fink, D., *Changing Our Schools: Linking School Effectiveness and School Improvement,* Buckingham, Open University Press, 1996.

20. Hargreaves, D., "The new professionalism: The synthesis of professional and institutional development," *Teaching and Teacher Education* 10(4), 1994, 423–438.

21. See especially Helsby, G., *Changing Teachers' Work: The Reform of Secondary Schooling,* Milton Keynes, Open University Press, 1999; Woods, P., Jeffrey, B., Troman, G. & Boyle, M., *Restructuring Schools, Reconstructing Teachers,* Buckingham, Open University Press, 1997.

22. On the egg-crate structure of schooling, see Lortie, D. C., *Schoolteacher: A Sociological Study,* Chicago, University of Chicago Press, 1975.

23. The other factors were time (almost everyone), implementation problems (48 respondents), insufficient or inappropriate professional development (48 respondents), problems of motivation and morale (45 respondents), and mistrust of the political reasons for change (43 respondents).

24. Capra, F., *The Web of Life: A New Synthesis of Mind and Matter,* London, HarperCollins, 1997.

25. Oatley, K., *Best Laid Schemes: The Psychology of Emotions,* Cambridge, Cambridge University Press, 1991.

26. See Hargreaves, Earl, Moore & Manning, *op. cit.,* note 16. I am grateful to the work of Susan Lasky of the International Center for Educational Change for drawing this point to my attention.

27. Scheff, T. J., *Bloody Revenge: Emotions, Nationalism and War,* Boulder, CO, Westview Press, 1994.

28. Troman, G. & Woods, P., "Careers under stress: Teacher adaptations at a time of intensive reform," *Journal of Educational Change* 1(3), 2000, 253–275.

29. Sikes, P., Measor, L. & Woods, P., *Teacher Careers: Crises and Continuities,* London, Falmer Press, 1985.

30. Huberman, M., *The Lives of Teachers,* London, Cassell and New York, Teachers College Press, 1993.

31. For a discussion of the nature of betrayal and its implications in teaching, see Hargreaves, A., "Teaching and betrayal," *Teachers and Teaching: Theory and Practice,* in press.

32. See the references listed in chapter 3, notes 1 and 2, for summaries of the field.

5

THE KNOWLEDGE-SOCIETY SCHOOL

An Endangered Entity

(with Corrie Giles)

THE SCHOOL AS A LEARNING COMMUNITY

The Blue Mountain secondary school in Ontario is the epitome of a knowledge-society school. Only eight years old at the time of writing, Blue Mountain stands out as a school that has operated from the outset on the principles of a learning organization and a learning community.

Since the emergence of Peter Senge's influential management text *The Fifth Discipline,* many writers have advocated that schools in complex, knowledge-using societies should become effective learning organizations.[1] If schools were learning organizations, they would develop structures and processes that enabled them to learn in and respond quickly to their unpredictable and changing environments. They would operate as genuine communities that drew on their collective intelligence and human resources to pursue continuous improvement. All their members would be able to see the "big picture" of their organization, understanding how parts and whole were interrelated (what is known as "systems thinking"), and how actions in one domain created consequences in another. They would see the connection between their own personal learning and how the organization learned collectively as being the key to change and success.[2]

Linking these ideas to the writing of Etienne Wenger on communities of practice,[3] school-improvement advocates have gone on to recommend that effective schools do and should also operate as strong professional learning communities.[4] Professional learning communities in schools emphasize three key components: collaborative work and discussion among

127

the school's professionals; a strong and consistent focus on teaching and learning within that collaborative work; and gathering assessment and other data to inquire into and evaluate progress and problems over time.[5] Professional learning communities lead to strong and measurable improvements in students' learning.[6] Instead of bringing about "quick fixes" of superficial change, they create and support sustainable improvements that last over time, because they build the professional skill and capacity to keep the school progressing.[7]

Professional learning communities are especially difficult to establish and maintain at the secondary-school level because of a long legacy of departmentalization and even balkanization of teachers' secondary-school subject communities.[8] It is at the high-school level in particular that Michael Fullan's complaint that "the school is not yet a learning organization" retains a strong and disturbing ring of truth.[9] This is what makes the Blue Mountain secondary school's status as a learning organization particularly exceptional. With its charismatic founding principal and carefully selected staff, and with the advantage of three years' preparation by the principal and extensive advanced planning with the original "pioneer" staff and community, the school has established great technological, structural, and curriculum innovations that challenge the standard "grammar of secondary schooling."[10]

Situated in a middle- to upper-middle-class neighborhood, Blue Mountain has been open for eight years. It started with 600 students in 1994; that number had rise to more than 1,200 at the end of the century. Architecturally, the school has a tiered "forum" that encourages interaction among staff, students, and visitors. Its main hallway resembles a commercial shopping mall, with the main school office, student guidance, and "business" studies area all accessed "boutique-style" from the main street. The cafeteria is open-plan, and the gymnasium is widely used by the staff and community as well as by the students for personal fitness.

Emphasizing its knowledge-society orientation, Blue Mountain was one of the first schools to be fully integrated for technology. From the beginning, every student had access to the Internet, and all staff members were given laptop computers and e-mail accounts and were expected to model the use of technology to students. The assessment and reporting system at the school has always been computerized, and achievement data are regularly collated, analyzed, and shared with parents—in relation to their own children and the school's performance overall.

The school is designed and operated as a learning organization. For example, leaders model "systems thinking" in staff meetings (all announcements are distributed electronically to make space for this). Teachers also model "systems thinking" in classrooms when school issues are discussed. The founding principal is an instructor in the province's leadership-development program, and his postgraduate study focused on schools as learning organizations. The second principal (also the founding vice-principal) possesses a doctorate in educational administration, as does the head of business studies, whose topic was self-managing work teams. Many of the highly dedicated and enthusiastic staff are omnivores of personal and professional learning outside school as well as within it. They include teachers who write detective novels, train in and practice massage therapy, participate in managing a construction business, offer guidance services to the corporate world, are involved in the city stock exchange, contribute to writing curriculum documents for the Ministry of Education, or have extensive involvement in the arts. Blue Mountain is built around extraordinary people who are or have become voracious personal and professional learners.

The nature of Blue Mountain as an effective learning organization is reflected in many different aspects of its creation and its continuing operation: the nature and distribution of its leadership; its goals and vision; the organization of curriculum and teaching; its innovative structures and processes; and the teachers' orientation to personal and professional learning.

Founding Leadership

Blue Mountain's founding principal brought an unconventional background to the school. As a former head of special needs, principal of a vocational school, educator with experience in elementary as well as secondary settings, and professional athlete and coach, he straddled conventional leadership categories and favored a collaborative approach to working with teachers and staff. The founding principal's experience of sports coaching was morally chastening and professionally salutary:

> One of the things I learned was how *not* to treat people if . . . you wanted to motivate them and you wanted to engage them around anything. . . . That's because of the somewhat abusive nature of coaches in those days and the tactics that they used which included basically . . . harassment tactics, punitive tactics, embarrassment. All of that kind of thing [that] they used on a daily basis in an attempt to motivate people, in fact had the opposite effect.

Through and beyond his postgraduate study, the founding principal of Blue Mountain was an avid reader and user of organizational and leadership theory: W. E. Deming on continuous improvement and the conscious management of quality,[11] Peter Senge on systems thinking and learning organizations,[12] and Margaret Wheatley on the need for fluidity and ambiguity when leading in complex systems.[13]

Exemplifying one of the key ideas of effective professional learning communities, the principal was strongly student-centered. He believed that schools should model the life and work that students would experience when they graduated. He also believed that achieving this vision required a "systems-thinking" professional culture that engaged teachers, support staff, students, and the wider community in defining the organization's goals and how to achieve them. The founding principal, in other words, subscribed to the principles of what is now called distributed leadership.[14]

The idea of organizational learning and systems thinking permeated almost everything the founding principal did. When the school district unexpectedly encountered hostility after announcing its plans for the new school in a top-down way, the founding principal set up monthly meetings with the community, "simply . . . establishing relationships with them." This led to the creation of a school council in 1992–93, long before school councils became official policy within the province. Parents were asked to work with the school to define the graduating outcomes—the knowledge, skills, and values they wanted their young people to have when they left the school. The work of John Carver on prudence and ethics was invoked to help the school council determine how to undertake an annual assessment of the organization and its effectiveness.[15] Open information and data sharing as a basis for this evaluation was influenced by the writing of Wheatley.[16]

When staff were hired, the founding principal used systems thinking to consider the interrelationships with and consequences for other schools. To avoid accusations of "stealing all of the good people from all of the other schools," he negotiated selection criteria with the district ensuring that his school would match the general teacher demographic profile in the district, and that "no other school would end up being burdened by the loss of too many people."

Sustainability of the school's success over time, as well as the school's interrelationships with others across space, was another key systems issue the founding principal considered. In a district that regularly rotated its principals, he worked hard to create a school structure that would survive his departure and "perpetuate what we are doing." He was also alert to the threats posed by leadership succession in which an ensuing principal might import a different philosophy.[17] He therefore "negotiated very strongly to have my vice-principal . . . be appointed as principal." One of the pioneer teachers recalled that the staff, along with the school council, "penned a very strong letter to the district administration, the superintendent of the school at the time, basically saying, 'That's all we would accept.'"

When the initial leadership team of ten teachers was established, the staff were not allocated specific roles. It was important "not . . . to compartmentalize," the founding principal said, and to ensure that the staff "had a schoolwide perspective from the very beginning." In future years, he would defend his school's designation of broad leadership roles against the district, which continually pushed for subject-based, department-head categories until imposed reforms and the resulting downsizing of middle-level leadership structures moved the rest of the district in the same direction as Blue Mountain.

Staff meetings, as well as school-council and leadership-team meetings, were carefully shaped according to learning-organization principles, as described by the founding principal:

> All our meetings started with systems issues where people were free to identify problems they were having at a systems level so that we could deal with them and remove fear from the organization. To say that there's something not working is what we wanted to promote so that we could deal with it as opposed to hiding it for fear that you might be blamed for it.

These principles extended to individual advisory sessions and collective meetings with students, which "became an opportunity for kids to accept responsibility for the organization and to provide input into concerns that they might have and to make recommendations for change."

All these sentiments regarding the value of the systems-thinking approach and a positive approach to problem-solving were echoed by Blue Mountain's pioneer staff:

> Philosophically, [the founding principal] and I were totally in line. We used to share books back and forth, so the philosophy, the systems thinking, the continuous-improvement approach, the teacher-leadership concepts, rather than [being] top-down, [provided] the freedom to initiate, carry through, with [the founding principal] sort of being there as a coach but staying out of the way and letting you do your job and be a leader with others and work collaboratively— that's the attraction.

I couldn't believe [the founding principal's] philosophy and the philosophy of the school was so in tune with what I absolutely believe
in and have lived [in] my teaching career. It was just fantastic. . . . It
was about the importance of relationships in education. It was about
process. It was about not just what we do but how we do it and how
we get that across and the interaction. It was about living with ambiguity. . . . We have the permission to fail and learn from our failures.
All this stuff I just love, because that leaves you the opportunity to
try. And I'm passionate about this, so excuse me.

In the midst of all this intoxication with systems theory and complexity, and
the opportunities it offered to staff to take risks and show responsibility, the
principal never lost sight of the students. As one teacher commented, "I'd
never been in a place where the priority was so much the student, and for
me, that's it—all that matters is the student."

Vision and Goals

The founding principal was careful to avoid a trap into which many previous innovative schools have fallen. Instead of developing the school's goals
and vision alone, he created them patiently with his staff and the community, gaining their vital support in establishing a school that was different
from a conventional secondary school. As a result, Blue Mountain has seven
defining goals (known as "exit outcomes") that serve as guiding principles
for the school and stand as criteria against which the school's performance
is self-assessed. The idea of the learning community is at the core of the
school's mission: "To be a center for lifelong learning responding to the
community." Among the school goals are:

- To provide high expectations for learning for all students and staff.
- To provide all students with the knowledge, skills, and values needed
  to be successful.
- To provide a culture that fosters cooperation and collegiality.
- To provide the opportunity for direct input from the community.

The mission and goals, in other words, stress high-quality, lifelong learning for students, learning for and among staff, and learning from the community. They are, in one teacher's words, "the philosophical glue that defines
the place."

Teachers

The teachers who came to work at Blue Mountain were literally exceptional. A number were known to, and specifically invited to apply for a position by, the principal. Unusually, eight had backgrounds in special education, and a disproportionately high number of others came from vocational schools. One was an art consultant in the school district who somewhat anxiously re-entered the classroom when the district downsized; he was not only given a home by Blue Mountain's principal, but was encouraged to develop, close to his retirement, an innovative computer-based graphic-design course. As the teacher recalled, this also helped him develop skills he could use in his post-institutional career. The principal had the insight to help this impending retiree to connect his professional learning to his personal learning.

The selection process was rigorous. One member of the staff recalled that it had taken "five meetings and four interviews to get to this building." The principal recalled that two selection criteria had been paramount for him: teachers' unswerving commitment to students and their capacity to live a balanced life. As noted earlier, most staff seemed to have active outside interests, and sometimes parallel careers, that energized rather than enervated them in their teaching work. Many staff had been drawn into the profession from other walks of life—radio broadcasting, flying helicopters, steelwork, communications consulting, and automobile sales, for example. This brought diverse experiences and a rich source of outside learning into their teaching work. Just as the school was focused on producing self-skilling, continuously learning students for the knowledge society, the staff were also self-skilling and self-renewing teachers who had other life and career options that fed their work and provided a balance to it. This kept them committed to their teaching, not merely committed by it.

In the school's early years, Blue Mountain teachers valued their autonomy and responsibility—how "you could be as creative as you could possibly be and it was valued." Most teachers described their experiences at this stage in the development of the school as "exciting," "having fun," "wonderfully creative," "electrifying," even "heaven." As one teacher put it, "It was like, I get paid for this? This is a great place to be."

Teachers saw the new opportunities for additional responsibility, problem-solving, decision-making, and planning as ways to achieve their personal visions of student-centered teaching and learning, which had not been possible in more traditional high schools. Teachers were excited about interacting with colleagues, engaging in "risk-taking" and experimentation in their teaching so they could develop innovative ways to engage students in their learning. As one teacher expressed it, "This school gave me the opportunity to experiment. I was a traditional teacher, I think, . . . so it's been a wonderful catalyst for me to grow and learn."

Many teachers felt that they had experienced accelerated professional growth through belonging to a community of learners in which new ways of working and thinking were internalized and rapidly became recognizable as their "philosophy in practice." A new teacher was especially appreciative of this strong professional culture:

> One of the things this school has done for me is, because my philosophy is not only supported by administration, but that is the way they see education as well, I think my ability to integrate my philosophy into my classroom has sped up. I've been able to accelerate my own professional development because I am sitting around a community of teachers that all share my philosophy and that have the philosophy of sharing materials and talking about lesson plans. In a lot of schools you don't see that. In a lot of schools, each teacher just goes to their classroom and teaches their class and doesn't really share how they go about it, or how they get good results unless you pry it out of them.

Blue Mountain not only provided a culture of rapid personal and professional growth. It was a fast-paced environment in general. One teacher described the formative years in the school as being like"a revolving door— going through the door, not really sure where you are going to stop. Everything was always kind of moving, swift pace, going fast. Sometimes you didn't know whether you were coming or going." Another commented on the scope as well as the speed of school change in Blue Mountain's early years:

> I think the biggest challenge at that point was, How you do manage everything? A new curriculum, new kids, new school, nothing was in place. We had the key processes, but what exactly are they and what do we do with them? We didn't have any rules, and sometimes that is more difficult.

Despite all the difficulties of creating a new, innovative school together— developing a vision, writing new curriculum, managing multiple innovations, and forming new relationships—Blue Mountain's pioneer teachers embraced the autonomy, creativity, and energizing "rush" that this professional opportunity gave them.[18]

Curriculum, Teaching, and Learning

The enthusiasm and excitement of working at Blue Mountain was reflected in the innovativeness and inventiveness of its teachers' curriculum and classroom teaching. Teachers integrated their classes and used team teaching. They talked about sharing classes of 50–60 students: "When you teach a class of 60 kids as opposed to a class of 25, of course, your teaching methods change." Integration and a global outlook were central features of Blue Mountain's early curriculum model. Efforts were made to integrate English with history and math with science; personal and career counseling with business studies; construction classes with community studies; and so on. The school also experimented with a "global camp," which took all Grade 10 students out of the school for a week. This global perspective was an extremely important aspect of the school's "learning-organization" orientation and underpinned the design and delivery of the curriculum. As the founding principal explained, "That perspective . . . is an inclusive one. It reflects all kids, it opens up learning, it talks about the interconnectedness of everything we do." An international expert in global education from the nearby university as well as a district consultant were both used to assist the school in this part of its work. This global emphasis made students aware of the chains of care that stretched across the world and of the importance of developing their own cosmopolitan identity as global citizens.

Teachers at Blue Mountain also made extensive use of alternative assessments, especially portfolios and exhibitions. Assessment targets were shared with students ahead of time. Computer technology was not locked into segregated laboratories. Students had free movement around the school to use whatever technology was available.

One mathematics teacher exemplifies the kinds of innovative teaching and learning that took place routinely at Blue Mountain. This teacher emphasized performance exams in which students presented their research on mathematical problem-solving. He let students undertake independent studies (common in other subjects but not in mathematics) to encourage problem-solving approaches. He even integrated mathematics into some French classes, where

I learned a lot more about how language teachers work. I learned that they involve kids with a lot more verbal skills, a lot more projects, a lot more presentations to the class . . . quite foreign to a math teacher. I used that opportunity to enlarge my teacher repertoire.

Innovative Structures and Processes

Much of Blue Mountain's innovative energy—its capacity to balance complexity with coherence[19] and creative tension with security—resulted from applying systems thinking to the task of developing distinctive, enabling structures that would promote personal and organizational learning throughout the school. As one teacher described it:

> Initially, the structure, everything was congruent. The [founding principal's] philosophy ensured that. We designed the school on systems, whole school processes that we should all be involved in. [We] broke down subject departments in the traditional sense. Yet we all had to have subject expertise because it was through the strength of our subject expertise that we brought to the system that we could work in a continuous improvement mode. Everything was congruent—the role, how we worked together, the organization of the school—and philosophically it was supported by [the founding principal]. We were given the responsibility to embed the philosophy.

Systems thinking increased personal learning, opened up information, valued differences and disagreements, made everyone aware of the school's "big picture," and drove each staff member to see and take responsibility for the consequences that his or her actions and preferences had for people elsewhere in the organization. In the words of one of the school's pioneer teachers:

> This is a systems school, and because it's a systems school . . . it works much better for students and for staff because we're not out of the loop. We know what's going on. . . . We're aware of the whole dynamic of the building, and it makes a huge difference, whereas in my old school I only knew what was happening in my department. . . . So it makes a big difference when the organization of the school is different. This organization fits my approach to teaching far better.

These principles and processes are clearly and consistently represented in the school's enabling management structure. Decision-making and planning occur in cross-departmental teams that include student representatives and that increase cross-school communication, as well as promote opportunities for deep-seated rather than superficial learning.[20]

Key Process Teams drive the organization and philosophy of Blue Mountain and are a powerful sources of continuous learning about the core work of teachers and everyone else at the school. All teachers are required to join at least one of the Key Process Teams, which meet a minimum of once a month and sometimes weekly. Administrators also attend these meetings, which determine directions by consensus while providing professional learning and development. The team structure represents a deliberate effort to create generative learning opportunities for everyone connected with the school by placing problem-solving and decision-making as close as possible to the people responsible for implementation.[21]

Key Process Teams are chaired by middle-level leaders (heads) who report back to the Leadership Team and act as a vital integrating force within the school. The number of process teams has varied over the years. Originally, there were ten, then eight, Four teams were in operation at the time of writing: assessment and evaluation; curriculum review and instruction/education from a global perspective; recognition, attitude, and morale; and teacher advisory groups/personal and career counseling.

Management Teams are temporary and event-driven task groups. They last a maximum of two months and consist of faculty and students who volunteer to undertake specific tasks that emerge from Key Process Teams or more predictable rituals and ceremonies, such as convocation, that are part of the life of any school. The group leaders of each team are volunteers who have an interest in or experience with the specific task in hand. Management Teams free the administration and middle-level leaders from much of the day-to-day management work that so often interferes with the strategic leadership necessary in rapidly changing circumstances.

The Leadership Team meets weekly and consists of the principal, vice-principal, and Key Process Team heads. This group plays a central role in maintaining the vision of the school and ensuring consistent communication across other teams. In addition, the Leadership Team helps identify issues for the Key Process Teams or Management Teams to consider. The team does not operate as a conventional senior-management team or secondary-school heads of department group. It works in partnership with the principal and vice-principal, performing both advisory and executive functions.

Other teams also operate within the school. These include the School Advisory Council mentioned earlier. Because of its creation and evolution before the school's opening, the School Advisory Council had the time and opportunity to develop a clear definition of its role as well as a sense of purpose that was based on the principle of inclusiveness for all students and the importance of anticipating and responding to the needs of a rapidly changing society. The School Advisory Council monitored and advised on student-graduating outcomes and worked with the newly appointed faculty to convert this philosophy into practice.

Subject Discipline Groups meet, as is customary in other secondary schools, but also include the interdisciplinary Education for Global Perspective program and the Teacher Advisory program. Curriculum integration, the integrating influence of the use of technology, and the cross-faculty composition of the Key Process and Management Teams and faculty workrooms tend to encourage subject-discipline groups to adopt more of an overview of all aspects of the school and to forge stronger cross-department and cross-curricular links than is typical in other secondary schools.

The Student Parliament has a staff adviser, eight elected student members, and 50 more student members (one from each teacher-advisory group), of whom 25 attend on a regular basis. The Parliament meets every Wednesday and considers systemwide issues first before moving to other concerns.

Finally, Professional Learning Communities were initiated in September 1999 to promote professional learning and development. All faculty participate in these communities, which are deliberately mixed in age, experience, gender, and subject discipline. They are chaired by one of the school's five middle-level heads. According to the second and current principal, the purpose of this new process is to ensure the sustainability of the school's distinctive approach beyond her departure by embedding the learning "deeply in our school's culture."

THE SCHOOL AS A CARING COMMUNITY

In so many ways, Blue Mountain School exemplifies how to be an exciting and effective learning organization. Its emphasis on systems thinking in all its structures and processes, its extensive processes of collaborative decision-making and inquiry, and the value it places on putting students and their learning first are highly consistent with the principles of strong professional learning communities.

Yet learning organizations and learning communities are not without critics. Wenger warns against romanticizing them. They can just as easily be a "cage for the soul" as a "cradle for the self," he says.[22] School-based learning communities have sometimes been mandated on schools rather than evolving from them, with predictably disappointing consequences.[23] They are often prone to surface friendliness and interactional congeniality, or "contrived collegiality,"[24] rather than probing deeply into issues that sometimes divide educators. Like all communities, learning communities can become victims of so-called "groupthink," where members of these communities insulate themselves from alternative ideas, turning shared visions into shared delusions.[25] The literature on learning organizations and learning communities has also been criticized for overemphasizing formal cognitive processes of problem-solving, systems thinking, and collective inquiry at the expense of the informal relationships that bind a group together.[26] In addition, learning-organization principles are normally addressed to the core organization, and particularly to management employees, but tend to exclude the parts of the organization that have been contracted out. The outsourced worker, contracted laborer, or child worker in less-developed countries—these groups are mystifyingly absent from or "out of the loop" of learning-organization advocacy, displaying a politically convenient absence of the systems thinking that is at the heart of learning organization practice.[27]

These criticisms seem to have limited application to Blue Mountain. The school's professional learning community was not imported as a mandate from elsewhere but evolved in the establishment of the individual school. Its staff spoke of spirited disagreements and debates about the school's future. The school had a "grown-up" professional culture, and we saw it in several of the meetings we attended. There may have been some vulnerability to groupthink—perhaps indicated in the repeated emphasis that administrators and pioneering staff placed on socializing newly appointed "settler" teachers to Blue Mountain's existing vision, getting them "on board"—or ensuring that they were "absorbed," in the current principal's terms—when the vision should perhaps also have been modified as a result of these new teachers' arrival. But it is particularly in its capacity to move beyond the rational, to balance cognitive problem-solving and systems thinking with an emphasis on caring cultures and human relationships, that Blue Mountain seems to excel. In addition to being a learning community, Blue Mountain is indisputably a caring community.

The founding principal's emphasis on the value of systems thinking was matched only by the importance he attached to relationships as a driving force behind Blue Mountain's capacity to keep improving. While still working as a professional athlete, he took one of his first teaching positions "with a group of boys (street kids) who were out of control." Instead of acting like a charismatic sports star or controlling the students with rigid discipline (taking a "heavy-handed approach"), however, he took "a counselling approach and a personal approach to the kids." This enabled him to "engage them around relationships," which further consolidated "the importance of that in working with anyone."

Establishing genuinely reciprocal relationships, not merely rational communication plans, with parents and the community when the school was first established was vital in gaining their support for and actively involving them in setting the school's innovative direction. With staff, an initial retreat was designed, among other reasons, to build relationships. Indeed, staff discussion was focused on "removing barriers to effective relationships in schools." One teacher described the founding principal's vision as, "If you are not happy as an individual, then you are not happy as a professional."

The school's pioneering system of Teacher Advisory Groups (an innovation that was subsequently adopted and implemented as a provincewide reform) was designed to ensure that, in the principal's words, all of the students "would have a significant adult contact in the building" who would care for them and guide them in setting and reflecting on their goals and give them a voice in the community. In this initiative, each teacher initially committed an additional 100 minutes per week to advise and support 20 students throughout their time at school (this was later adjusted to 80, 40, and finally 50 minutes as teachers searched for the optimum time period).

Blue Mountain's second principal (also its founding vice-principal) continued to stress the relationship theme. She and her leadership team were described by many of the staff as "wonderful," "supportive," "spectacular," and "amazing" people who were "still teachers at heart." She was highly valued as being "very caring" and as someone who recognized that "family comes first." The principals she had worked with and been influenced by in the past "were always very visible. There was a real sense among the students that they were important. That really helped with the open-door policy." The current principal also emphasized the importance of family: "We ask so much of our teachers and we try [in scheduling meetings] to attend to the fact that the time they need to spend with family and friends is important and comes first." The families included not only include conventional two-parent families but also single-parent families and same-sex relationships.

The principal's days, as she typically described them, were spent with people, often outside her office. She was rarely out of the school. She spent the first half-hour in the office and around the photocopier, chatting with students and staff; mixed with students in the entranceways; and walked the corridors to ensure that everything was settling down. She visited three or four classroom every day, tried to see and hear music performances and artwork three times or so per week, was often invited into classrooms to see students' presentations, and taught classes and course units from time to time. "It sort of raises you in [the students'] eyes to be their teacher as opposed to being their principal," she reflected. The library was visited everyday, creating opportunities to chat with individual students. Although not an athletics aficionado herself, she also watched afterschool teams, taking pleasure in her students' indulgent explanations of what the games and the moves actually meant.

Staff retreats, increasingly difficult to organize under the competing pressures of external reform, exemplified the learning and caring aspects of the school's mission:

> I think that it is a crucial emotional experience that people have where they laugh together at a number of things, where they share ideas so there's a lot of learning that goes on, but there's also a rebonding of the relationships that are so very, very important.

The teachers spoke freely about the caring nature of Blue Mountain's culture and its positive influence on collegial as well as classroom relationships. A teacher new at the school remarked:

> You can't work in the school and not care about your colleagues. That's just the way the school works. Those are the types of people that were hired. And so you hire people that care about you and worry about you and when you are stressed out, you talk to them, because people feel very free in expressing ideas in small forums. When your colleagues are stressed out, you are part of that.

Because of the care and support they receive from their colleagues, teachers at Blue Mountain feel less guilty than their counterparts elsewhere about taking time away to look after their families when they are ill or when they have other personal difficulties. For example, one teacher talked about how she and a colleague split the class of a sick colleague between them, taught the students, and marked their work. "I think we are all very supportive of each other's lives in that way, and so is our administration," she said. "It's always been family first. And then you can come and focus on your job. So that would be a story about the culture that we have . . . that supports one another."

This vision of caring for one another as individuals has also spilled over into the development of mutually supportive working practices, with teachers and staff working together and caring for one another professionally. With the active support of the administration, this has created an enabling culture in which professional risk-taking is always encouraged. At Blue Mountain, the intellectual and emotional work of teaching, the business of learning and of caring, are not contradictory or even philosophically in tension. They are integrated into a single, all-embracing approach of effective education.[28] Among its staff and students, Blue Mountain develops skilled problem-solvers and effective teamworkers, as well as people who build strong relationships and support one another over the long term and in effective groups. Knowledge and nurturing, learning and development, teamwork and group work, teaching for the knowledge society and beyond it— these are complementary principles and practices at the Blue Mountain secondary school.

There is disagreement and sometimes dissension among advocates of professional community in schools about whether a strong professional community should be based on informal collaboration or more formal kinds of discussion in a "Collegium."[29] There are also arguments about whether good colleagues should be good friends or whether the bonds of friendship among teachers inhibit principled disagreements about the best ways to teach.[30] One teacher's extended description of her positive relationships with her colleagues eloquently reveals how Blue Mountain challenged many of the binary distinctions that plague educational-change literature and practice: personal or professional relationships, consensus or conflict, and being a rigorous colleague or being a supportive friend.

> I work very closely with my colleagues here. We all do. We work very well together, and just about everything we do is positive. I think that's because all of us have similar beliefs in education. When the principal hired us, he asked that we all think about our philosophy of education and submit it. . . . Because we all know that we're here for the students, because we all have similar beliefs in education and because we all came in here through choice, I think we work very well together.

What we've discovered we do need here, probably a lot more than at other schools, is we every now and then have to stop and say, "Where are we? Where do we want to go? How do we get there?" We do that a lot. Two or three times in a year we just sit down and try to regroup.

Another thing that is very important for us is we don't have staff meetings like other schools, where you get a lot of information. We're very fortunate here—we all have laptops, so information comes to us daily on e-mail. We don't need that for staff meetings. So we have staff sessions where we discuss teaching, systems issues, what is it about this school that's working? What is it about this school that's not working? How can we continue this? How can we fix this? Very important, because you are constantly looking at the big picture and being brought back to, "Why are we here?" "Then let's get back on task." I think there's less strife here. And when there is stress here, we have probably . . . the most compassionate administrative team in the world. I'm sure the principal and vice-principal together are a formidable force, because they respond very quickly to our needs.

Family comes first at this school, first and foremost. You know, if there's a family situation, nothing else is as important, because the belief is here that if you're happy, then you can make others happy. But when you're not happy, obviously you're not going to be as effective, like when my father-in-law passed away.

So, you know, I have this feeling in me that I never want to leave this school, which is unusual for me, because I like change. Right now, I want to stay forever. I want my children's education here. I have such faith in this process. There's this trust, this loyalty, this faith, this positive—You know, you want to give back constantly. And that's how you feel here.

THE PRESSURED COMMUNITY

Blue Mountain's overall culture of learning and caring and its interrelated elements is summarized in Figure 5.1. Like all innovative schools, or newly created organizations, Blue Mountain has had to deal with and respond to a set of predictable problem in its evolution.[31] As the school grew, it lost some of its original intimacy and had to try to socialize new staff (not always

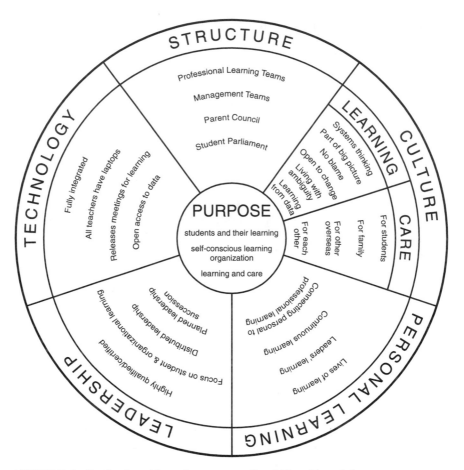

FIGURE 5.1. Professional learning community at Blue Mountain

successfully) into its distinctive culture and mission. Securing community understanding and support for innovative schools is always vital, and the founding principal needed to make a systematic and sustained effort to establish and rebuild community trust and involvement after the school district's initial communication gaffe. Sustainability of early momentum and success is always at risk when charismatic founding leaders leave, but the planned succession of appointing the incumbent vice-principal largely avoided this difficulty—although at the time of writing, she, too, is moving to another school. Continuing district support is also essential, as is the maintenance of good relationships with surrounding schools. The founding principal therefore worked hard to appoint staff according to equitable formulas when the school was established so it could not be accused of being the beneficiary of district favoritism.

Yet despite efforts not to "brag too much," as the second principal put it, the advantage of the new building, with its receipt of "money up front [so] all new teachers got laptops, became a point of jealousy" (founding principal). The school has tried not to hog the limelight, but its staff feel as if they are regarded by colleagues in other schools as "a favored cousin." Although they have been asked to provide expert professional development across the nation, they receive almost no invitations locally, confirming that "it's hard to be a prophet in your own land," the second principal said.

With reflectiveness and tenacity, Blue Mountain so far has been able to stave off most of the predictable problems in the evolution of innovative schools to a point at which, at worst, they have been temporary threats or continuing irritations rather than major calamities that jeopardize the school's distinctive identity. This is a powerful testament, perhaps, to the enduring and sustainable power of the learning organization and learning (as well as caring) community model compared with previous models of innovative beacon or lighthouse schools elsewhere—at least, over an initial eight-year period.

Blue Mountain's fundamental problems and difficulties, which may well jeopardize its continuing success as a learning and caring community, come not from the evolutionary "attrition of change" that has tended to befall most innovative schools over time[32] but from the historically specific and serious impact of inflexibly mandated, standardized reforms. Blue Mountain was unfortunate to be born in a "false dawn" at the end of the lifespan of a government that advanced progressive educational ideas but was unable to back them up with resources or support. In 1994, the year Blue Mountain opened, burgeoning provincial debt led to deep cuts in educational funding, a wage freeze for teachers, increased class sizes, and cuts to teaching staff and administrative personnel in school-district offices. The "Transition Years" reform initiative, which had influenced the philosophy and the integrated outcomes-based curriculum model at Blue Mountain, was largely stillborn in other high schools as a result of fiscal realities and new political directions.

In 1995, the newly elected "cost-cutting" and "restructuring" Conservative government centralized power; removed the ability of school districts to raise tax revenues locally; downsized the roles, responsibilities, and duties of school districts; reduced overall budgets; and introduced a centralized, subject-based curriculum and province-wide testing, including the Grade 10 literacy test. These measures presented Blue Mountain with external mandates and austerity measures that ate away at the school's flexible capacity to continue realizing its founding vision.

As shown in chapter 4, government legislation increased teachers' time in the classroom to seven out of eight periods per day, which subsequently also included covering for absent colleagues ("on-calls") in the extra period available. When agreements between the school district and the local branch of the teachers' union were temporarily reached to soften this requirement, they were achieved at the cost of severe reductions in school support services, including guidance counselors, teacher-librarians, technology assistance, and substitute-teacher cover. Economies were also achieved by merging middle-level leadership positions into a smaller number of more expanded, generalist roles that lost all the time previously allocated for administrative duties. At Blue Mountain, this meant that while the school's student population doubled, the middle-level leadership team was almost halved to just five people; guidance counselors were reduced from four to two full-time equivalents (half of this coming from many small fractions of part-time commitment); teacher-librarians were cut by half; and all teachers were teaching more, covering for absent colleagues, and coping with little or no scheduled planning and preparation time during the school day.

These reform measures and the reform climate generally affected all aspects of Blue Mountain's work and culture: curriculum and teaching, technology, leadership, overall vision, organizational learning and decision-making processes, staff and student relationships, and teachers' professional and personal identities.

The Loss of Learning

Curriculum Recycling and Regression. Standardized reform has chipped steadily away at Blue Mountain's distinctive approach to teaching and learning, especially, as one teacher put it, in terms of the "attrition of the global focus." Another teacher remarked, "I think we have gotten away from the global learner philosophy or culture that we were trying to foster initially." Certainly, the more specialized emphasis of the legislated curriculum has enabled staff who never fully believed in integrated programs to question their continuance and push for modification. Standardized reform, in this sense, has encouraged some regression toward the conventional curriculum mean. By diluting the global focus, it has also weakened the school's capacity to develop cosmopolitan identity.

Second, legislated reform mandates have recycled Blue Mountain's groundbreaking ideas back into the school in ways that have undermined the intent and the professional belief system that spawned the initiatives in the first place. As one teacher noted:

> The reforms externally have been often the results of what we have been experimenting with here. So, for example, the move to a smaller sense of department heads in the school was something that we started with. The idea of having an advisory council was something we started with. The idea of having Teacher Advisory Groups and portfolios was something we started with. The idea of technology being really important in the school is something we started with.

Blue Mountain is featured in the Ministry of Education's promotional and implementation reform videos. Several of its faculty were involved in writing the new centralized curriculum. But the very things it invented have often re-entered the school in ways that are educationally questionable or unworkable. School councils that depend on relationships have been re-imposed as formal procedures. Enlightened cross-disciplinary roles for department heads have been turned into downsized management measures with hugely expanded roles and less administrative time to fulfill them. Fifty-minute or longer Teacher Advisory Groups that fostered intensive mentoring of students in sustained relationships are now less effective because they were legislatively reduced to 30 minutes. Moreover, the integrated support in personal and career education that the guidance department provided to teachers and their classes can no longer be provided by the skeleton guidance staff who remain.

This pattern of recycled change, as I call it, has wider implications for how innovative schools and pilot projects are often used or misused as test beds for broader system mandates. The essence of recycled change was once expressed to me by a waste-management specialist. His company, he explained, recycles a large proportion of the paint in the region. "What happens to the paint when it's recycled?" I ask him.

"Well, it gets recycled into more paint," he responded.

"But is it just as good as the original paint?"

"No. You get faded blues and muddy greens. It doesn't retain the original full spectrum of color. Also, you can't quite get all the lumps out."

"Who do you sell it to, then?"

"Mainly poor countries, like Cuba."

This is how recycled reform seems to work. If the school is not already engaged in the practice that the reform stipulates, then mediocre practice, like dull, lumpy paint, may be better than none at all. But if the school already has a full spectrum of sophisticated practice, recycling this practice back in through inflexible legislation will make its standards worse, not better. Sadly, the effects of legislated educational reform on Blue Mountain have been ones of recycling and regression rather than improvement and renewal.

Technology. Loss of time and resources have also affected Blue Mountain's ability to retain its lead as a "high-tech" school. Reduced preparation time has meant that the school can no longer provide in-school technology training for teachers or compensate for the district's inability to provide its own training or maintain equipment in good time (due to its own support services' being downgraded). There are insufficient resources to upgrade equipment and reduce breakdowns. There is also less time for the key technology person in the school to provide the necessary support:

> I have gone from having two or three support "sections" [of time] to none this year. And I think the first year I had three [sections] at one point. So, I was only teaching three classes [and] . . . I had less than half of the computers we now have to look after. So things break, and things are not repaired or responded to at nearly the rate that they used to be. I was bragging the first year that the network was never down for the entire year. Now it's down frequently.

With little upgrading of technological hardware or software, staff are beginning to worry that Blue Mountain is no longer on the leading edge.

Professional Community and Decision-making. Work overload, shortage of time, and the unstoppable pace and astounding scope of imposed reform have seriously affected decision-making processes at Blue Mountain. Teachers at the school use the staff lunchroom less, stay in their workrooms more, and increasingly operate more like overwhelmed individuals than reflective groups. As one teacher remarked, "This year, especially, hardly anybody goes to the staff room for lunch. Everybody is working right through their lunch. People pretty much stay in their workrooms for lunch, and we've formed more isolated groups." Meetings are periodically canceled because staff are tired and need time to concentrate on pressing short-term issues. There is little time to visit other classes, to interact professionally with colleagues, or to assist new teachers. There is also no time to train new staff in the use of technology or to involve them fully in curriculum development.

Scarcity of time constantly threatens to undermine the school's collaborative team approach to planning and decision-making. It "suck[s] the creative time away from the building dramatically," in one teacher's view. Ironically, another teacher commented, collaboration and teamwork are crumbling just at the point that they are needed the most. With less collaboration, fewer people know what is "going on" in the school. "There's just so much to do, it's easier to take a task on, do it yourself, get it done, and then you can get at the next thing," the teacher said. As a result, another teacher remarked,

> More decisions have to be made without consensus because of time constraints. One can't possibly do everything. It takes a lot of time to meet with groups, to listen to everyone's ideas, to reformulate what's been said and do it over again. It's still done, but I don't think to the same extent as it was. . . . I think the time really forces your hand a bit.

Reflecting on these changes gave teachers a sense of actual or impending loss of their distinctive identity as a pioneering learning community:

> The philosophy that we started with—and we had collaborative teams, etc.—that's what we need now, because that's where teachers support each other, and that helps them through. Even though it's a negative environment, there's still so much creativity. But we're being fragmented, and we're backing into our own little territory. This is the time when we shouldn't. We should more than ever be on collaborative teams, action research, continuous improvement process, reflecting. This is when we need to do all this. But we're not. And in some ways, not to place blame, [but] I feel that there isn't the administrative support to do that.

Leadership. The school's leadership is unavoidably embroiled in, and some-times seen as the source of, these communication problems. One teacher emphasized that "the leaders that we have are great. I really admire and respect them. They do an awful lot of hard work." In many ways, the school's innovative structure and tradition has made it more able than many of its counterparts to weather the reduction in the number of middle-level heads' positions. But at the same time, some teachers did not "think that they can do the job they [have to] do, because the job description is too big. . . . As a result of the changes, they are getting stretched so much that they can't be effective".

The principal tries valiantly and often successfully to sustain a caring and inclusive approach in difficult times. But several teachers pointed out that, in the new reform climate, the school was having to be more "top-down." One teacher described a key moment when courses were canceled without consultation:

> It's because so much has to be done in so little time. We [used to] meet to decide as a group how best to go about a process. Well, there's been no meeting. We've just been told these classes are closed. . . . And never in my whole career has that ever happened. . . . There isn't that opportunity to share information. . . . Now it's just sort of "top-down" because there's only time for top-down.

Other staff members perceived the way the principal tried to "talk up" change as being somewhat forced and not fully sincere—the effect of hav-ing to engage in the emotional labor of manufacturing optimism in a pol-icy environment that repeatedly seemed to defeat it. They recognized her dilemma but also saw its effects.

> I think we've gone from an organization that was very, kind of, shared responsibility—at least, in appearance—to a very linear one now, . . . because of time. And perhaps the [second principal is] fairly directive and likes to be in control of lots of things, but she's also a humanist with you on that. But I think we've lost some of that shared responsibility because of direction and so on.

As a self-conscious learning organization and professional learning com-munity, the Blue Mountain secondary school has spent its recent years swimming against a policy tide of tsunami proportions. Accelerated and inflexible curriculum change, reductions in teacher time, and downsizing of intellectual leadership have led many teachers to retreat to their subject groups, to forsake long-term planning for short-term implementation, and to reduce their professional interaction with colleagues. Decisions are sometimes made without consultation; learning process teams have been halved; and staff feel compelled to focus more exclusively on their own curriculum and their own classes. Much professional interaction across different groups and teams remains—far more than in almost all other schools. But because of standardized reform, Blue Mountain as a learning community and as a shining example of a knowledge-society school is undoubtedly endangered. One of the school's teachers perhaps put it best when he said, "Regressive policies and bureaucracy are stifling the release of intellectual capital in our schools."

The Corrosion of Caring

In addition to being an organization that learns, Blue Mountain is a community that cares. Caring depends on possessing and acting on emotionally sympathetic dispositions. To Adam Smith, sympathy was the fundamental sentiment that made it possible for people to commit to the public good.[33] Caring depends on people having a sufficiently secure sense of themselves that their reserves of emotional energy are not completely consumed by their own needs and enough is left to serve the needs of others. Caring depends on the organization, as well as on the self. It is important that the organization enable and encourage people to build relationships and connect with those who are the focus of their caring efforts.[34] In its short history, Blue Mountain has built a strong and enviable reputation for caring among students and staff alike. But the secure selves and relationships on which effective caring depend are being consistently undermined by the effects of large-scale, standardized reform.

Relationships. Blue Mountain is a highly student-centered school. For its teachers, therefore, some of the most pernicious effects of the government's legislated mandates have been on their relationships with their students. Foremost among these was the stipulation that all teachers teach an additional 125 minutes each week, not including individual mentoring of or support for students. At the same time, the government mandates included the imposition of Teacher Advisory Group responsibilities for 30 minutes per week. At Blue Mountain, this incurred a double loss—of the additional minutes that teachers already spent with their advisory groups on top of the 30 that were mandated, and of individual contact time with students because they were now required to cover extra classes.[35] One teacher who always helped students and was involved with their learning and their lives was exasperated that individual mentoring of students did not count in the 125 minutes:

> It's ludicrous. That's my job—to help these kids, to mentor them in situations that are unique to the individual. . . . That has changed me, because I am forced to give up a lot of my time during my spares to cover classes where I am not doing a lot of instruction. . . . Most of the time, the kids just want to talk to you about something, and not to be available to them hurts me, because I only have so much time available during the day to give to these kids. I can't do stuff because I have to cover, because I have to put in my 125 minutes. I think it challenges my integrity as a professional, which I don't like.

Another teacher also found the new regulations regarding time hurtful:

> In the last two years [there have] been a lot of outside influences that don't let you get to the business of teaching kids, and maybe people would be more amenable to spending more time with kids if they weren't told that they had to do it for 125 minutes. As soon as the word *"minutes"* came into our jargon, it was the kiss of death for us. Until we get rid of that word [from] our vocabulary . . . you can't discuss care and talk about minutes. It just . . . it will not work. . . . What 125 meant to me was a legislative caring and you cannot legislate caring. You can't do it.

Some teachers were so overwhelmed that they were refusing to volunteer for coaching because they did not have the time. As one teacher said of his colleagues: "You know what? That's it. I'm doing the best I can in my classroom, but I'm not going to do the extras." In secondary schools, extracurricular activities are key places, outside of subject teaching, where teachers can form good relationships with their students and get to know them well. With the loss of teachers' involvement in extracurricular work, partly because of union work-to-rule action, but also because of time, the guidance teacher noted that discipline problems and referrals of students to the office were sharply on the increase. The reduction of his own role as sole remaining full-time guidance teacher to crisis management of students with severe problems, rather than one where he could also work proactively with students in the classroom, had made it difficult for him to avert major crises, to nip discipline problems in the bud.[36]

Teachers at Blue Mountain repeatedly complained that the reforms were "not good for kids." They did not help teachers maintain strong relationships with their colleagues, either. The tendency of teachers to retreat to the immediate demands of curriculum implementation in their own classrooms, and away from staff-room conversation and collaborative teamwork in general, has always been noted. As one staff member put it:

> I just see many teachers here as being simply individuals . . . [It used to be] like a family. I just don't see it that way now, because there have been too many changes. . . . I see the school as being a group of individuals, all with different agendas.

The debts of time that teachers were made to pay to the government mortgaged their relationships into the future. One effect of this was on the support teachers could provide for new faculty. Teachers at Blue Mountain placed a high value on getting to know and offering to help teachers who were new to the school. In highly innovative schools, paying attention to supporting and socializing new teachers into the school, its culture and mission, is essential for making its progress sustainable. But since the impact of standards-based, legislated reform, there was no time to induct new faculty into the Blue Mountain culture: "We don't have the in-service for them. We just assume that here's somebody new, life goes on, and we absorb them and then wonder why there is some difficulty." As one teacher put it:

> We don't really meet them until they're here and they stand up and introduce themselves. Then, by the time the semester's over, you're lucky if you've run into them once or twice because you're so busy. . . . You don't know everybody; you don't have that bond with people that you started off with. . . . So . . . some of the new teachers [who] have been here for this semester I know I've never talked to. And sometimes you even have to ask the kids in my adviser group, "What does this teacher look like?"

Mandated reform not only strained the connections and communications among teachers at Blue Mountain. Sometimes it began to drive wedges between them. When Blue Mountain was first affected by government economies, the seniority rules governing teacher layoffs meant that teachers with 10 years' experience or less had to leave the school, and some experienced teachers surplus to requirements in other schools with shrinking student populations were transferred in.[37] Not only were these teachers often unfamiliar with or sometimes unsympathetic to Blue Mountain's mission; a number of them were also angry about the conditions and very existence of their forcible transfer. For example, on a day that a teacher and two colleagues were supposed to be informed of their transfer fate at noon, they were given the message at just five minutes to the hour. "It was brutal. . . . I'll never forget that," the teacher said. As Blue Mountain's first two principals both related, this created real challenges in integrating staff into the school who were not only new but also disaffected with their transfer.

The effects of reform sometimes set teachers against one another, creating great emotional turmoil and resentment among teachers who cared for their colleagues but attributed personal blame to them for making their own work harder (especially when they had to cover classes during absence), even when they knew that this ultimately was not their colleagues' fault:

> This has done a couple of things, in terms of change, for me personally. . . . It makes me resent the people that are away. [Then] I feel guilty for resenting them because they are sick. But you resent people who are constantly doing PD [professional-development] stuff, which is ultimately beneficial to you, you resent that and that bothers me. . . . It also bothers me that if I am away, I can't have a lesson plan that runs through the babysitting. You have two people in there, and they are not area specialists, like a substitute would be. So you can't leave a lesson plan; you have to leave an independent module.

Teachers' Selves. Like their colleagues elsewhere in Ontario, many teachers at Blue Mountain felt that the reforms and the derogatory tone in which reformers and some of the media described teachers and their work affected their motivation and morale. Some talked about how the fun, spark, and creativity had gone out of their work; about feeling angry, resentful, unappreciated, and not valued. Endless negative media characterizations and policies that seemed to promote no learning or growth for teachers at all made teachers feel cynical and disillusioned. As one teacher said, "I'm thinking, no PD, [from] eight heads to five, extra 125 minutes! Where is the positive growth in any of that?"

Teachers felt they were losing their resilience. "How often can you be emotionally hurt and pull yourself back together again?" one teacher noted."What the heck, I am not trying to bother next time! We may just be on the edge of that." Another teacher felt that the profession's public image had sunk so low that "I hate it when I have to confess my occupation to strangers." Several of the initial group of teachers we interviewed were taking or had taken early retirement, had moved into the business world, or were going on sabbatical leaves from which they were unlikely to return. As the second principal acknowledged, in somewhat understated terms, the school was "in a little bit of dip."[38] With her staff, she had therefore established one of the Professional Learning Community Teams as RAM (Recognition, Attitude, Morale), because "we have to work on morale and attitude for teachers, as well."

LEARNING, CARING, AND SURVIVING

Innovative schools always have to swim against tides of jealousy, suspicion, loss of leadership, fading energy, waning enthusiasm, and the shifting attention of their political sponsors to other bright, shiny objects elsewhere in the district firmament. Blue Mountain is no different from its many predecessors in this respect.

But the school's self-conscious identity as a learning organization and caring community has given it notable resilience in withstanding the usual flood of difficulties—by involving the community early, planning ahead for leadership succession, and building process teams and multiple professional communities of learning and support into the school's ongoing structures. Despite the very real effects of, and teachers' complaints about, the impact of reform, Blue Mountain has seemed better equipped than most of its other high-school counterparts to withstand the worst effects. This echoes the historical tendency for innovative schools with highly collaborative cultures to be able to absorb and rework externally imposed changes in ways that protect and preserve their own mission better than more conventional schools seem able to do elsewhere.[39] After a training session shared with other schools, one teacher commented that we all came back and said, "Thank God . . . we're home! . . . in a place where you come and live and the kids live and learning lives . . . and we interact and we care for each other, and it's really great." One teacher may have exaggerated this point a little in her own remarks, but she still captured an essential truth when she said:

> What I think all of us agree is that what we're doing here is very, very good and allows us to change and flex much more easily than other

people. . . . Definitely I don't see the changes that are coming down the pipe being very difficult at all. . . . Change isn't harder for the people in this building. Change is what we do everyday. Change is the way we are.

Yet loss of time, overstretched leadership, recycled change, reduced support, and a dispiriting climate of shame and blame that are all the results of market fundamentalism have taken the edge off Blue Mountain's most exciting programs, hindered the maintenance of its technological capacity, undermined relationships with students, and put dents in the collaboration and teamwork that have been the backbone of the school as a professional learning community. Judging by this critical exceptional case, an inflexible, standardized reform agenda not only fails to create schools that develop young people for the knowledge economy or that prepare them to participate in community and public life beyond the knowledge society. Standardized educational reform also is actively undermining the efforts and success of those few true knowledge-society schools that already exist.

NOTES

1. Senge, P., *The Fifth Discipline: The Art and Practice of the Learning Organization,* New York, Doubleday, 1990. See also Senge, P., Cambron-McCabe, N., Lucas, T., Smith, B., Dutton, J. & Kleiner, A., *Schools That Learn: A Fifth Discipline Fieldbook for Educators, Parents, and Everyone Who Cares about Education,* New York, Doubleday/Currency, 2000; Leithwood, K. & Louis, K. S. (eds.), *Organizational Learning in Schools,* Lisse, The Netherlands, Swets and Zeitlinger, 1998; Fullan, M., *Change Forces: Probing the Depths of Educational Reform,* London, Falmer Press, 1993; Retallick, J., Cocklin, B. & Coombe, K. (eds.), *Learning Communities in Education: Issues, Strategies and Context,* New York, Routledge Press, 1999.

2. Mulford, W., "Organizational learning and educational change," in A. Hargreaves, A. Lieberman, M. Fullan & D. Hopkins (eds.), *International Handbook of Educational Change,* Dordrecht, The Netherlands, Kluwer Academic Publishers, 1998.

3. Wenger, E., *Communities of Practice,* Cambridge, Cambridge University Press, 1998.

4. Cochran-Smith, M. & Lytle, S., "Teacher learning communities," *Review of Research in Education* 24, 1999, 24–32; Louis, K. S. & Kruse, S. D., *Professionalism and Community: Perspectives on Reforming Urban Schools,* Thousand Oaks, CA, Corwin Press, 1995; McLaughlin, M. & Talbert, J., *Professional Communities and the Work of High School Teaching,* Chicago, University of Chicago Press, 2001.

5. Newmann, F. & Wehlage, G. *Successful School Restructuring,* Madison, WI, Center on Organization and Restructuring of Schools, 1995; Newmann, F., King,

B. & Youngs, P., *Professional Development That Addresses School Capacity,* Paper presented at the American Educational Research Association annual conference, New Orleans, 2000.

6. Newmann & Wehlage, *op. cit.,* note 5.

7. Stoll, L., Earl, L., & Fink, D., *It's about Learning: It's about Time,* London, Routledge/Falmer Press, 2002.

8. Talbert, J., "Boundaries of teachers' professional communities in U.S. high schools: Power and precariousness of the subject department," in L. Siskin & J. W. Little (eds.), *The Subjects in Question: Department Organization in the High School* (pp. 68–94), New York, Teachers College Press, 1995; McLaughlin & Talbert, *op. cit.,* note 4; Hargreaves, A., *Changing Teachers, Changing Times: Teachers' Work and Culture in the Postmodern Age,* London, Cassell and New York, Teachers College Press, 1994; Siskin, L., *Realms of Knowledge,* New York, Falmer Press, 1994.

9. Fullan, *op. cit.,* note 1.

10. Tyack, D. & Tobin, W., "The grammar of schooling: Why has it been so hard to change?" *American Educational Research Journal* 31(3), 1994, 453–480.

11. Deming, W. E., *Out of the Crisis,* Cambridge, MA, MIT Press, 1988.

12. Senge, *op. cit.,* note 1.

13. Wheatley, M., *Leadership and the New Science: Discovering Order in a Chaotic World,* San Francisco, Berrett-Koehler Publishers, 1999.

14. Spillane, J. P., Halverson, R. & Diamond, J. B., "Investigating school leadership practice: A distributed perspective," *Educational Researcher* 30(3), 2001, 23–28; Crowther, F., Kaagan, S., Hahn, L. & Ferguson, M., *Developing Teacher Leaders: How Teacher Leadership Enhances School Success,* Thousand Oaks, CA, Corwin Press, 2002.

15. Carver, J., *Boards That Make a Difference: A New Design for Leadership in Nonprofit and Public Organizations,* San Francisco, Jossey-Bass, 1990.

16. Wheatley, *op. cit.,* note 13.

17. Fink, D., *Good School/Real School: The Life Cycle of an Innovative School,* New York, Teachers College Press, 2000; Hargreaves, A. & Fink, D., "Three dimensions of educational reform," *Educational Leadership* 57(7), 2000, 30–34; Macmillan, R., "Teachers' negotiation of change," in N. Bascia & A. Hargreaves (eds.), *The Sharp Edge of Educational Change: Teaching, Leading and the Realities of Reform,* London and Philadelphia, Routledge/Falmer Press, 2000.

18. This is characteristic of the early phases of innovative schools. See, for example, Smith, L. & Keith, P., *Anatomy of Educational Innovation: An Organizational Analysis of an Elementary School,* New York, Wiley, 1971; Sarason, S., *The Creation of Settings and the Future Societies,* San Francisco, Jossey-Bass, 1972.

19. Fullan, M., *Leading in a Culture of Change,* San Francisco, Jossey-Bass/Wiley, 2001.

20. Argyris, C. & Schön, D. A., *Organization Learning: A Theory of Action Perspective,* Reading, MA, Addison-Wesley, 1978.

21. Garms, W. I., Guthrie, J. W. & Pierce, L. C., *School Finance: The Economics and Politics of Public Education,* Englewood Cliffs, NJ, Prentice-Hall, 1978.

22. Wenger, *op. cit.,* note 3.

23. Bryk, A., Camburn, E. & Louis, K. S., "Professional community in Chicago elementary schools: Facilitating factors and organizational consequences," *Educational Administration Quarterly* 35 (special issue), 1999, 751–781.

24. Lima, J. de, *Colleagues and Friends,* unpublished Ph.D. diss., University of the Azores, 1997; Hargreaves, *op. cit.,* note 8; Hargreaves, A., "Fielding errors? Deepening the debate about teacher collaboration and collegiality: Response to Fielding," *Australian Educational Researcher* 26(2), 1999, 45–53.

25. Hord, S. M., *Evaluating Educational Innovation,* London and New York, Croom Helm, 1987; Fielding, M., "Radical collegiality: Affirming teaching as an inclusive professional practice," *Australian Educational Researcher* 26(2), 1999, 1–33.

26. Hargreaves, A., "Cultures of teaching and educational change," in B. J. Biddle, T. Good & I. Goodson (eds.), *International Handbook of Teachers and Teaching* (pp. 1327–1350), Dordrecht, The Netherlands, Kluwer Academic Publishers, 1997; Mulford, *op. cit.,* note 2.

27. Fenwick, T., "Questioning the concept of the learning organization," in C. Paechter, M. Preedy, D. Scott & J. Soler (eds.), *Knowledge, Power and Learning* (pp. 74–88), London, Paul Chapman Publishing, 2001.

28. On the intellectual and emotional work of teaching and change, see Hargreaves, A., Earl, L., Moore, S. & Manning, S., *Learning to Change: Teaching beyond Subjects and Standards,* San Francisco, Jossey-Bass/Wiley, 2001.

29. Hargreaves, D. "The new professionalism: The synthesis of professional and institutional development," *Teaching and Teacher Education* 10(4), 1994, 423–438; Fielding, *op. cit.,* note 25; Little, J. W., "Colleagues of choice, colleagues of circumstances: Response to M. Fielding," *Australian Educational Researcher* 26(2), 1999, 35–44; Hargreaves, A., "The emotional practice of teaching," *Teaching and Teacher Education* 14(8), 1998, 835–854; Hargreaves (1999), *op. cit.,* note 24.

30. Lima, J. de, "Forgetting about friendship: Using conflict in teacher communities as a lever for school change," *Journal of Educational Change* 2(3), 2001; Hargreaves, A., "The emotional geographies of teachers' relations with colleagues," *International Journal of Educational Research,* forthcoming.

31. Sarason, *op. cit.,* note 18; Smith & Keith, *op. cit.,* note 18; Hargreaves & Fink, *op. cit.,* note 17, pp. 30–34.

32. Fink, *op. cit.,* note 17.

33. Smith, A., *The Theory of Moral Sentiments* (12th ed.), Glasgow, R. Chapman, 1809.

34. Noddings, N., *The Challenge to Care in Schools,* New York, Teachers College Press, 1992.

35. However, there was a benefit for teachers for nine weeks of the academic year. Normally, under a semestered system, they had taught four out of four periods per day, with a 50-minute lunch period in between. The new legislation therefore reduced teachers' total amount of out-of-class scheduled time across the whole year but improved it a little in relative terms during this nine-week commitment of their time.

36. Four full-time guidance teaching equivalents had been reduced to two—one full time, and the remainder formed from fractions of remaining teacher time. Fur-

ther evidence of the negative impact of reduced extracurricular activity on student discipline, relationships, and achievement in Ontario is documented in Earl, L., Freeman, S., Lasky, S., Sutherland, S. & Torrance, N., *Policy, Politics, Pedagogy and People: Early Perceptions and Challenges of Large-Scale Reform in Ontario Secondary Schools*, Toronto, Ontario Secondary School Teachers' Federation, 2002.

37. The school's appointment policy of striking a balance in the composition of the staff meant that it had appointed one-third of its staff with 5–10 years prior experience. The school was unsuccessful in using this policy as a reason to warrant being treated as an exception when teachers with the least experience were declared surplus to requirements in the district.

38. The principal stated that these perceptions were also echoed by several staff.

39. Ball, S. & Bowe, R., "Subject departments and the implementation of the national curriculum," *Journal of Curriculum Studies* 24, 1992, 97–116.

6

BEYOND STANDARDIZATION

Professional Learning Communities or Performance-Training Sects?

TOWARD A LEARNING PROFESSION

Teaching today is increasingly complex work. It requires the highest standards of professional practice to perform it well. Teaching is the core profession, the key agent of change in today's knowledge society. Teachers are the midwives of the knowledge society. Without teachers, their confidence and competence, the future will be malformed and stillborn. On entering office, George W. Bush's educational slogan was to "leave no child behind." Leaving no child behind means leaving no teacher or leader behind either.

Yet teaching is in crisis. The demographic turnover among teachers, along with years of burnout and disillusionment with large-scale reform, is draining the profession. The attractiveness of teaching as a career among actual and potential new recruits has been fading fast. Chapter 4 laid out the depressing evidence of good teachers' retiring early, dedicated young teachers' leaving for something that was more emotionally uplifting, and teachers advising their own children not to follow in their footsteps.

Teaching has to compete much harder against business and other professions for-high caliber candidates than it did in the last period of mass recruitment in the 1960s and '70s, when able women were led to feel that nursing and secretarial work were their only other options. Teaching may not yet have reverted to being an occupation for "unmarriageable women and unsaleable men," as Willard Waller described it in 1932,[1] but many American inner cities now run their school systems on high numbers of uncertified teachers, and more and more school systems depend on endless streams of the increasingly casualized, contracted labor of temporary teachers from overseas or on endless streams of substitute teachers whose quality administrators have no time to monitor.[2] In Ontario, the reform processes

160

described in Chapter 4 led to a 20–25 percent drop in applications to teacher-education programs in a single year.[3]

Amid this danger and despair, though, there are signs of hope and reasons for optimism about a future of learning in the knowledge society that is tied to more empowering, imaginative, and inclusive visions for teaching and learning. The reduction of educational standards to soulless standardization in many places has generated public dissatisfaction with teacher shortages in schools, and the loss of creativity and inspiration in classrooms.[4] In Australia and elsewhere, adolescents' alienation from overly specialized content-driven schools has created growing support for the resumption of more humane middle-years philosophies in the early years of high school. School districts in the United States, and the philanthropic foundations that support some of their efforts, are increasingly seeing that high-quality professional development for teachers is indispensable in bringing about deep and lasting changes in students' achievement.[5] England, meanwhile, is creating the incentive of more "earned autonomy" and freedom from curriculum constraints and inspection requirements for schools and teachers who perform well.[6] Almost everywhere, governments are beginning to talk up teachers and teaching, bestowing honor and respect where blame and contempt had prevailed.[7] TV drama series are even being made about teachers, not just about lawyers and doctors.[8]

The time is ripe to rethink what teaching and learning for students and professional learning and support for teachers should look like for the new generation of educators who will shape the next three decades of public education. Educational reform can no longer be built on the backs of teachers. Improved learning must be achieved through methods that inspire good teaching and that retain good teachers. If schools are to become real knowledge communities for all students, then teaching must be made into a real *learning profession* for all teachers.

FUTURES FOR TEACHING IN THE KNOWLEDGE SOCIETY

The Organization for Economic Cooperation and Development (OECD) has sketched out six likely scenarios for the future of public education in the knowledge society.[9] Two of these presume an unraveling of existing arrangements that will lead to either more entrenched bureaucracy in school systems or increasing emphasis on market and choice-based solutions as people's dissatisfaction with public education spreads. A second pair of options presumes a shrinkage of public schooling either by atrophy as teacher shortages and a desperate proliferation of innovations create panic and "meltdown" in educational policy or by investment in other alternatives outside the school in e-learning and non-formal learning.

Just two scenarios, which the OECD labels "Re-Schooling," assume that public schooling can be saved and improved for the better. One of these sees the school being reinvented as a focused learning organization that emphasizes learning for the knowledge society, on the lines of Chapter 5. The other envisions schools as focal points for broader community relationships and networks, developing students' social capital and enabling them to live well and work productively in the knowledge society. This last pair of recommendations amounts to teaching for the knowledge society and beyond it. But how can schools become learning and caring communities, given everything that teachers and their systems have experienced and endured in the past 15 years of educational upheaval and reform? We might be able to see the destination, but where is the path toward it?

CULTURES, CONTRACTS, AND CHANGE

In Chapter 4, I looked at the fate of Britain's Railtrack as a metaphor for understanding how and why public education has been going off the rails. The collapse of Railtrack and its record of standards, safety, and security was the result, in many ways, of the railway service's abandoning a system of regulation by cultures of knowledge and experience, in which workers knew and trusted their local "patch" of railway, the people who worked there, and the practices that maintained and sustained it. Instead, Railtrack introduced a system of regulation by contracts of performance, in which quality assurance through mutual obligation, trusted relationships, and local knowledge was replaced with detailed performance targets imposed on a mobile, low-cost, flexible workforce of contract labor.

Similar patterns have characterized more than a decade of public-education reform. Teaching standards for students, performance standards for teachers, an increasingly casualized teaching force, more and more contracting out of professional development and other support services, and the rise of charter schools and other private options have replaced the forms of accountability that used to be embedded in the long-standing relationships and experiential knowledge of local school districts.

Yet, we must not get too nostalgic about the loss of local cultures to impersonal contracts in education. Local educational cultures can be paternalistic, even feudal, in the ways they cultivate compliant loyalty among their teachers and principals. Too often they have camouflaged incompetence, moving problem teachers and principals (including abusive ones) around the system instead of confronting them and their unions. More than a few school districts cross the thin line that divides collaboration from cronyism and corruption. Strong local cultures in the form of old boys' networks kept women out of educational administration for years. To say that moving from cultures of knowledge and experience to contracts of performance represents only a turn for the worse oversimplifies the issues.

We need a more sophisticated understanding of how cultures and contracts can contribute to reinventing public education in the knowledge society so that it combines the mutual personal trust of relationships with the professional trust and accountability of performance contracts.

Stronger and weaker versions of contract-based and culture-based regimes for regulating quality and standards can and do interact with each other in different ways to create different patterns and emphases of school reform and different types of teaching communities. If we consider two types of contract regimes (strong and weak) and three kinds of culture regimes (strong-mutual, strong-hierarchical, and weak), this highlights six possible future scenarios for teachers in the knowledge society (see Figure 6.1).

CULTURE REGIMES

The first three combinations in the left-hand column assume weak contractual systems in which performance data are in short supply, testing is only lightly emphasized, and accountability relies more on personal judgment than formal procedures and quantifiable results. I have described these three regimes, which preceded the emergence of the new educational orthodoxy of standards, tests, inspections, and choice, elsewhere, so I will review them only briefly here.[10]

Permissive Individualism

The professional regime of permissive individualism preceded not only contract regimes but also efforts to *re-culture* schools into more collaborative workplaces for teachers.[11] In the era of permissive individualism, most teachers taught alone, away from scrutiny, in insulated classes. Their formal qualifications as teachers licensed their right to autonomy and protection from interference for the duration of their careers. Under permissive

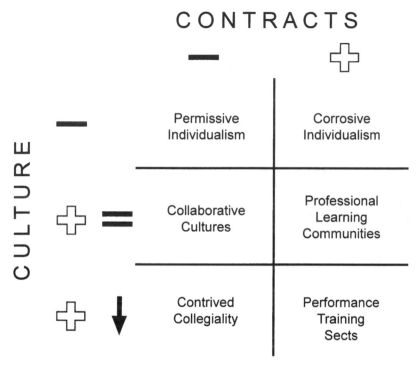

FIGURE 6.1. Culture and Contract Regimes

individualism, teachers sometimes combined their efforts to spearhead innovations—and this was an age in which there were many—but most curriculum innovations and projects that relied on teachers' voluntary commitments did not last. Further qualifications and in-service education were typically pursued individually, away from the school site, and had little chance of influencing others in the school who had not shared the experience. Without opportunities to learn from colleagues or benefit from their encouragement to take risks in trying new practices, individualism in teaching created decades of barriers to widespread and sustained positive educational change and classroom improvement.

Collaborative Cultures

In the 1980s and beyond, efforts to eliminate the effects of individualism and isolation in teaching led to widespread attempts to re-culture schools along more collaborative lines. Although it could never be legislated, re-culturing was strongly supported and encouraged in many schools and their districts. Teachers were encouraged to work together and interact more. Sharing resources and planning together started to emerge as acceptable norms for the job. In-service education was directed at school teams, often at the school site. Effective leadership also promoted informal as well as formal collaboration among teachers, embedding joint professional efforts in a web of long-lasting and trusted relationships.

At their best, when teachers' collaborative efforts focused on ways to improve teaching and learning, the effects on students' achievement and school improvement were strong. In other cases, though, collaborative efforts could be superficial, concentrating on student discipline, staff socializing, or task coordination rather than on teachers' making demanding improvements together that would benefit students' learning. In some cases, collaboration could become comfortable and rewarding for the staff without any check on whether this really benefited students. Without some external or independent reference points, collaboration could perpetuate ineffective practices as easily as effective ones.

The results of building effective collaborative cultures therefore have not been consistent. In addition, there have been only weak strategies to spread them beyond a few enthusiastic and well-led schools and districts so they benefit students and teachers across entire regions and nations. Re-culturing holds great promise as an improvement strategy, but by itself it sometimes fails to make real improvements in student achievement and is hard to generalize across a broad system. Re-culturing in the knowledge society is only part of the solution of effective school change and teacher development.

Contrived Collegiality

Collaborative cultures can also create problems when they are hijacked by hierarchical systems of control. Here, collaboration among teachers becomes forced, or artificial. It turns into what I call *contrived collegiality*. Contrived collegiality is collaboration imposed from above about what to plan or learn, with whom to plan or learn it, and where and when to undertake the planning and learning. Contrived collegiality is more than a scaffold of structures and expectations that promotes and supports collaboration. It is a prison of micromanagement that constrains it.

Contrived collegiality neglects, crowds out, or actively undermines opportunities for teachers to initiate their own joint projects, shared learning, and collective inquiry in such areas as action research, team-teaching, and curriculum planning. By crowding the collegial agenda with requirements about what is to be done collectively and with whom, contrived collegiality inhibits bottom-up professional initiative. Unlike knowledge-economy corporations, which are supposed to devise general knowledge goals centrally that inspire people locally to develop their own solutions, contrived collegiality micromanages the collaborative process, setting strict boundaries around it and limiting room to maneuver. As a result, teachers may actually collaborate less, or they may abandon collaborative ways of working altogether once the urgency of implementation or creating a school-improvement plan has passed., or a leader who had been breathing down their necks has left. Whether it is introduced by overzealous principals or devious districts, contrived collegiality can produce temporary surges of teamwork under pressure, but it rarely produces sustainable improvement.

CONTRACT REGIMES

On their own, culture regimes provide weak assurances of quality. When they are voluntary, their effects can be weak or inconsistent. When they are imposed, their consequences can be counterproductive and perverse. This is partly why another kind of regulation by contract and performance has been introduced.[12]

Contract regimes have brought about three kinds of measures.[13] First, they have increased consumer choice of schools among parents through charter schools; increased public funding and tax relief for private schools; support for magnet schools, or other schools of choice and special emphasis; publication of school-performance results as a basis for parent choice; and competition among schools for the highest-achieving students and their parents.

Second, more public provision is being taken over by or outsourced to private companies. In some cases this has involved sole or joint private running or sponsorship of curriculum programs, technology innovations, and even entire schools or their districts when they have had a history of poor performance. In other cases, a range of school and district services has been outsourced to private companies—from cleaning and catering to professional-development services, school-improvement support, evaluation and inspection in relation to achievement of performance standards, and the supplying of temporary or substitute teachers.

Third, diverse and fragmented "flexible" groups of contractors and "deliverers" can no longer assure quality through the mutual trust of valued relationships, so these are replaced with common, detailed, "high-stakes" standards of performance that all providers and contractors must meet.

Corrosive Individualism

A regime of contracts and competitive individualism in schools has spread around the world since the 1990s. S. Lindblad and T. Popkewitz have identified this new regime in all the cases of school governance they studied in North America, Britain, Scandinavia, Spain, Portugal, Greece, and Australia.[14] Through the funding priorities of global financial organizations, which favor movement of money from public service to private investment, elements of contract regimes are also becoming widespread in much of the less-developed world, especially South America.

Contract regimes in education operate as quasi-markets.[15] Consumer choice and flexibly organized provision are typically organized within detailed legislated frameworks of student testing, curriculum standards, and high-stakes processes for inspecting, monitoring, and intervening in school performance. The new educational orthodoxy is, in this sense, a paradoxical combination of choice that is supposed to promote diversity with standards that impose uniformity.

The result of these influences has been the emergence of a culture of competitive individualism in schools and teaching. School competes with school, outbidding its competitor for the best students and families in a Darwinian struggle for survival and success. Schools try to be different, but because of imposed standards framework, they ultimately look the same. I once met with the principals of several neighboring secondary schools in Victoria, Australia, that were in competition for students in a standards-based system. They advertised in the newspapers to market their schools. One morning, the schools' principals opened their newspapers and saw all the schools' ads. They were exactly the same. All the schools represented themselves as having high standards and expectations, but not at the expense of caring and relationships. They valued school uniform and tradition but also embraced computers and technology. The rhetoric of the market was difference; the reality was sameness. So they abandoned their advertisements, pooled their resources, formed a federation, and decided to collaborate instead of compete.

Elsewhere, though, competition prevents schools and teachers from learning from one another. People keep their best ideas to themselves. Districts become the antithesis of learning organizations. Social exclusion increases as those parents with the economic and social capital to choose and move around for the best deal cluster in schools that pull away from those where choice is not an option. Chapter 3 showed how magnet schools and systems can polarize their schools and their students. Social division follows the new social geographies of the contract and the market. In his compelling analysis of the human consequences of globalization, Zygmunt Bauman puts it this way:

> Those "high up" are satisfied that they travel through life by their heart's desire and pick and choose their destinations according to the joys they offer. Those "low down" happen time and again to be thrown out from the site they would rather stay in.[16]

The middle classes, middle America, and middle England enjoy the globalization of choice and the chance to educate their children in the best schools. The lower classes and many minorities are condemned to what Bauman calls "enforced localization"—to the poorly resourced ghettos, housing projects, and hinterlands of the market economy of schooling.[17] Interestingly, according to recent OECD studies of literacy achievement at age 15 in 31 developed countries, those Anglophone countries that have invested most heavily in the new regimes of contracts, choice, and performance score among the poorest in terms of social inclusion and their capacity to secure achievement among the most disadvantaged students.[18]

In response to years of coercive reform, more and more parents have taken flight from the public to the private system, with proportions of children in private education expanding rapidly in virtually all Anglophone countries. David Hargreaves fears that, if these trends persist, public schools will become little more than a safety net for those without the financial or cultural capital to choose the private option.[19]

The paradoxical policy response to this very real threat has been to keep the middle classes in public education by creating elite enclaves, schools, or classes of distinction for them within the system. Middle-class families can then continue to feel that their children's education is excellent and even exclusive while keeping their conscience clear about committing to the public good. Gifted and talented classes, higher tracks, honors programs, schools serving only wealthy neighborhoods, and schools of choice—these are the "business class" sections of public education to which the middle classes can sign their name without having to participate more inclusively in the comprehensive and diverse realities of public life.[20] Meanwhile, defining failure in terms of schools that have the weakest test scores and dealing with this through forceful intervention ensures that the teeming masses back in economy class, whose failure must be combated and whose violence must be given zero tolerance, exist as objects of pity or disgust to more privileged parents. This emotional economy of distinction and disgust self-righteously reminds, reassures, and provides relief among the middle class about their own more fortunate distinction.[21] This growing divide between the business- and economy-class categories of education (including school improvement and professional development) is the enemy of an innovative knowledge society and a just democracy.

The regime of contracts and competitive individualism also consumes teachers' time, intensifies it to cut costs, and fills it up with meeting short-term performance targets. Competitive individualism, then, becomes corrosive individualism that wears down teachers from the outside and eats away at their sense of community from within. As we saw in chapters 3 and 4, teachers start to retreat to their classrooms, keeping their heads down and concentrating on the short term. They withdraw from pursuing self-initiated, long-term, sustainable improvement with their colleagues. Initiative disappears; creativity is lost; and ingenuity goes walkabout. Teaching for the knowledge society becomes a distant dream. A world in which contracts eliminate cultures is a toxic and corrosive one for sustainable school improvement.

The positive legacy of contract regimes is that they have led schools and teachers to treat achievement data and other evidence seriously—to take a reality check and rely on more than their experience and intuition as a basis for improvement. But contract regimes have exacted too great a cost on cultures of experience and understanding and on the chance for long-term improvement among teachers. Can these two worlds of contracts and cultures be brought together in ways that preserve their strengths and minimize their weaknesses?

Professional Learning Communities

Professional learning communities add contracts to culture. They put a premium on teachers' working together, but they also insist that this joint work consistently focus on improving teaching and learning and use evidence and data as a basis for informing classroom-improvement efforts and for solving whole-school problems. In their research on school and departmental communities, M. McLaughlin and J. Talbert found that strong professional learning communities

> centered their work on students and shared responsibility for students' mastery of content and progress in the curriculum. They developed "innovative" methods of instruction that achieved a better "fit" of course work to students without compromising expectations for students' conceptual learning.[22]

As we saw in chapter 5, a strong professional learning community brings together the knowledge, skills, and dispositions of teachers in a school or across schools to promote shared learning and improvement. A strong professional learning community is a social process for turning information into knowledge. It is a piece of social ingenuity based on the principle that, in Michael Fullan's words, "new ideas, knowledge creation, inquiry and sharing are essential to solving learning problems in a rapidly changing society."[23]

Professional learning communities promote and presume key knowledge-society attributes such as teamwork, inquiry, and continuous learning. Unlike regimes of competitive and corrosive individualism, which use data to inflict embarrassment on underperforming teachers, professional learning communities use data to support and promote joint improvement among them. As the Blue Mountain school demonstrated (see chapter 5), professional learning communities work best when they are combined with cultures of caring and are grounded in long-term relationships of trust, foundations of security, and commitments to active care among teachers and others.

Professional learning communities do not flourish in standardized systems that severely restrict teachers' discretion for decision-making and self-initiated change. Nor do they flourish in a workforce of transient teachers who are only in teaching for the short-term. Reforms that drive teachers to teach to the test or tie them to scripted programs of literacy and other curriculum areas prevent long-term development of competence and confidence in the teaching force. The results reported in chapters 3–5 show that standardized educational reform damages rather than develops strong professional learning communities. As McLaughlin and Talbert put it:

> [S]chools and teachers sanctioned on the basis of standardized test scores are drilling their students to pass the test even when they believe the learning is of limited enduring value and the practice is educationally unsound.[24]

To build strong professional learning communities, they advocate a "shift from system policies that seek to provide standardized practice to those that aim to strengthen teachers' judgement and opportunity to learn."[25]

This tide is already turning. In the United States, Steve Anderson, Shawn Moore, and I have been working with the Learning First Alliance, a consortium of some of America's leading educational organizations, to help identify which kinds of professional-development strategies in school districts are associated with long-term, sustainable improvements in students' achievement. In several of the districts we have studied, we have uncovered a wide range of high-quality practices that build strong professional learning communities. These include professional learning teams, teacher networks, and action research groups.

Looking at five districts that had been selected because they had demonstrated three continuous years of improved student achievement, the Learning First Alliance project found that district-level improvement was associated with urgently driven, commonly agreed, and specifically focused strategies that promoted

- *Professional development* that was continuous, shared, job-embedded, and closely connected to teaching and learning.
- *Instructional leadership* through intensive training, mentoring, and coaching for school leaders.
- *Evidence-informed decision-making* where multiple kinds of data were consulted to inform improvement decisions. Data were interpreted intelligently, not treated uncritically.
- *Distributed leadership* where improvement became a shared commitment and responsibility.
- *Local creativity and flexibility* where there was high scope at school level for deciding the best way to achieve improvement.

All five districts studied by Learning First Alliance were also characterized by three crucial conditions for supporting professional learning communities:

- *Access to external resources* through successful grant-writing, suggesting that existing levels of baseline public funding in poorer school districts are often inadequate for sustaining professional learning communities.
- *Stability of district-level leadership* that puts the goals of long-term improvement ahead of short-term reform.
- *Multiple indicators of accountability* to create sophisticated images of change, rather than single scales of failure and success.

In England and Wales, meanwhile, educational-policy statements are responding to the crisis of teacher recruitment and the over-reaching of standardized reform by emphasizing:

- Substantial reductions in the National Curriculum to give more flexibility and discretion to teachers.
- Permission to move even further away from the National Curriculum when schools are performing exceptionally well "to free the best secondary schools from constraints which stand in the way of yet higher standards."
- "Earned autonomy" for teachers in high-performing schools, where the demands of external inspection will be eased as standards rise.
- Government seed money to support school-based teacher-research projects that are designed to improve practice.[26]
- Professional networks to connect teachers and schools that are inquiring into and improving their practice.

These frameworks of incentive and flexibility provide significantly increased opportunities for building strong professional learning communities among teachers, especially in schools that are performing well. They are meant to

> develop the strengths of every school, and help schools to learn and work together . . . [as well as] to free the energies, talents and professional creativity of [principals] and teachers . . . to lead a program of innovation and transformation.[27]

Professional learning communities exert their effects slowly, yet sustainably, over time. They have clear links to improved standards of learning. Their success depends on continuing support from outside the school, compatibility with external reform imperatives, strong support in terms of instructional materials and leadership development, and a staff with sufficient levels of knowledge, competence, and skill to share with their colleagues.[28]

Professional learning communities are also important beyond the school in terms of face-to-face and virtual professional learning networks such as subject associations, the thousands of teachers in the National Writing project in the United States, the California New Teacher Mentor program that now operates nationwide, many districtwide professional learning networks that are springing up in the United Kingdom, the Thousand Schools projects in Mexico and South Africa, and so on. They can also give coherence to contracted services for professional learning and development and inspection and accreditation if these services are clustered regionally beyond the local district itself. This regionalization of professional learning and development releases outside support from the grip of local micromanagement while preventing it from degenerating into a chaos of unknown and poorly regulated providers. Robust regionalization offers the capacity to build cultures of understanding and experience with a manageable range of providers over time while maintaining the integrity and independence of the best kinds of contract relationship.[29]

Some of the ways in which policy can promote strong professional learning communities within and beyond schools include:

- *Leadership development,* emphasizing the importance of professional learning communities and developing the specific skills to build them in the education of school leaders.
- *School inspection and accreditation,* building indicators of professional learning communities into processes of school inspection and accreditation—for instance, whether the school has professional learning teams that include all staff, whether teachers use data as a basis for improvement, the extent to which decision-making teams include teachers with relevant experience and interest and not just the dominant cliques in the school, etc.
- *Recertification and performance management,* linking evidence of commitment to professional learning communities to performance-related pay and to measures of competence that underpin recertification of teachers over time. This means moving far beyond the outdated and ineffective models of professional development in which teachers accumulate required numbers of individual course credits off-site, like frequent-flyer points, to maintain their salary or professional standing. This system degenerates into little more than "bums on seats"—teachers reluctantly showing up just to notch up their course credits. Instead, certification, professional standards, and performance-related pay should be linked more to professional learning experiences undertaken with colleagues in ways that are designed to improve teaching and learning, such as school-based teacher research, peer coaching in a new classroom practice, active participation in a professional learning team, etc.
- *Seed money for self-learning,* in which small amounts of government or district funding are provided to individuals and schools to pursue their own professional learning in ways that are planned to improve teaching and learning within people's own practice. This provides a framework of support and accountability criteria without micromanaging the outcomes.

- *Professional self-regulation,* in which teachers' organizations of professional self-regulation that include *all* teachers are established and
  strengthened (unlike the National Board of Professional Teaching Standards in the United States, which is merely voluntary) and that extend
  beyond issues of licensing, discipline, and ethical codes of conduct
  (unlike the Scottish Teachers' Council) to embrace setting, raising, and
  enforcing agreed professional standards in teaching that include principles of professional learning community. In England, the General
  Teaching Council does not yet have the power to define and regulate
  standards through a model of professional accountability. Instead,
  teacher standards remain under the government-controlled Teacher
  Teaching Agency and its model of bureaucratic accountability. The
  Ontario College of Teachers currently comes the closest to being a self-
  regulating professional body that has compulsory membership, a broad
  professional mandate, and power to regulate and raise standards for all
  teachers. However, no bodies of professional self-regulation for teachers and no governments that have established their terms of reference
  have yet been able to define, raise, and enforce improved professional
  standards for all teachers that are appropriate within a knowledge society. Unions are reluctant to let their members' terms of employment
  fall into the hands of another representative teacher body. Governments are unprepared to yield their grip on micromanagement and
  give teaching back to teachers. Someone, somewhere, needs to find the
  moral courage and social ingenuity to break through this impasse.
- *Professional networks,* providing initial financial and logistical support
  for teachers to establish and maintain their own professional networks
  of learning and advocacy. These are more than membership organizations of school principals or staff developers, but diverse bodies that
  promote genuine learning opportunities in curriculum, leadership,
  pedagogy, and other areas. Although the emergence of such networks
  might be facilitated by government, they should operate independently
  of it. This means, importantly in a democratic learning society, that
  governments help create networks and organizations in education that
  from time to time will make life difficult for it—that is, that will provide the necessary irritation of the flea to make the government elephant move around a little more.[30]
- *Regionalization of professional development and support services* by creating regional professional learning centers that bring together contractors and clients (school clusters etc) in genuine, long-term communities of interest, learning, and support. As I have explained, there is

more at stake here than providing menus of in-service courses. The opportunities and expectations should be to make generic connections to schools and districts in ways that strengthen their capacity to operate as professional learning communities.

- *Grown-up norms of professional community,* building communities among teachers that develop and pursue broadly shared goals focused on improving teaching, learning, and caring through respectful and sometimes spirited disagreement and debate about the best ways to do this. Developing these grown-up norms is a responsibility of teachers themselves—to become as comfortable and assertive in a vigorous and rigorous culture of sometimes argumentative adults as they are with a class of subordinate children. Grown-up norms also depend on leadership and government. Can grown-up leaders cultivate a climate of challenge and disagreement that will sometimes rebound on them? Are grown-up governments prepared to absorb the democratic dissent they will sometimes create? Can governments and leaders communicate that there are many ways to excel as a teacher (not just one)? Imposing single best ways of teaching excellence inevitably polarizes teachers who disagree into those who are good, right, and strong and those who are bad, weak, and wrong. Singular strategies of imposed success discourage the long-term development of grown-up cultures of teaching.

Together, these policy measures can help reinvent teaching as a learning profession that is based on grown-up norms that recognize that teachers' commitments to their students create obligations to engage with their colleagues and to regard continuous professional learning as an individual and collective duty that, if not performed, makes teachers a liability to their students. At the same time, these measures also signal that continual and connected professional learning is an institutional right that deserves time, support, and flexibility from government.[31]

Professional learning communities are not an attractive improvement strategy for policymakers and school leaders who face pressure and demands for quick results in raising achievement levels. They do not fit well with the soulless standardization of testing regimes or highly prescriptive curriculum frameworks. They are difficult to develop where teachers or leaders still lack minimal levels of knowledge or expertise on which a professional learning community might be built. In these conditions, policymakers and administrators tend to turn to another reform strategy, which I call *performance-training sects.*

Performance-Training Sects

In the face of what Tom Sergiovanni calls the "standards stampede," educational reformers have armed themselves with strongly asserted claims from parts of the educational-research community that certain teaching practices are highly effective for improving students' learning, and that there are proven methods to manage the educational change process effectively.[32] Reformers have then launched a set of large-scale reform strategies that combine a strong insistence on performance standards and prescribed classroom techniques with measures to re-culture teachers' working relationships more collaboratively.

The large-scale initiatives include Peter Hill's groundbreaking work with literacy reform in Catholic school systems in Australia;[33] Robert Slavin's high-profile Success for All program and the strongly promoted Open Court program of scripted phonics instruction within the United States;[34] the widely publicized success of New York District 2 and its superintendent, Tony Alvarado, in dramatically turning around its students' performance in reading and mathematics[35] and Alvarado's follow-up impact on the much larger school system of San Diego;[36] and England's massive National Literacy and Numeracy strategy, which has legislated literacy and math reform in the form of daily hours for literacy and math in all of the nation's primary schools.[37]

Although these large-scale initiatives vary in their details and emphases, they and their advocates are tightly linked in networks of mutual influence, and key similarities run through all of them. The similarities include:

- Making instruction the central focus of improvement efforts.
- Concentrating attention on high-profile areas of instruction, especially literacy and math.
- Setting ambitious targets for improved achievement results across the whole system that will produce large gains with rapid success.
- Giving particular priority to low-achieving students to narrow the achievement gap between students from advantaged and less-advantaged homes.
- Expecting all students to achieve higher standards (with greater support for those who need extra help)—no excuses, no delays.
- Providing clearly defined, closely prescribed, and sometimes tightly scripted programs of instruction for teachers to follow that ensure compliance and consistency (although the actual degree of prescription varies).

- Providing intensive training for teachers in workshops and summer institutes in the core instructional priorities to establish large-scale competence in them.
- Creating a strong and generous support structure of trainers, coordinators, and consultants to work with teachers on implementing the priorities within their schools.
- Providing intensive one-to-one peer coaching support for teachers within the classroom, on the basis of evidence that this is one of the key factors that gets more teachers to use and persist with the change over time.
- Insisting that principals become instructional leaders, including being directly involved in all relevant training activities within their school.
- Having teachers examine achievement data together to make adjustments in their instruction when necessary.
- Aligning the improvements in instruction with the evaluation and testing system.
- Involving parents and the community in supporting their children's learning within the selected initiative.

The emphasis throughout is on providing the pressure and support to train teachers intensively in a limited number of given instructional priorities that will deliver rapid and significant increases in measured learning performances for all students. This strongly supported, closely aligned, and intensively applied strategy has already yielded important benefits for students and their teachers.

First, almost all the initiatives have shown significant early success in improving students' achievement results, including narrowing the achievement gap among students from different social backgrounds. Second, the reforms have led all teachers and schools to treat literacy and math seriously when this had not always been the case. Third, the achievement gains have challenged the views of some teachers that their poor or minority students could not learn to significantly higher standards, and for the first time many teachers have started to believe that all their students have the capacity to learn. This reinforces the well-established principle that, with imposed change, most teachers have to change their practices before they will change their beliefs.[38] These breakthroughs in teachers' belief systems make them more receptive to further professional learning.

Fourth, the scripted materials and strong support structures can benefit teachers who lack confidence at the beginning of their careers; uncertified or underqualified teachers who work in poor school districts; poorly paid and trained teachers in less-developed countries; and other teachers whose knowledge, skills, and overall expertise are weak or underdeveloped. A tightly driven program of instructional change equips these teachers with a repertoire of strategies that is inalienably theirs for life and that can provide a strong platform for further improvement. Last, teachers who have endured years of unwanted reform and worsening working conditions finally find themselves being offered generous levels of support and release time from the classroom to learn things that make a real difference with their students. The forceful pressure to improve is undeniable, but the support is significant, too.

These benefits are real and significant. There is much to learn from the progress these programs are achieving. However, the regime of intensive performance training also raises serious problems. Like the Railtrack contract workers who repaired only the rails but not the rest of the track, performance training might get quick results, but it seems to be less successful in securing sustainable improvement. In December 2001, England's early gains in literacy scores as a result of its National Literacy project suddenly reached a plateau. Tightly regulated regimes of performance training also achieve less success at the high-school level, where students' learning is more complex, as is their school as an organization. In England, improving literacy among high-school students is more challenging than with younger children. Interestingly, Alvarado's success in New York was achieved in a district that did not include high schools. Not only is the instruction more complex in high school, but, as I showed in chapter 3, many students have difficulties not so much with the instruction as with the fragmented organization of high-school life. When literacy skills or learning in general become more sophisticated, performance-training regimes have less dramatic effects.

Second, the repeated stress on literacy and math in these programs draws attention and support away from other areas of the curriculum, such as social studies, arts, and citizenship, where critical thinking and creating and applying knowledge and other core competencies of the knowledge society are typically given greater emphasis.[39] Regimes of performance training may therefore improve results in basic skills in the short term but imperil more complex knowledge society objectives in the long run.

Then there are the effects on teachers. Research on the impact of performance-training initiatives indicates that many teachers dislike teaching highly prescriptive programs.[40] Even when teachers acknowledge the benefits for students, they dislike losing their classroom discretion by being locked into an instructional straitjacket.[41] They feel less satisfied, less professional, less motivated to teach overall. As Maurice Galton has argued, even if it is effective for students, mandating instructional change by force is undesirable because it can damage teachers' long-term commitments to their work. This is not wise in an era of teacher shortages.[42]

Of course, some teachers do like to have their teaching spelled out for them. Our Spencer Foundation study *Change over Time?* suggests that they include newer, younger teachers who patrol their time and commitments more carefully than do many of their older colleagues. Pandering to the preference for prescription runs the risk of cultivating compliance and recycling professional dependence on the external authority of bureaucrats, on scripted texts, or on the "incontrovertible" results of research. In performance-training sects, there is little opportunity to promote continuous professional learning among reflective teachers who can exercise discretionary judgment. Over time, teachers inducted into performance-training sects can lose the capacity or desire to make professional judgments and become more reflective.

Alvarado's successor, Elaine Fink, has described continuing developments in New York District 2 with Lauren Resnick.[43] Their article appeals to the idea of learning community where leaders engage in "reading and thinking all the time" and where "intellect is valued in its own right." There is a clear focus on instruction in principal meetings; data are treated seriously, and problems are shared among principals openly. District 2's successes have taken a decade to evolve and have produced sophisticated practices and not just scripted performances of learning and teaching in balanced literacy. At the same time, even here, when Fink and Resnick refer to how "new instructional initiatives may be introduced," all examples used are specifically in literacy and math, and it is clear that these initiatives are externally inserted, more than internally developed. The external thrust and concentration on results-driven literacy and math to the exclusion of other, more creative learning areas, along with the intensive support of training, learning, and group disclosure of "problems," points to this system as conforming to the characteristics of a performance-training sect as well as those of a professional learning community.

In other cases, the evidence is less ambiguous. Stein, Hubbard, and Mehan show how the carefully evolved practices that promote deep literacy in New York District 2 failed in many ways to transfer successfully with Alvarado and many of his staff to San Diego. San Diego's larger and more bureaucratic system, combined with intense political and corporate pressure to produce quick achievement gains in two years, substituted District 2's decade of trust building and deep understanding of change, with a hierarchical demand for urgency and compliance that produced rushed and superficial understandings of the practices that were being promoted. If more and more districts and governments insist on quick achievement-gain fixes, strong professional learning communities that produce deep and sustainable interpretations of teaching and learning will be replaced by rigid perform-ance training sects that secure only fleeting and superficial compliance.[44]

This does not mean that reflective professional learning is always better than directive training. When I was in my early 40s, I decided to try a new skill—scuba diving. I had been a complete non-swimmer until my late 20s, so I did not take this learning lightly. In my first lesson, I had to learn how to remove and replace my mask and breathing tube while submerged—a terrifying prospect for as poor a swimmer as I am. Five meters underwa-ter, I was relieved to be doing this in the hands of a very directive (as well as calm and supportive) coach and trainer rather than with someone who wanted to engage me in underwater critical dialogue and reflective practice. Training will always be a necessary component of professional learning.

Training and coaching are rarely as straightforward as this, though. Indeed, the use of *"coaching"* as a metaphor for professional and instruc-tional development is itself controversial. Bruce Joyce and Beverley Show-ers, two of the leading experts in this area, relate that much of their inspi-ration for devising ways of coaching teachers came from athletics and sports, especially tennis and football.[45] Some aspects of sports coaching do trans-fer reasonably well to in-service teacher training—particularly the idea of applying and developing skills in real "game" contexts while still under supervision. However, what is to be coached is usually more contentious in teaching than in sports or scuba diving. Teachers are much more likely to disagree about the value, importance, and practicality of computer tech-nology or approaches to literacy, for example, than aspiring tennis players will disagree about the virtues of developing a good backhand. What is being coached in teaching is not only a matter of technical skill and com-petence. It also involves personal, moral, and political choices. It raises questions of values.

Even sports skills are less ideologically neutral than they first seem. The double-handed backhand would never have evolved without challenging the dominant assumptions of coaches, for example. Some years ago, when I moved to Canada, I served as a soccer coach to a team of 10-year-old boys. There were problems with one of the players. He had excellent ball control. He was easily the side's top scorer. He had boundless energy and running power. In almost every respect, he was a "star" player. Yet for much of the time, he could not or would not pass the ball to his teammates. Indeed, in his eagerness to gain possession of the ball, he often took the ball from them. I tried many of the things a good coach is supposed to do. I stressed the importance of passing and explained the rationale for it: that "we have to give the ball away if we want to get it back." I demonstrated various kinds of passing and set up drills in which they could be practiced. I ran alongside players during practice games, advising them when and how to pass. I praised successful passing or worthy attempts at it. When the skills of passing were overlooked, I withdrew this child or other children from the game, explained what was required and why, then put them back to practice the skills once more. Despite all these interventions, the player continued not to pass.

Only after extensive conversation with the player and his father (also the team's commercial sponsor and coach for another team) did it become apparent that the boy was not short of passing skills at all. He simply disagreed about their importance in the game. For the father and his son, the game of soccer was like the popular North American sport of hockey: The idea was to get the ball toward the opposite goal as quickly and directly as possible. For me, with my European and lifelong soccer background, the sport was a more patient passing game whose point was to keep possession of the ball until opportunities opened to move it forward and score—more like chess on grass. What appeared as a technical problem of skill and competence requiring technical coaching support was therefore a fundamental ideological, cultural, and aesthetic problem rooted in disagreements about the purpose and style of the game being coached. The implication of this is that in education, teachers must be allowed and encouraged to question and critique what they, as professionals, are being coached in, and not just practice exactly what the coach directs them to do.

If extensive support addresses only issues of technique, and not those of context and values, teachers are put in a position of dependence on and submission to other people's questionable certainties of effective teaching that claim universal applicability without any adjustment to context. This is an insult to teachers' professionalism. Professional development becomes like being inducted into an evangelical sect whose message of instructional salvation is presented as a divine and universal truth—the truth of government wisdom, of allegedly incontrovertible scientific research, or of the leading "gurus" of classroom learning, staff development, and change management.[46] As Anthony Storr argues, gurus do not promote professionalism. They perpetuate dependency by "awakening" the child that is latent in us all.[47]

In general, systems of performance training in education have many of the characteristics of religious sects.[48] According to the Oxford Concise English Dictionary, a sect is "a religious group or faction regarded as hierarchical or as deviating from orthodox tradition" that has "separated from an established church." In his classic work on the definition and classification of religious sects, Bryan Wilson identified eight explicit and all-encompassing characteristics of sects and implied two others.[49] Only three of these do not apply or have particular relevance to performance training.[50] The remaining seven characteristics of sects are:

- *Exclusivity.* "A sectarian is committed to only one body of . . . teaching and has only one membership."[51] You can't embrace 'Open Court' or England's National Literacy Strategy at the same time as, say, critical literacy. "They do not admit of dual allegiances."[52]
- *Monopoly on truth.* "Sects tend to claim that they have a monopoly of the complete . . . truth which others do not enjoy. This truth provides a framework of understanding"[53] for members of the sect. In performance-training sects, the truths of teaching effectiveness are monopolized by gurus of particular initiatives, governments that impose them, and oligarchies of effectiveness researchers who justify them.
- *Demanding standards.* "Sects exercise concern for sustained standards among their members . . . [including] sanctions against the inadequate or wayward, to the point of expelling such individuals from the sect."[54] Fail to comply with the content of performance training in literacy or math and you will risk being labeled a failing teacher or failing school and have to face the ultimate sanction of excommunication from the profession.
- *Total allegiance.* This "is "expected to be evident in its influence on all areas of life."[55] It is made manifest in the required "observation of strict rules of behavior and belief."[56] Performance-training sects countenance few or no deviations or exceptions.
- *Fundamentalist orientation.* "Some sects represent a powerful return to what they regard as having been the pristine message of the faith, in response to which they call for a new level of dedication and performance."[57] Contemporary performance-training sects complain that the vague cults of progressivism that became part of the educational establishment corrupted the rigors of teaching and learning. They demand that we go back to basics—to literacy and math being taught in highly structured ways and to particular times in the day when this is assured.
- *Ascetic origins.* Historically, sects often have been recruited from and formed among lower classes who resisted the domination of traditional church hierarchies.[58] The origins and characteristics of sects, in this sense, are often ascetic and self-denying compared with contemporary New Age cults, which have more self-expressive elements. In educa-

tion, performance-training sects of literacy and math have a strong ascetic emphasis on earnest performance, focused achievement, and productive, results-driven activity.
• *Equal obligations*. This is demanded from all members of the sect, irrespective of hierarchy. In performance-training sects, the truth belongs to everybody, and everybody is beholden to the truth.[59]

Performance-training sects possess the "essential totalitarianism" of all sects, which

> consists in the reorganization and reorientation of the ideals, values and sentiments of its members: the dictation of just what are accepted as "facts", and the insistence on an ethic divergent from the wider society [or, in this case, profession].... The sect seeks the total organization of the lives of its members, at least in the intellectual sphere.[60]

Teaching should not be driven by the false certainties of gurus, governments, or research oligarchies but by a combination of and creative tension between commitment and doubt. In his reworking of Cervantes' classic novel *"Don Quixote,"* Graham Greene tells the story of two men who are expelled from their village.[61] One is the village's Catholic priest; the other is its Marxist mayor. In their flight, they find themselves compelled to take a long journey, cramped in a tiny car. Their physical journey soon becomes a spiritual one. As time unfolds, the mayor proclaims his Marxist commitments but also comes to doubt the value or the likelihood of the revolution. The priest professes his devout Catholicism but also acknowledges inner doubts about the existence of God. Both learn and grow from their conversations, keeping their commitments but also revising them as they engage their doubts. Their commitments and beliefs drive them to talk to each other. Their doubts make talk between them possible. Charles Handy reflects that

> [r]eligion like this is a great aid to self-responsibility.... It is religion without the creeds and without the hierarchies. It is the religion of doubt and uncertainty, offering one the strength to persevere, to find one's own way.... I find it necessary to reject the false certainties of both religion and science in order to discharge what I feel to be the responsibility for my own destiny. I believe this to be a responsibility which falls on all of us. We cannot duck out of it.[62]

The evangelical nature of performance-training sects deprives teachers and principals of this responsibility. Their job is to follow, not question. They

Professional Learning Communities	Performance-Training Sects
Transform knowledge	Transfer knowledge
Shared inquiry	Imposed requirements
Evidence informed	Results driven
Situated certainty	False certainty
Local solutions	Standardized scripts
Joint responsibility	Deference to authority
Continuous learning	Intensive training
Communities of practice	Sects of performance

FIGURE 6.2. Professional Learning Communities and Performance-Training Sects

cannot challenge the versions of literacy or other curriculum changes they are required to teach. Although more reflective and challenging forms of coaching exist, performance-training sects promote strictly technical kinds of coaching as unreflective practices. For all their technical complexity and their sophisticated systems of mentoring and support, sectarian impositions of performance training can make support look more like suffocation.

This point is even more important when we recognize that no written reform is completely explicit and unambiguous; no mandate is unmodified; and no local circumstances and difficulties can ever be completely predicted by the planners. Everything is always open to interpretation. If teachers are led to believe otherwise, their habits of learned dependency will prevent them from making the creative modifications for their own students that externally introduced changes always require. In educational change, context always makes a difference.

The differences between professional learning communities and performance-training sects can be summarized as follows (see Figure 6.2):

- Professional learning communities transform knowledge and learning among community members. Performance-training sects transfer unquestioned canons of research knowledge and instructional beliefs that are defined by administrative and research authorities.
- Professional learning communities promote shared inquiry. Performance-training sects pursue imposed requirements.

- Professional learning communities use evidence and data to inform the improvement of practice. Performance-training sects employ achievement results as the sole arbiter of approved practice.
- Professional learning communities encourage teachers to devise local improvement in a context of unpredictability and uncertainty. Performance-training sects require teachers to implement standardized scripts of change in an authoritarian system of false certainty.
- Professional learning communities get groups to engage in continuous learning about their teaching. Performance-training sects promote groupthink and loyalty to external prescriptions through intensive training.

Sectarian approaches to performance training are not only ethically and morally problematic; they are also technically inflexible. They are ill-suited to differences of context, and they are inadequate tools for producing the higher levels of learning and development that are essential in a knowledge society. Their record of early success suggests that they may sometimes provide a necessary platform for improvement in circumstances of extreme adversity and low teacher capacity, but in a knowledge economy and an inclusive society, they should never be embraced as the end of improvement itself. Our efforts and energy must be directed toward something higher than this, something that embodies greater social and political ingenuity and integrity.

NOTES

1. Waller, W., *The Sociology of Teaching*, New York, Russell & Russell, 1932.
2. Townsend, J., "It's bad—trust me, I teach there," *Sunday Times*, December 2, 2001, p. 10; Dillon, J. & Berliner, W., "Amy didn't help: Estelle thinks she can," *Focus, Independent on Sunday*, February 10, 2002, p. 22.
3. Hargreaves, A. & Fullan, M., "Mentoring in the new millennium," *Theory Into Practice* 39(1), 2000, 50–56.
4. Department for Education and Skills, *Achieving Success*, London, Her Majesty's Stationery Office (HMSO), 2001.
5. Steve Anderson, Shawn Moore, and I are learning this in a study of the long-term impact of professional-development strategies in several school districts that is being supported by the Learning First Alliance, a consortium created by some of the United States' most influential educational organizations. For other examples, see Fullan, M., *Leading in a Culture of Change*, San Francisco, Jossey-Bass/Wiley, 2001.
6. Department for Education and Skills, *op. cit.*, note 4.
7. The Australian state of Victoria, for example, now puts reward and respect high on its priorities for reforming the teaching profession.

8. "*Boston Public*" is the key series in the United States. "*Teachers*" is showing in the United Kingdom.

9. Organization for Economic Cooperation and Development (OECD), *Schooling for Tomorrow: What Schools for the Future?* Paris, OECD, 2001.

10. The nature of the new orthodoxy of educational change is discussed more fully in Hargreaves, A., Earl, L., Moore, S. & Manning, S., *Learning to Change: Teaching beyond Subject and Standards,* San Francisco, Jossey-Bass, 2000. For the more extended account of cultures of teaching, see Hargreaves, A., *Changing Teachers, Changing Times: Teachers' Work and Culture in the Postmodern Age,* London, Cassell and New York, Teachers College Press, 1994. The detailed references on which this part of the discussion is based can also be found there.

11. As far as I can tell, I was the first person to discuss the concept and strategy of re-culturing as an alternative to the reform strategy of restructuring. This discussion first appeared in publication in Hargreaves, A., "Restructuring, restructuring: Postmodernity and the prospects for educational change," *Journal of Educational Policy* 9(1), 1994, 47–65. Before that, it appeared in a paper presented to the Second International Conference on Teacher Development, Vancouver, British Columbia, February 1991.

12. Another significant reason, of course, is simply the cost reduction achieved by moving the cost of overhead, benefits, and so on from government to contractors.

13. For more details on the measures that make up what Geoff Whitty and his colleagues call quasi-markets in education, see Whitty, G., Power, S. & Halpin, D., *Devolution and Choice in Education: The School, State, the Market,* Buckingham, Open University Press, 1998.

14. Lindblad, S. & Popkewitz, T., *Education, Governance and Social Integration and Exclusion: Studies in the Powers of Reason and the Reasons of Power* (Uppsala Reports in Education), Uppsala, Sweden, Department of Education, Uppsala University, 2001.

15. On the concept of quasi-markets, see Whitty, Power & Halpin, *op. cit.,* note 13.

16. Bauman, Z., *Globalization: The Human Consequences,* Oxford, Basil Blackwell, 1998.

17. Ibid., p. 93.

18. OECD, *Measuring Student Knowledge and Skills: The PISA 2000 Assessment of Reading, Mathematical and Scientific Literacy,* Paris, OECD, 2000.

19. Hargreaves, D., "The occupational culture of teaching," in P. Woods (ed.), *Teacher Strategies,* London, Croom Helm, 1982.

20. Oakes, J., Quartz, K. H., Ryan, S. & Lipton, M., *Becoming Good American Schools: The Struggle for Civic Virtue in Education Reform,* San Francisco, Jossey-Bass, 2000.

21. This argument is developed more fully in Hargreaves, A., *Distinction and Disgust: The Emotional Politics of School Failure,* unpublished manuscript, Ontario Institute for Studies in Education, University of Toronto, 2002.

22. McLaughlin, M. & Talbert, J., *Professional Communities and the Work of High School Teaching,* Chicago, University of Chicago Press, 2001.

23. Fullan, M., *Leading in a Culture of Change,* San Francisco, Jossey-Bass/Wiley, 2001.

24. McLaughlin & Talbert, *op. cit.,* note 22, p. 129.

25. Ibid., p. 135.

26. Department for Education and Skills, *op. cit.,* note 4.

27. Ibid.

28. Fullan, *op. cit.,* note 23.

29. An earlier version of this case for the regionalization of professional development is found in Hargreaves, A. & Evans, R. (eds.), *Beyond Educational Reform,* Buckingham, Open University Press, 1997.

30. The philosophy of the elephant and the flea is drawn from Handy, C., *The Elephant and the Flea: Looking Backwards to the Future,* London, Hutchinson, 2001.

31. See Day, C., *Developing Teachers: The Challenges of Lifelong Learning?* London, Falmer Press, 1998.

32. Sergiovanni, T., *The Lifeworld of Leadership: Creating Culture, Community, and Personal Meaning in Our Schools,* San Francisco, Jossey-Bass, 2000.

33. Hill, P. W. & Crévola, C., "The role of standards in educational reform for the 21st century," in D. Marsh (ed.), *Preparing Our Schools for the 21st Century,* Alexandria, VA, Association for Supervision and Curriculum Development, 1999.Peter Hill's work has now extended into the Calgary School district in Canada where, in a higher-capacity system, its performance-training emphases are being blended more thoroughly with the principles of professional learning community.

34. Slavin, R., Madden, N., Dolan, L. & Wasik, B., *Every Child, Every School: Success for All,* Thousand Oaks, CA, Corwin Press, 1996.

35. This is evaluated in Elmore, R. F. & Burney, D., *Investing in Teacher Learning: Staff Development and Instructional Improvement in Community School District #2,* New York, National Commission on Teaching and America's Future and the Consortium for Policy Research in Education, 1997.

36. This is reviewed extensively in Fullan, *op. cit.,* note 23.

37. The broad strategy, its rationale, and the policy context for it are described in Barber, M., "High expectations and standards for all, no matter what: Creating a world class education service in England," in M. Fielding (ed.), *Taking Education Really Seriously: Four Years' Hard Labor,* New York: Routledge/Falmer Press, 2001. The strategy is being evaluated by my colleagues Michael Fullan and Lorna Earl at the International Center for Educational Change. An interim evaluation can be found in Fullan, M. & Earl, L., "Large scale reform," *Journal of Educational Change* 3(1), 2002.

38. See Wideman, R., *How Secondary School Teachers Change Their Classroom Practices,* unpublished Ed.D. diss., University of Toronto, 1991.

39. See Fullan & Earl, *op. cit.,* note 37.

40. See especially the research of Amanda Datnow evaluating the impact of Success for All and other reforms in the United States, in Datnow, A. & Castellano, M., *An "Inside Look" at Success for All: A Qualitative Study of Implementation and Teaching and Learning* (45), Baltimore, Center for Research on the Education of Students Placed at Risk, Johns Hopkins University, 2000.

41. Ibid.

42. Galton, M., "'Dumbing down' on classroom standards: The perils of a technician's approach to pedagogy," *Journal of Educational Change* 1(2), 2000, 199–204.

43. Fink, E. & Resnick, L. B., "Developing principals as instructional leaders," *Phi Delta Kappan,* 2001, 598–606.

44. Stein, M. K., Hubbard, L. & Mehan, B., "Reform ideas that travel far afield: The two cultures of reform in New York City's District #2 and San Diego," Paper presented at the American Educational Research Association annual conference, San Francisco, 2001.

45. Joyce, B. & Showers, B., *Student Achievement through Staff Development,* New York, Longman Press, 1988.

46. See Massey, D. & Chamberlain, C., *Perspective, Evangelism and Reflection in Teacher Education,* Paper presented to the International Study Association of Teacher Thinking, University of Nottingham, England, September 1988.

47. On the influence of gurus, see Storr, A., *Feet of Clay: A Study of Gurus,* London, HarperCollins, 1997.

48. They are, however, less like cults. The Oxford Concise English Dictionary defines a cult as "a system of religious devotion directed toward a particular figure or object." Cults, however, tend to be small and localized, highly personalized in their leadership, and somewhat vague in their systems of belief (as in several of the New Age religious movements). In this sense, apart from their required devotional elements, cults have limited applicability to performance-training regimes.

49. These are the fact that sects are lay organizations (true but not really helpful); the criterion of voluntary membership (most performance-training regimes of large-scale reform have mandatory membership, although some, such as Success for All, are in principle voluntary); and their identity as protest groups against secular society or the state (although some performance-training regimes originate in the state, they do claim to challenge the established wisdom of the profession: It is the profession here that is being challenged by the state, not vice versa).

50. Wilson, B., *Sects and Society,* London, Heineman, 1961; Wilson, B., *Religion in Sociological Perspective,* New York, Oxford University Press, 1982.

51. Wilson (1982), *op. cit.,* note 50, p. 91.

52. Ibid.

53. Ibid., p. 92

54. Ibid.

55. Wilson (1961), *op. cit.,* note 50, p. 4

56. Wilson (1982), *op. cit.,* note 50, p. 95.

57. Wilson (1961), *op. cit.,* note 50.

58. Ibid., p. 4.

59. Ibid.

60. Ibid.

61. Greene, G., *Monsignor Quixote,* London, Bodley Head, 1982.

62. Handy, C. B., *The Hungry Spirit: Beyond Capitalism: A Quest for Purpose in the Modern World,* New York, Broaday Books, 1998.

7

THE FUTURE OF TEACHING IN THE KNOWLEDGE SOCIETY

Rethinking Improvement, Removing Impoverishment

Professional learning communities and performance-training sects each combine contracts of performance with cultures of commitment, but in different ways. There is growing recognition in the field of school improvement that "one size does not fit all."[1] Different kinds of schools and systems need different ways to tackle improvement. The same strategy will not suit all of them. In this respect, professional learning communities and performance-training sects can offer complementary, not competing, routes to improvement beyond standardization.

Sophisticated professional learning communities seem to work best with high-capacity teachers in high capacity systems, where teachers are highly skilled and qualified, the schools are already reasonably effective, leaders are capable of motivating and engaging their teachers, and sufficient resources are available to provide teachers and schools with the time and flexibility they need to work together professionally. M. McLaughlin and J. Talbert note that "the most qualified teachers are attracted to the most favorable professional environments, often in districts serving relatively affluent communities."[2]

By contrast, improvement through performance training seems to yield results in low-capacity systems, where large numbers of teachers are uncertified and underskilled, where schools have a record of poor performance and many teachers have lost belief in their capacity to make a difference, where too many leaders see themselves as managers more than as instructional leaders, or where resources have been scarce or spread too thinly across too many initiatives—the plague of projectitis, as I call it. Given the schools and the systems we have and the differences among them, perhaps

189

a differentiated rather than "one-size-fits-all" approach to school improvement and to professional learning and development offers an effective and pragmatic solution.[3]

However, there is more than one way to interpret and implement the idea of differentiation in professional growth and school improvement. Not all differentiated approaches are equally desirable. I will examine three of them: professional-development apartheid, developmental progression, and complementary growth.

DIFFERENTIAL DEVELOPMENT

Professional Development Apartheid

One danger of differentiating approaches to school improvement and professional growth is that this strategy can easily create deep-seated divisiveness between communities. Amanda Datnow and her colleagues have found that, among a range of federally approved and funded U. S. Comprehensive School Reform models of change from which districts could choose, those that operated from broad principles, guiding frameworks, and the promotion of open-ended teacher collegiality and networking tended to be adopted by schools in affluent communities. Meanwhile, the tightly scripted, closely monitored programs that involved intensive training in given methods were mainly adopted by poor districts, often dealing with high proportions of minority students.[4]

England's educational policies may generate similar divisions. Schools that are performing well according to inspection evidence and test results, it is said, will enjoy "earned autonomy" in terms of freedom to maneuver beyond the prescribed curriculum.[5] However, because the United Kingdom has one of the most stubborn ties between educational achievement and students' social background, and still operates a competitive market system of school choice that reinforces these ties, "earned autonomy" will be enjoyed mainly by schools and teachers in affluent communities.[6] Meanwhile, schools and their teachers who are categorized as failing or close to failing will remain tied to prescribed programs, endlessly intrusive monitoring and inspection, and sectarian performance training in mandated methods of teaching. The definition of failing schools in raw terms (i.e., in comparison with test scores in all other schools) also means that "failure" becomes an official problem only in poor, disadvantaged communities, which often have high concentrations of racial and ethnic minorities. The cruising schools with coasting teachers who ride in the slipstream of their middle-class academic achievers get off scot-free.[7]

Separate communities, separate teachers, separate development—this is nothing less than an apartheid of professional development and school improvement. Schools and teachers in relatively affluent communities such as Blue Mountain (see chapter 5) enjoy all the benefits of professional learning networks and communities. Their self-skilling teachers engage in professional learning teams and generate student exit outcomes with parents to produce self-skilling students who see the "big picture," employ systems thinking, and receive excellent preparation to work in the high-skills, higher echelons, and "weightless work" of the knowledge economy. Schools in those affluent communities are exempted from scripted literacy programs because they seemingly do not suffer the "deficits" in phonological awareness of their urban counterparts.[8]

Meanwhile, schools and teachers in poor communities in the desolate sprawl of housing projects, the decaying ghettos of the inner city, or the fourth world of less-developed nations struggle in the shadow of failure—watchful of test scores, fearful of intervention, and with a bellyful of imposed requirements and restrictions. These teachers and schools are thrown into performance-training sects in which their instructional options and professional learning choices are restricted. They teach the basic skills of math and literacy that get their students to improve to a point in elementary school, only to see their achievements plateau in the high-school years. These schools and systems prepare students to participate in very different sectors of the knowledge economy. Students learn not to create knowledge, develop ingenuity, or solve unfamiliar problems in flexible formats. Their destiny is to be literate and mathematically competent enough to serve and support the "weightless work" of their affluent superiors in restaurants, tourist hotels, health spas, and other service work, where understanding instructions, obsequious communication, and urging others to turn over or have a nice day have far greater importance than inventiveness or ingenuity. In the name of "one size does not fit all," these separate systems and forms of separate development prepare students from more and less privileged backgrounds, respectively, for two very different sides of the knowledge economy: those who create the knowledge economy and those who cater to it.

In Zygmunt Bauman's terms, students, teachers, and parents in affluent, high-achieving communities become the "tourists" of knowledge-society schools who enjoy flexibility, autonomy, freedom of movement, networking, and mobility as they are drawn toward magnets of excellence, opportunity, and organizational learning.[9] By contrast, students, teachers, and parents in poor, low-achieving communities become Bauman's "vagrants" and "vagabonds" of the knowledge society—immigrant, racial minority, or working-class students and their casualized, uncertified, or demoralized teachers, whose mobility must be monitored and movements must be watched through endless surveillance and evaluations and whose learning is restricted and regulated as they are left behind in the enforced localization of the "special-education magnets" of the system.

If we want to prepare all young people to have the chance to be among the most successful, high-skill workers within the knowledge economy, as well as decent, democratic citizens beyond it, this new social geography of divisive improvement that offers professional learning communities to the advantaged and imposes performance-training sects on the rest is one of our most disturbing threats.

Developmental Progression

Still, different kinds of schools do benefit from different approaches to improvement. For example, in small elementary schools, the principal can play a vital, hands-on role as a leader of learning, visiting classrooms, understanding learning, participating in training, and doing some teaching. In large high schools, the principal must work more through other adults, exercising an indirect effect on learning through the staff, particularly key teacher leaders. The same strategies do not suit all schools.

Another argument is that schools are not only of different types but at different stages in their levels of effectiveness and improvement. The school-improvement expert David Hopkins, now the standards adviser to the Ministry of Education in the United Kingdom, puts it this way:

> Schools at different levels of effectiveness require different school improvement strategies. . . . When circumstances exist that are less supportive of change, it is necessary to concentrate much more in the initial stages of development work on creating those internal conditions within the school that facilitate development.[10]

Hopkins describes three types of schools: failing/ineffective, underachieving, and good/effective, along with three types of strategies that are most suited to their improvement efforts:

Type I strategies help failing schools become moderately effective. These
   schools need high levels of extensive intervention and support and
   usually new leadership. They focus on a limited number of organizational issues, such as school dress codes, attendance, student behavior,
   and the appearance of the school. They also concentrate on building
   teachers' competence and confidence by helping them develop a limited but specific repertoire of effective teaching strategies.
Type II strategies help moderately effective schools become more effective.
   These schools, says Hopkins, need to build the capacity of teachers
   and others in the school to make improvements in specific areas of
   teaching and learning. Much can be achieved with existing leadership
   and the school's own resources, but some outside help is usually
   needed. Lengthening lesson periods to generate more creativity in
   instruction; broadening teacher leadership; listening to students and
   their concerns; motivating disillusioned staff; and remaining centered
   on values and purposes are key priorities in these schools.
Type III strategies try to ensure that good schools stay effective. External
   support is less necessary, because these schools are able to create and
   sustain their own networks. External partnerships and exposure to
   new ideas and practices keep the school stimulated, as do making
   continuing efforts to raise expectations for achievement, undertaking
   structural change to improve collaboration, and dedicating time to
   celebrating successes.

Hopkins applies his insights to recommendations for change in England's
National Literacy Strategy. Instead of adopting the strategy's uniformly prescriptive framework, he advises, schools "at the bottom end of the performance cycle"[11] might benefit from something even more prescriptive,
such as Slavin's Success for All program. Schools that already have outstanding results might benefit from having flexibility to move beyond the
framework. Meanwhile, schools in the middle, Hopkins says, might be best
suited to the framework as it is. Evaluations of the National Literacy Strategy have made similar recommendations: that intervention and prescription should be inversely related to success.[12]
   This analysis recognizes the reality that schools are different in their initial levels of effectiveness. It acknowledges that trying to create professional
learning communities among teachers whose skills and confidence are
underdeveloped is not a practical option. It is no use sharing knowledge
until there is something worthwhile to share. There is also a suggestion that,
although schools and teachers in disadvantaged districts may have fallen

into failure, there is no reason that they should stay there. Developmental strategies exist not just to get schools out of failure but also to take them far away from it in order to offer them increasing success.

Hopkins's developmental view is a significant breakthrough in school-improvement thinking. It moves school-improvement strategy beyond simple quick fixes to long-term sustainable change in a model that recognizes that schools and their needs are not all the same and vary over time. However, as it stands, this developmental model still contains some important limitations.

First, the model is based on snapshot research of different kinds of schools in terms of their levels of effectiveness. Insights from these different types are then glued together in a hierarchical sequence to make an overall developmental model. As yet, however, there is no longitudinal evidence that demonstrates, over time, how particular schools can be moved successfully from Type I to Type III solely on the basis of the improvement strategies that are used (rather than, say, increased resourcing or better-qualified staff). We do not know whether, once a school has been taken out of the failure zone, it can use these strategies to move sequentially into the highest levels of effectiveness. We do not know whether performance-training sects can be treated as a necessary first stage of development on the way to building more sophisticated professional learning communities or whether they are a trap of prescription and dependency that takes schools and their teachers out of immediate failure but does not allow them to progress toward achieving and maintaining the knowledge-society fruits of sophisticated success.

Second, this developmental model is a continuum. As representational devices, all continuums are misleadingly simplistic.[13] They are normative, managerial devices as much as conceptual, analytical ones. Their purpose is to organize understanding on a single linear scale, which is used to locate where schools are and to move them along it. The continuum is a simple tool that helps administrators measure and manage improvement. But in the interests of management, continuums do great injustices to complexities of meaning. There are many different types of schools—large and small, urban and rural, poorly staffed but competently managed, resource-rich but badly led. These cannot all be collapsed into a single continuum of development. Schools do not all progress along the same path. The continuum of development denies the very complexity and acknowledgement of difference it is meant to establish. Better to recognize, perhaps, that there may be different paths of development appropriate to different types of school rather than insisting, ironically, that one scale fits all. Real school improvement may be more like a multitrack digital sound system than a single, sliding scale.

Third, part of the problem of defining school differences depends on how we define failure and success. If failure is defined in terms of raw achievement scores with no allowances for differences in wealth and poverty or varying levels of financial support in the community, schools in affluent districts will consistently appear at the top of the tables and schools in poor ones at the bottom. By comparison, if success and failure are defined in clusters of schools that are like one another in terms of the kinds of communities they serve (called *statistical neighborhoods*), then, relatively, there will always be underachievement (as well as success) in affluent communities that warrants intervention and public outcry, along with great success (as well as failure) in the poorest communities. Then again, if failure and success are defined in relation to schools' past performance, or in relation to the kinds of achievement students initially bring to the school (in what is called *value-added improvement*), then affluent schools can be backsliders (i.e., cruising or coasting schools) just as much as those in poor areas.

These forms of defining school failure through statistical neighborhoods, in relation to past performance, or through value-added achievement are politically controversial and typically resisted by elites who do not want their schools to be branded with the stigma of failure.[14] By relying on the first definition of failure (raw score comparisons across all types of schools, irrespective of context), almost all schools that fall in the lowest developmental stage, and that are deemed to be fit only for sectarian performance training, are schools in poor communities. In this way, only the poor end up being officially underdeveloped. School failure becomes a proxy for poverty. The middle classes enjoy their self-defined educational distinction and make the schools and teachers of the poor the object of their contempt and disgust.

Combining a definition of failure that restricts it to poor and disadvantaged communities, with a developmental model of school improvement that reduces complex differences among schools into a single continuum of progress or retardation, turns the politically contentious issues of poverty and inequitable funding that afflict "failing" schools and their communities into misleadingly neutral technologies of development and improvement.[15] Ineffective schools may well be developmentally different from effective ones and therefore may need different improvement strategies. But in terms of the measures of achievement and improvement that are used, only poor

schools fail. In this way, policymakers convert economic and political problems of impoverishment into technically neutral strategies of improvement.
Dealing with the problems of impoverishment in urban schools and communities must be made part of all reform efforts to achieve equitable school
improvement. I return to this important matter in the closing section.

This book has shown that standardized reform in education undermines
teachers' capacity to teach for the knowledge society and beyond it. Standardization magnifies educational exclusion. Differential strategies of
improvement offer one way to move beyond the flaws of the one-size-fits-
all approach of soulless standardization. But the way in which difference is
being defined locks poverty and failure together within a neutral language
of "underdevelopment" that is as politically evasive and misleading in school
politics as in world politics. With no longitudinal evidence that prescriptive strategies of change will enable schools and their teachers to move to
higher levels of improvement later, performance-training sects may well
trap "underdeveloped" schools and their teachers within cycles of minimum
competence and dependency, producing students who are just good enough
to work at the low levels of the knowledge economy but not beyond that
point. Perpetuating underdevelopment in teaching takes us little further
than maintaining an apartheid of separate development.

Complementary Growth

How can one avoid the problems of standardization and recognize that
schools are developmentally different without trapping schools and their
teachers in poor communities within performance-training sects of pre-
scriptiveness and dependency? How can students and teachers in poor communities get their fair chance to be at the apex of the knowledge society
along with their peers who are in schools that have flexibility and earned
autonomy and operate as learning communities?

One answer might be to pursue what I call *complementary strategies*
for school and teacher growth. These might take two forms: vertical and
horizontal.

Vertical Complementarity. Vertical strategies would involve schools that are
"failing" or in trouble, embarking simultaneously on a short-term rescue
plan for immediate survival combined with a long-term strategy for sustainable improvement. Investing both stages of this change effort in one

heroic principal would almost certainly be a mistake. The principal who can rustle up a rapid response to a crisis is not usually the principal who can patiently build teachers' capacity for commitment to long-term improvement. Appointing a succession of leaders with different strengths and styles appropriate to each sequential stage of development might help, but this runs a risk encountered in all leadership succession events, in which the new leader misunderstands, disregards, or overturns what has been achieved by his or her predecessors. A better strategy is to compose a leadership team of complementary strengths—some who are managers, some who are leaders; some who can bring about short-term efficiency, others who can secure long-term improvement. Then, norms and processes need to be established that ensure that members of the leadership team understand one another, respect one another's different contributions, and work together effectively.

North Ridge school (see chapter 4) for many years was a "cruising school" (as identified by its staff) that was led by an efficient principal who was more of a manager than a leader. His customary response to external reforms was to closet himself in his office and write a detailed response, which he then sent out to staff for comment. Unsurprisingly, feedback was scant. The principal complained that his teachers were apathetic, but he did his staff's thinking for them.

Shaking the school up did not require a change of principal. The arrival of two new assistant principals with great strengths in team-building and instructional leadership suddenly propelled the school forward. The principal's greatest act of leadership was to recognize his own limitations as an innovator and give the assistant principals freedom to spearhead ambitious improvement efforts in curriculum and assessment on behalf of the school. It was the leadership team that made the difference, not the principal alone.

In a failing school that is facing short-term survival, and that ultimately needs long-term improvement, an effective leadership team should comprise people with complementary strengths. Some may be able to remove ineffectiveness quickly by insisting on clear teaching plans, setting up specific training, improving behavior and attendance, and so on. Other people may have the strengths of developing trust, creating collaboration, and involving staff in the bigger picture of change to build longer-term capacity among the staff to secure sustainable improvement. Some team members can initiate immediate changes and act on them; others can help devise longer-term improvements and articulate them (leaving much of the action until later). Once the immediate changes prove effective, then the longer-term improvements that have been articulated can also be implemented—and the staff will already be aware of them. As this next stage takes prominence, other team members will come to the fore, knowing that they are building on and working with their predecessors, not despite them. Sustainable improvement toward knowledge-society goals therefore depends less on heroic individual leaders than on shared or distributed leadership.[16]

Horizontal Complementarity. Performance-training sects provide some necessary elements of training to achieve effectiveness quickly on a large scale. They provide an invaluable repertoire of teaching skills, and by demonstrating early success, they push some teachers into acknowledging that all of their children can learn—irrespective of social background. Performance-training sects presume that more sophisticated processes for building professional learning communities will come at a later developmental stage, if at all. The basics must be established before more complex skills can be indulged.

How accurate are these assumptions? There is a wealth of evidence that, with the right teaching and curriculum, even the most disadvantaged children and adults can learn to engage in critical thinking and complex learning. Paulo Freire demonstrated this in his literacy work with adults among some of South America's most deprived peoples, involving them in literacy by engaging them in controversial issues in their community.[17] Reuben Feuerstein's work on instrumental enrichment helped "less able" students around the world to be successful in high-level critical thinking and problem-solving.[18] Henry Levin's accelerated learning in accelerated schools pursues similar goals.[19] Reform efforts in some of the world's poorest and "least-developed" countries, do not follow standard Western models of school effectiveness but involve communities closely in the critical work of pursuing improvement. They deal explicitly with values, not just technically with results.[20] The Comer Schools and other projects in the United States follow a similar philosophy.[21]

If we believe and have evidence to show that almost all students can learn to a complex and critical degree that meets the demands of the knowledge society, why should we not also believe that all teachers can learn, as well—and not just in the basics, but in the most complex knowledge-society skills?

Knowledge-society skills are the new basics. Neither students nor teachers should be denied them. Gross ineffectiveness may call for emergency measures in performance training, tight planning formats, and intensive monitoring, but not necessarily in all curriculum areas. Outside the areas of immediate training focus, such as literacy and math, there is no reason that other curriculum subjects should be left to fall by the wayside. Instead, it is here that a stronger emphasis on creative and critical thinking among teachers and students, exploring collaborative planning and shared professional learning, might reasonably begin. This is where the seeds of professional community can be sown. Instead of leaving the knowledge society to wait (perhaps forever) until the basics are mastered, the capacity to engage with it can be built among all teachers and students, even the most challenged, at the outset, in parallel with emergency initiatives in performance training. Alongside performance training in literacy and math (where this is regarded as necessary), it is also important to concentrate on initiating creativity and critical thinking in at least one other focused area of change in the curriculum. This maintains a focus on a school's change efforts but ensures that creativity is not completely sacrificed to compliance.

This balance between performance training and professional learning community can vary among schools. Like lunar cycles, it can also vary over time as the school becomes a more sophisticated organization, so that, in the end, the performance-training regime is scarcely necessary and "earned autonomy" prevails. What this idea of complementary growth represents is that professional learning communities and performance-training sects are parallel, not just sequential, categories of development. Their sequencing over time is a matter of changing the balance between the two components, with the training element diminishing as the school progresses. However, from the very beginning, when training needs are dominant and pressing, there should always be an element of more critical reflective community-building that is given priority among the staff. Indeed, once this is present, the performance-training emphasis no longer takes the form of a sect at all. It becomes a collective priority with which there is always some critical engagement.

An increasingly popular argument is that the successful school should be the one that is granted earned autonomy. To those that have, more shall be given. A compelling counter-argument is that it is at the bottom, not the top, where creativity, flexibility, and ingenuity in school improvement are most needed—in schools that are repeatedly in the failure zone or on the edge of it; in schools where relentless intervention, desperate acts of school reconstitution, and revolving doors of principal replacement are failing to produce sustainable change. Instead of persisting with the misdirected methods of micromanagement, there is a powerful case for attracting high-caliber principals and teachers to schools in demanding communities with incentives that are intrinsic to the nature of the work. Engaging educators in the task of engaging their students in learning that is challenging and meaningful, and that connects students to their own culture, is a direction of proven success that is worth pursuing here.[22] This still begs the question of the point in the school's and the teacher's development at which engagement-based strategies first become feasible. But the more that incentives of flexibility, excitement, support, and reward are offered to educators to attract them to inner cities (instead of subjecting them to relentless regimes of inspection and surveillance), the earlier it will be possible for engagement-based strategies to be initiated. It is increasingly clear that in school improvement, there needs to be room at the bottom as well as at the top.

These different scenarios for the future of teaching in the knowledge society can be represented diagrammatically, as shown in Figure 7.1.

CONCLUSION

Values and Vision

> *There is a crack in everything.*
> *That's how the light gets in.*
>
> —Leonard Cohen, *Anthem*,
> Leonard Cohen Stranger Music, 1992

My purpose in this book has been to outline the nature and significance of the knowledge society, of the world in which teachers now do their work. I have argued that teachers must prepare their students to have the strongest chances of success in the knowledge economy as a matter of sustaining their own and other's prosperity and as a matter of fairness and inclusiveness where these opportunities are made available to students of all races, backgrounds, and initial abilities. Our future prosperity depends on our ingenuity; our capacity to harness and develop our collective intelligence in terms of the central knowledge-economy attributes of inventiveness, creativity, problem-solving, cooperation, flexibility, the capacity to develop networks, the ability to cope with change, and the commitment to lifelong learning. Market fundamentalism and soulless standardization will ensure that we fall tragically short of this goal.

I have also drawn attention to the costs of the knowledge economy—of how the fragmented, frenetic world it has brought into being weakens communities, undermines relationships, spreads insecurity, and damages public life. As one of our last surviving public institutions, public education and its teachers must preserve and strengthen the relationships and the sense

1. Professional Development Apartheid

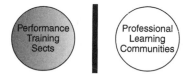

Separate schools, separate teachers,
separate development

2. Development Progression

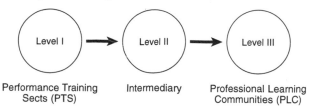

Performance Training   Intermediary   Professional Learning
  Sects (PTS)   Communities (PLC)

Different strategies for different stages of development

3. Complementary Growth

Professional learning and performance training, from the beginning,
with a shifting emphasis over time

4. Achievement through Engagement

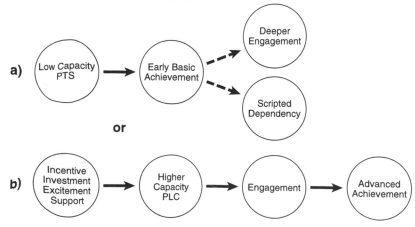

FIGURE 7.1. Models of Differential Development

201

of citizenship that the knowledge economy threatens. It must deal with the human consequences of the knowledge economy, teaching beyond as well as for it and adding values to the agenda of reform that build community, develop social capital, and forge cosmopolitan identity.

This means making teaching into a moral, visionary profession once more in which teachers know and care about their world as well as, and as part of, their work. It means teachers' recapturing their status and dignity as some of society's leading intellectuals, not being the mere technicians and instruments of other people's agendas. It means teachers' being active in the world of adults as much as being committed to their kids.

Teachers are not deliverers but developers of learning. Those who focus only on teaching techniques and curriculum standards and do not also engage teachers in the greater social and moral questions of their time promote a diminished view of teaching and teachers' professionalism that has no place in a sophisticated knowledge society.

The women's and civil-rights movements called for teachers who knew what they were fighting for. For them, making a difference was not just about helping a few individuals wherever they could. It was also about helping to change their world. Teaching was an instrument of social change. In *Change over Time?* Ivor Goodson and I, along with our other colleagues, saw how a great many teachers who had entered the profession in the demographic boom of the 1960s and early 1970s brought these great social missions into their teaching. They were motivated and animated by them. Much of their recent disillusionment with teaching, as shown in chapter 4, is less a result of aging and weariness than of their reaction to loss of vision within the public-educational system and its narrowing sense of purpose. These teachers are demoralized because they have had their purposes stolen from them.

We live in a time when great vision is called for again—when our prosperity and security depend on our capacity to develop students and teachers who can understand and engage with the dramatic social changes, and their human consequences, that today's knowledge society represents. My endowed Chair in Education at Boston College is named after Thomas More Brennan. He was working on the 104th floor of the World Trade Center on September 11, 2001, when terrorism brought his life to a tragic end and left his wife bearing their unborn child. The enlightened mission of the Chair, as defined by Thomas More Brennan's mother, herself a dedicated educator, is to promote social justice in public schools and connect theory and practice in doing so.

In recent years, we have become too coy about openly promoting social justice in public schools. Instead of race or social class, we talk about "diversity." The injustices of exclusion are replaced by the technicalities of achievement gaps. Political and moral outrage about impoverishment have given way to technical debates about improvement. Educators preach the importance of having a moral purpose but, beyond a few cliches, they dare not say what it is. Our diluted vocabulary betrays a lack of courage and a loss of nerve.

The gaps between rich and poor are widening. In government, in teaching, and in teacher education, there has never been a greater need for social ingenuity and moral integrity. Now that we have started to establish some standards, it is also time to redefine our vision and reassert some values.

A massive new generation is entering teaching and will shape the profession for the next three decades. We cannot afford for this generation to be bereft of a wider vision or for teacher educators and government officials to conspire in creating such a void. Engaging with the knowledge society and its human consequences calls on us to make teaching into a social mission and a creative, passionate profession once again.

Improvement and Impoverishment

We have seen that standardized educational reform has made it almost impossible for many teachers to teach for the knowledge society or beyond it as part of a broader social mission. Affluent schools and magnet schools such as Barrett (see chapter 3) find that the standards are irrelevant because they are already meeting them. Knowledge-society schools such as Blue Mountain (chapter 5) discover that, once the initiatives they have created are adopted as policy, their standardized formats make them unworkable when they are recycled back into the school. Meanwhile, vocational schools and disadvantaged schools in urban areas quickly realize that their students have no chance of passing the standardized tests that are set for them or of graduating on the basis of those tests. Soulless standardization becomes irrelevant and offensive to them, too. In a rapidly changing world of work, vocational education is becoming the lost continent of late adolescence.

By insisting on the inclusion of all students within standardized reform policies that, at best, address the needs of only students and schools in the middle, standardization actually creates greater exclusion by denying disadvantaged students opportunities to graduate and by branding lower-class and minority students with the stigma of public failure. Standardization is not only the educational opposite of what the knowledge society needs. It is also a direct consequence of the public costs of the knowledge economy itself as market fundamentalists have interpreted it. Teachers are having to teach despite these misguided interpretations of knowledge-economy needs.

Although standardization and quick-fix changes seem to be throwing teaching and learning off the rails, the emergence of professional learning communities promises a way to secure longer-term, sustainable improvements in our schools, serving as the ties and the ballast of educational change. In addition to securing sustainable change, professional learning communities exemplify and promote key knowledge-society characteristics, such as learning in teams, involving the entire school in the big picture, using technology to enhance everyone's learning, and engaging in systems thinking. Schools as professional learning communities also work best when they not only process knowledge and learning effectively but also attend to the social and emotional aspects of teaching, learning, and caring and build social capital among students and teachers as a way to strengthen relationships, community, and cosmopolitan identity. Professional learning communities demand that teachers develop grown-up norms in a grown-up profession in which difference, debate, and disagreement are viewed as the foundation stones of improvement. Blue Mountain is a striking example of a knowledge-society school.

In reality, though, professional learning communities are hard to create. They presume and demand qualities of leadership and levels of teacher capacity that are not always available, especially in schools in poor communities with long legacies of failure and hopelessness. In desperation, reformers in some poor communities have turned to implementing tight regimes of performance training in a limited number of curriculum areas and instructional strategies, supported by coaching, curriculum consultants, and the involvement of school leaders. These strategies have produced demonstrable gains in achievement results, changed many teachers' beliefs about their capacity to make a difference to disadvantaged students' learning, and given teachers a toolbox of techniques that is theirs for life. But they have also created as many problems as they have solved.

When it is applied to all of a system's schools, sectarian performance training repeats the familiar problems of micromanagement and standardization. It demands uniform loyalty and compliance; it is insensitive to the needs of different schools; it crowds creativity and inspiration out of the curriculum; and it diminishes teachers' capacity for professional judgment. Performance-training sects foster basic learning and competent teaching but not the kinds of teaching and learning that fuel the knowledge society or that make people want to teach.

When they are applied only to districts in difficulty, these strategies perpetuate an apartheid of classroom learning and professional development in which professional learning communities are enjoyed by schools and teachers in affluent communities and performance-training sects are inflicted on the rest. These differential strategies of improvement run the risk of creating divided strata of development in which underdevelopment is associated only with and recycled among minorities and the poor, separating those who create the knowledge society from those who merely cater to it.

I therefore propose more sophisticated strategies for improvement in the knowledge society that combine elements of performance training and professional community in almost all schools so that critical dialogue exists from the outset and prevents performance training from becoming a compliant sect. A strategy of complementary growth recognizes that elements of training almost always need to be combined with those of learning community, and vice versa. How and in what proportion this balance works depends on the type of school and its stage of development. Critical dialogue is never something we should leave until later; it belongs at the beginning, too. Reform in urban schools needs to promote students' engagement as well as achievement. Schools at the bottom need more opportunity and flexibility to engage these critical capacities, not less.

Alongside all this attention to strategies of improvement in the context of a knowledge society, it is important to remember that many of the basic challenges of schools and teaching in poor communities come not from a lack of strategies for improvement but from having to endure the scourge of impoverishment. Nations that care about including everyone in the knowledge society as a matter of economic development and social justice, and that care about averting the worst human consequences of the knowledge economy, must face the challenge of redistributing economic and social resources across the society to those who have the greatest need. We will never have a fair or fully effective knowledge society. and we will never draw on and develop our rich reserves of collective intelligence, until the poor can enjoy more generously equipped schools, highly qualified teachers, and extensive outside support just as much as their more comfortable neighbors.

School Improvement and Social Movements

When political will does not support redistribution of support toward the public sector and the poorest groups of public schools, it is not our role to capitulate to its lesser morality. As governments, teachers, and citizens, our task is to create a visionary social movement that will provide opportunity for the weak, safety and security for everyone, and community for all of us in a more dynamic and inclusive society that harnesses the collective intelligence of all people and cultivates the social capital and cosmopolitan identity that will enable people to live and work together.[23]

Social movements in education today are often created by the privileged against the wider public interest, promoting subject-based standards against more inclusive outcomes or gifted and honors classes for affluent children so they will not have to mix with the rest.[24] But in the late 1990s, a small group of mothers with no training or resources managed to galvanize public opinion and support, helping to stall the march of market fundamentalism and standardization in Ontario's educational reform by publicly documenting its effects on teachers, schools, and students. They stood up for an inclusive idea of public education, appealing to basic human values of fairness, decency, and commitment to the public good and undermining the claims of government policy with a relentless assault of evidence to the contrary. Their network, People for Education, now has a Web site—just one aspect of its influence on the public-education debate in the province of Ontario.[25] The easing of pressure and change of tone that has emerged in Ontario's educational system in the short time since the evidence for this book was collected is due, in no small part, to this group's remarkable efforts.

One of the greatest tasks of educators is to help build such a social movement for a dynamic and inclusive system of public education in the knowledge society by

- Rekindling their own moral missions and purposes in a system that has begun to lose sight of them.
- Opening their actions and minds to parents and communities and engaging with their missions.
- Working with their unions to become agents of their own change, not just opponents of changes imposed by others.
- Courageously speaking out against injustice and exclusion wherever they see it.
- Recognizing that they have a professional responsibility not just to their own children, but also to other people's children, in chains of care that extend to the neighboring school that is not the magnet, that does not have a special emphasis, or that is in the poor district next door.

The knowledge society belongs to everyone. All of our children should have an opportunity to reach the highest and most creative levels of it. Each of us should be protected from its potentially damaging human consequences of insecurity and lost community. Our schools, teachers, and students need massive injections of social ingenuity and the courage to reactivate their educational integrity. We cannot afford to risk a future in which teachers have prepared students neither for the knowledge economy nor for the social and moral challenges that lie beyond it. If they are to be successful—to reach the peak of their powers in teaching for and beyond the knowledge society and not be dragged down by the base concerns of soulless standardization or growing social division in education—five things will be required from us:

- We will need to revive and reinvent teaching as a passionate *social mission* that is about creating an inclusive, ingenious, and cosmopolitan knowledge society, and that is about changing teachers' world as much as their work. Governments, teacher educators, and others will need to help with this.
- We will need to help build a *social movement* that galvanizes public opinion in favor of investing in an ingenious and inclusive educational system and society that benefits everyone rather than a divided system that suits only those who have the privilege of mobility and choice.
- We will need to develop more *sophisticated strategies* of school improvement that acknowledge the differences among teachers and schools and construct distinct paths of development for all of them, without locking problematic schools in poor communities into cultures of compliance and dependency.
- We will need to acknowledge that the greatest ingenuity, experimentation, and flexibility should not be offered solely as rewards to affluent schools and teachers who perform well at the top. They should also be offered as powerful incentives to the best teachers and leaders to undertake the challenge of transformative work with students and schools in poor communities at the bottom.
- We will need to show political courage and integrity by reconnecting the agenda for educational improvement with a renewed assault on social impoverishment.

The knowledge society is beckoning. It is time that everyone in education be granted his or her right to have access to and engage with the highest levels of it. Ingenuity, investment, and integrity, as well as cosmopolitan identity, are required from all of us. Otherwise, insecurity and worse will be all that we have, and no less than we deserve.

NOTES

1. Hopkins, D., *School Improvement for Real,* London, Routledge/Falmer Press, 2001.

2. McLaughlin, M. & Talbert, J., *Professional Communities and the Work of High School Teaching,* Chicago, University of Chicago Press, 2001.

3. Hopkins, *op. cit.,* note 1.

4. Datnow, A., Hubbard, L. & Mehan, H., *Extending Educational Reform: From One School to Many,* London, Falmer/Routledge Press, 2002.

5. Department for Education and Skills, *Achieving Success,* London, Her Majesty's Stationery Office (HMSO), 2001.

6. The evidence on the United Kingdom's comparative literacy attainments comes from Organization for Economic Cooperation and Development (OECD), *Knowledge and Skills for Life: First Results from the Program for International Student Assessment,* Paris, OECD, 2001.

7. This definition of cruising schools in relation to other kinds of school failure was first established by Stoll, L. & Fink, D., *Changing Our Schools: Linking School Effectiveness and School Improvement,* Buckingham, Open University Press, 1996.

8. Gee, J. P., "Literacy, schools and kinds of people in the new capitalism," in T. McCarty (ed.), *Language, Literacy and Power in Schooling,* Albany, State University of New York Press, in press. See also Cummins, J., "Deconstructing the literacy crisis: Scripts, imagination, power and identity," in B. Cope & M. Kalantzis (eds.), *Learning for the Future* (proceedings of the Learning Conference, Spetze, Greece), 2001.

9. Bauman, Z., *Globalization: The Human Consequences,* Oxford, Basil Blackwell, 1998.

10. Hopkins, *op. cit.,* note 1, p. 162.

11. Ibid., p. 175.

12. See the evaluation of the National Literacy Strategy by Fullan, M. & Earl, L., "Large-scale reform," *Journal of Educational Change* 3(1), 2002, 1–5.

13. I develop this argument more fully in Hargreaves, A., "Development and desire: A postmodern perspective," in T. Guskey & M. Huberman (eds.), *Professional Development in Education: New Paradigms and Practices,* New York, Teachers' College Press, 1994.

14. Amanda Datnow and I have come across this phenomenon in our work supporting four U.S. state departments to rethink how they categorize and improve failing schools in their states. This project was initiated and funded by the Appalachian Educational Laboratories, Washington, DC.

15. For wider critiques of schools' effectiveness and some of its problematic political emphases, see Slee, R., Weiner, G. & Tomlinson, S. (eds.), *School Effectiveness for Whom?* London, Routledge/Falmer Press, 1998.

16. On distributed leadership, see Spillane, J. P., Halverson, R. & Diamond, J. B., "Investigating school leadership practice: A distributed perspective," *Educational Researcher* 30(3), 2001, 23–28.

17. Freire, P., *Pedagogy of the Oppressed,* Harmondsworth, Penguin, 1982.

18. Feuerstein, R., *Instrumental Enrichment: An Intervention Program for Cognitive Modifiability,* Baltimore, University Park Press, 1980.

19. Levin, H., "Accelerated schools: A decade of evolution," in A. Hargreaves, A. Lieberman, M. Fullan & D. Hopkins (eds.), *International Handbook of Educational Change* (pp. 807–830), Dordrecht, The Netherlands, Kluwer Academic Publishers, 1998.

20. These are discussed, for example, in Riley, K., *Schooling the Citizens of Tomorrow,* Paper presented at the International Conference for School Effectiveness and Improvement, Copenhagen, Denmark, January 4, 2002.

21. Comer, J. P., Haynes, N. M., Joyner, E. T. & Ben-Avie, M., *Rallying the Whole Village: The Comer Process for Reforming Education,* New York, Teachers' College Press, 1996.

22. See, as just one inspirational example, the case of a school in a poor community that creates achievement through student engagement, as described by Portelli, J. & Solomon, R. P. (eds.), *The Erosion of Democracy in Education: From Critique to Possibilities,* Calgary, Alberta, Detselig Enterprises, 2001.

23. I discuss the relationship of social movements to educational change more fully in Hargreaves, A., "Professional and parents: A social movement for educational change," in N. Bascia & A. Hargreaves (eds.), *The Sharp Edge of Educational Change,* London, Routledge/Falmer Press, 2000; and Hargreaves, A., "Beyond anxiety and nostalgia: Building a social movement for educational change," *Phi Delta Kappan* 82(5), 2000, 373–383.

24. One of the clearest examples of this is provided in Nespor, J., *Tangled Up in School: Politics, Space, Bodies and Signs in the Educational Process,* Hillsdale, NJ, Lawrence Erlbaum Associates, 1997. See also Oakes, J., Quartz, K. H., Ryan, S. & Lipton, M., *Becoming Good American Schools: The Struggle for Civic Virtue in Education Reform,* San Francisco, Jossey-Bass, 2000.

25. The Web site is available at: <http://www.peopleforeducation.ca>.

APPENDIX

TABLE 1. Teachers' responses to curriculum change

	Strongly agree (%)	Agree (%)	Dis-agree (%)	Strongly disagree (%)	Total responses
The new academic curriculum is appropriate to the learning needs of my students.	4	45	36	15	259
The new Grade 9/Grade 10 curriculum is diminishing my range of classroom teaching strategies.	9	39	41	11	255
The new curriculum makes it more difficult for me to engage students from different cultural backgrounds in their learning.	17	35	38	10	240
The new curriculum has prompted me to expand the variety of assignments I set for my students.	5	45	36	15	262
I would favor a return to the Common Curriculum for Grade 9.	13	28	38	21	208
I have a clear understanding of the curriculum that I am required to teach.	17	41	29	13	277

TABLE 2. Teachers' responses to changes in assessment

	Strongly agree (%)	Agree (%)	Dis-agree (%)	Strongly disagree (%)	Total responses
I understand the new assessment methods.	10	54	26	10	274
I support the new policy changes to student assessment.	4	29	39	28	255
The new Grade 9/Grade 10 assessment policies have improved my feedback to students about their learning.	2	27	42	29	249
I am using a wider range of student-assessment strategies since the introduction of Secondary School Reform.	3	41	41	15	259
Since the introduction of new assessment policies, I have involved my students more in the assessment process.	3	37	48	12	266
Since the introduction of new assessment policies, my communication with students has improved.	2	20	55	23	262
Since the introduction of Secondary School Reform, I am more confident of my assessment practices.	2	17	57	24	258

TABLE 3. Teachers' responses to literacy testing

	Strongly agree (%)	Agree (%)	Dis- agree (%)	Strongly disagree (%)	Total responses
I support the new policy changes to student testing.	3	20	38	39	266
The new Grade 10 Test of Reading and Writing Skills promotes my students' improvement.	4	17	35	44	249
The Grade 10 Test of Reading and Writing Skills has enhanced my confidence as a teacher.	0	10	40	50	233
Provincial testing of students makes me more accountable.	3	21	37	39	278
The Grade 10 Test of Reading and Writing Skills, and the preparation required for it, have stimulated my students' motivation to learn.	2	10	33	55	240
My classroom assessment strategies are consistent with the provincial Grade 10 Test of Reading and Writing Skills.	6	63	22	10	195
The new Grade 9/Grade 10 testing policies have reduced my range of classroom teaching strategies.	9	37	45	8	238
I have successfully integrated the skills required for the Grade 10 Test of Reading and Writing Skills into my classroom teaching.	4	48	34	14	208

TABLE 4. Teachers' responses to curriculum and testing reforms in relation to student differences

	Strongly agree (%)	Agree (%)	Dis-agree (%)	Strongly disagree (%)	Total responses
The new academic curriculum is appropriate to the learning needs of my students.	4	45	36	15	259
Judging from the students in my classroom, the expectations of the new curriculum are realistic.	3	23	48	27	270
The new applied curriculum is appropriate to the learning needs of my students.	3	25	41	32	215
My lower-ability students are especially anxious about how theywill perform on the Grade 10 Test of Reading and Writing Skills.	41	36	14	9	224
Results of the Grade 10 Test of Reading and Writing Skills have helped me identify the learning needs of students who scored below provincial norms.	2	18	38	42	209

TABLE 5. Responses of Mountain View teachers to curriculum, testing, and assessment items compared with responses aggregated for all other schools[a]

	Strongly agree (%)	Agree (%)	Dis-agree (%)	Strongly disagree (%)	Total responses
The new academic curriculum is appropriate to the learning needs of my students.	0 [4]	0 [49]	37 [36]	63 [11]	30 [235]
I would favor a return to the Common Curriculum for Grade 9.	13 [13]	58 [25]	26 [40]	3 [23]	31 [184]

(continued)

	Strongly agree (%)	Agree (%)	Dis- agree (%)	Strongly disagree (%)	Total responses
The new applied curriculum is appropriate to the learning needs of my students.	0 [4]	14 [26]	49 [39]	37 [31]	35 [186]
I support the new policy changes to student testing.	0 [4]	11 [21]	34 [39]	55 [36]	38 [236]
The Grade 10 Test of Reading and Writing Skills has enhanced my confidence as a teacher.	0 [1]	0 [11]	33 [41]	67 [47]	33 [204]
I support the new policy changes to student assessment.	0 [4]	18 [31]	26 [42]	55 [24]	38 [224]
The new Grade 9/Grade 10 assessment policies have improved my feedback to students about their learning.	0 [3]	10 [29]	44 [43]	46 [25]	39 [217]
My lower-ability students are especially anxious about how they will perform on the Grade 10 Test of Reading and Writing Skills.	68 [36]	20 [40]	5 [15]	8 [9]	40 [192]
The Grade 10 Test of Reading and Writing Skills, and the preparation required for it, has stimulated my students' motivation to learn.	— [2]	6 [10]	11 [37]	83 [51]	36 [211]
Since the introduction of new reporting policies, my communication with students has improved.	3 [0]	8 [14]	40 [48]	50 [38]	38 [236]
Since the introduction of new assessment policies, my communication with students has improved.	0 [2]	9 [21]	60 [55]	31 [22]	35 [234]
Since the introduction of Secondary School Reform, I am more confident of my assessment practices.	0 [3]	8 [18]	56 [57]	36 [23]	36 [229]

[a]Percentages and total responses for five other schools in the sample are in brackets.

TABLE 6. Teachers' responses to changes in reporting

	Strongly agree (%)	Agree (%)	Dis- agree (%)	Strongly disagree (%)	Total responses
"E-Teacher" has improved my process of marking.	3	9	30	58	258
I have had time to become comfortable with the new ways of assessing my students' learning—e.g., the new report card.	3	26	31	40	273
Since the introduction of new reporting policies, my communication with students has improved.	1	14	46	40	266

TABLE 7. Teachers' perceptions of changes in collegial communication and relationships

	Strongly agree (%)	Agree (%)	Dis- agree (%)	Strongly disagree (%)	Total responses
Communication with colleagues within my department has improved.	1	22	44	33	260
I am less involved in decision-making in my school.	24	46	22	9	256
Communication with my colleagues across departments has improved.	3	13	45	40	270
I work more collaboratively with my colleagues around issues of student learning.	3	30	39	28	269
I have reduced my involvement in activities outside the classroom.	45	40	10	5	290
I have received adequate professional development to help me implement the new curriculum effectively.	1	18	32	49	280

TABLE 8. Teachers' perceptions of the impact of reform on their selves and careers

	Strongly agree (%)	Agree (%)	Dis-agree (%)	Strongly disagree (%)	Total responses
Commitment to my career as a teacher has deepened.	3	11	49	36	271
I have been motivated to seek early retirement.	41	32	22	5	239
I am less likely to advise children of my own to go into teaching as a career.	45	33	18	5	266
The balance between my personal and work life has improved.	5	9	32	55	277
I have become hesitant to seek promotion to leadership positions.	45	40	11	4	258
My self-image as a professional has improved.	3	7	36	55	265

TABLE 9. Overall survey responses

	Strongly agree/ agree	Count
Curriculum		
1 The academic curriculum is appropriate to my students	48.3	259
2 The new Grade 9/Grade 10 curriculum diminishes my teaching range	48.2	255
3 The new curriculum expectations are realistic	25.2	270
4 The new curriculum does not engage students of different cultural backgrounds	51.3	240
5 The new curriculum uses more variety of assignments	50.0	262

(*continued*)

	Strongly agree/ agree	Count
6 I favor the Common Curriculum for Grade 9	40.9	208
7 The applied curriculum is appropriate to my students	27.9	215
8 I understanding the curriculum I teach	58.5	277
9 Community service in Secondary School Reform is positive	20.5	171

Testing and Assessment

	Strongly agree/ agree	Count
10 I support the new policy on student testing	23.3	266
11 The new Grade 10 literacy test helps students improve	21.3	249
12 I understand the new assessment methods	64.2	274
13 The Grade 10 Test enhanced my confidence as a teacher	10.3	233
14 I support the new policy on student assessment	32.9	255
15 The new Grade 9/Grade 10 assessment improves my feedback to students	29.3	249
16 My lower-ability students are anxious about the Grade 10 Test	76.8	224
17 The Grade 10 Test helps me identify learning needs	20.1	209
18 E-Teacher has improved my process of marking	12.4	258
19 I am becoming comfortable with the new assessment report card	28.6	273
20 Provincial testing of students makes me more accountable	23.7	278
21 The Grade 10 Test and preparation motivate students to learn	11.3	240
22 With new reporting my communication with students has improved	14.3	266
23 My assessment strategies are consistent with the Grade 10 Test	68.2	195
24 Grade 9/Grade 10 testing policies reduced my teaching range	46.6	238

(continued)

	Strongly agree/ agree	Count
25 I use a wider range of assessment strategies since Secondary School Reform	44.0	259
26 With new assessment I involve students more in assessment	40.6	266
27 With new assessment my communication with students improved	21.8	262
28 I integrate skills for the Grade 10 Test into my teaching	52.4	208
29 I am more confident about my assessment practices with Secondary School Reform	19.0	258
Communication and Relationships		
30 Communication and relationships with department colleagues improved with Secondary School Reform	22.7	260
31 Reporting to parents improved with Secondary School Reform	20.2	272
32 The Teacher Advisor Program improved my relations with students	6.9	275
33 The Annual Educational Plan improved my ability to help students plan	17.4	264
34 I am less involved in school decision-making with Secondary School Reform	69.5	256
35 Communication with colleagues across departments improved with Secondary School Reform	15.2	270
36 I have more collaboration with colleagues with Secondary School Reform	32.7	269
37 I have reduced involvement outside class with Secondary School Reform	84.5	290
38 Students have a greater voice in school with Secondary School Reform	11.9	243
39 I work well with parents to implement the mandates	9.4	265
40 I have less contact with parents	42.6	258
41 Work relations with school administration improved	20.5	22.

(continued)

	Strongly agree/ agree	Count
Self and Work		
42 My commitment to a career as a teacher is deeper with Secondary School Reform	14.8	271
43 I am motivated to seek early retirement with Secondary School Reform	73.2	239
44 I am less likely to advise children to teach with Secondary School Reform	77.4	266
45 The balance between my personal and work lives improved with Secondary School Reform	13.4	277
46 I am more hesitant to seek a leadership position with Secondary School Reform	85.3	258
47 My professional self-image improved with Secondary School Reform	9.8	265
Resources		
48 More money is available for textbooks with new funding formula	19.3	218
49 Adequate professional development is provided on new curriculum	18.9	280
50 More money is available for learning materials with new funding formula	4.1	242
51 I have lost access to counseling support staff with new funding formula	73.5	238
52 The school has sufficient funds to meet students' needs	6.2	242
53 I have experienced time constraints on my job	91.1	281
54 I have less access to academic support staff with new funding formula	86.5	252
55 Ontario College for Teachers has enhanced teachers' professional standing	10.1	258

INDEX

Italic letter *"t"* or *"f"* following a page number refers to a table or a figure. References to notes are indicated by page number followed by "n." (or "nn."), which is followed by the note number (or numbers).

221

ABOUT THE AUTHOR

Andy Hargreaves is the Thomas More Brennan Chair in Education at Boston College. The Chair has a mission of promoting social justice in public schools and connecting theory and practice in teacher education.

Professor Hargreaves has written or edited more than 20 books on education. His book *Changing Teachers, Changing Times* received the 1995 Outstanding Writing Award from the American Association of Colleges for Teacher Education. He is co-editor of the *International Handbook for Educational Change* (1998) and editor-in-chief of the *Journal of Educational Change*. In 2000, he received the Whitworth Award from the Canadian Education Association for contributions to educational research in Canada.

DATE DUE